Praise for HUNG__,

"Dr. Jody is courageous in exposing the personal challenges she faced while living in Thailand. She generously shares practical wisdom for navigating through life's challenges, which readers will easily be able to apply to their own life."

- Marcia Wieder, CEO/Founder, Dream University, top rated keynote speaker and author of 14 books

"I LOVE THIS BOOK! What a beautiful story of power, courage, & adventure. You'll feel like you're on a glorious vacation, while absorbing powerful life lessons, as you follow Dr. Jody on her incredible journey."

-Amy Ahlers, bestselling author of Big Fat Lies Women Tell Themselves

"With honesty, vulnerability and inspiration, Hunger shows us how to stop starving for the things we want most - love, recognition and security - by giving us a path to finding the bounty we seek from inside of ourselves."

-Christine Arylo, bestselling self-love author and founder of Madly in Love with ME

"On so many levels this book is a wonderful adventure. Dr. Jody takes you on an interesting journey through her year in Thailand, but that's only a start. Brilliantly woven throughout the book is the wisdom she gained from a life transforming 10-day silent meditation retreat. The life lessons she shares will inspire you to apply them yourself and experience your own personal transformation."

-Mary O'Malley, author of What's in the Way IS the Way

***

HUNGER

An Adventurous Journey of Finding Peace Within

By Dr. Jody Stanislaw

Written and developed by Dr. Jody Stanislaw

Sun Valley, Idaho

Copyright © 2012 Dr. Jody Stanislaw

Printed by CreateSpace
All Rights Reserved

ISBN - 13: 978-1478185840
ISBN – 10: 1478185848
First edition printed July 2012
Printed in the United States

***

Dedicated to my beloved aunt Mary,
the wisdom you have shared with me is one of the greatest
gifts of my life.

***

A note from the author...

Hello Readers!

Thank you for picking up HUNGER, An Adventurous Journey of Finding Peace Within. I hope you truly enjoy reading the pages that lie ahead. I'd like to start by telling you the story of how the idea for this book came to life...

The true stories I share throughout each chapter originated from a blog I wrote while working in Thailand in 2008. I started the blog simply for my friends and family to keep in touch with what I was up to while I was living halfway around the world in Asia.

As someone who has always considered herself a math and science person, much to my surprise, everyone really loved reading my blogs. My dad even called me one day to say, "Man, your latest blog was amazing! Did you really write that story? What a great writer you are!"

One friend told me she'd drop everything she was doing anytime a new post appeared in her inbox because my writing always enthralled her so much, often making her feel as if she were right there next to me experiencing the story first hand.

As I continued to post blog after blog, I started to really enjoy the writing process, as well as all the positive feedback I was receiving. I began carrying a little notebook around everywhere I went to capture the ideas that kept popping into my head for new blog entries. My list eventually grew so long that to this day, many exciting topics never made it into one of my blogs.

My newfound love for writing, combined with all the encouraging feedback I was receiving is how the idea to write this book was born, but I remained hesitant for many months. I would often think to myself, 'Who, me? Write a book?! I'm a doctor, not an author!'

After my time in Thailand came to an end, I had published over 50 blog entries and I eventually decided to follow through with the idea of writing a book. Being inspired by the popular book, Eat Pray Love, I moved to Bali to dedicate several months to transforming my diverse blogs into this very book you now hold in your hands.

(And for those of you familiar with Elizabeth Gilbert's story, I met both of the main characters she described during her time in Bali! I lived next door to Katut and visited Wayan at her herbal medicine shop regularly, and even saw the house she built as a result of Elizabeth's financial donation.)

As I wrote, two personal intentions for HUNGER surfaced. The first is for you to enjoy being captivated by the courageous and adventurous true stories from my time living in Thailand. The second, and more ambitious one, is the intention for you to be inspired to embrace and adopt the life lessons I present throughout into your own life…and as a result, experience greater peace, health, and happiness.

If I am successful with this latter, more profound and transformative intention, at the end of the book, you will find a list of several ways for how you can continue to be inspired by my messages of health and wellbeing…and I would be deeply honored if you did!

But without further adieu, please enjoy…
HUNGER, An Adventurous Journey of Finding Peace Within!

Sincerely,
Dr. Jody Stanislaw

P.S. The cover photo is one I took when in Bali. I am standing on one of the northern Gili islands, looking south to the mainland of Bali.

Table of Contents

Introduction:
The Birth of a Dream

June 1980

My hunger was insatiable. No matter how much food I ate, it was never enough...yet I kept losing weight. The nausea was relentless. My mouth was so dry it hurt. Every time my lips touched together, little bits of skin would rip off when I cautiously pried them back apart. I cried every night, desperate for water, but if I drank anything after eight o'clock, I would wet my bed, again. I don't remember for how long this went on...maybe a week, maybe longer.

Once my mom realized I wasn't getting any better we went to the doctor. I gave a urine sample and when the doctor came back into the cold exam room, after what seemed like hours later, he had a very stern look on his face. He said a word I'd never heard before that started with the letter 'D' and suddenly my mom started crying hysterically. The doctor told us we had to go to the hospital immediately. I wasn't sure what was going on but I knew it wasn't good. I started crying and yelled out, "I need my blankey!" My fear dissipated only slightly when the doctor gave us his approval to make a quick stop at home before arriving at the hospital.

My urine was apparently full of sugar and I was diagnosed with Type 1 Diabetes. That was June 12, 1980. I was just seven years old.

The next week of my life was spent at the famous Children's Orthopedic Hospital, luckily located in my hometown of Seattle. That week forever shaped my life...in more ways than one. In a time when most doctors didn't really know much about managing a disease as complex as juvenile diabetes (other than telling me to avoid sugar), this week probably saved my life in terms of getting the quality education I needed for knowing how to live with this condition for the rest of my life. For this, I feel very lucky.

We were given a crash course in how to become experts at knowing how much sugar is in every single type of food that exists, and subsequently, how to calculate the appropriate amount of insulin to give myself each time I ate in order to keep

1

my blood sugar levels stable. This would, of course, be done via poking my body with injections of insulin, something from that day forward was going to be a mandatory part of my daily life; more important than brushing my teeth; more important than sleep. Yep, even right now as you are reading this book, wherever you are and wherever I am, I am likely wondering what my blood sugar level is and if I need yet another injection of insulin.

In many ways, I remember having a lot of fun that week. I was (and remain) a very gregarious, little spirit. I would sneak out of my bed and wander the halls of the hospital just to chat with all the friendly nurses and doctors. I absolutely loved how they always greeted me with their exuberant enthusiasm (as they kindly walked me back to my room). As I skipped through the halls to the education room with my parents each day, I couldn't help but notice how serious their facial expressions were. I knew that whatever this 'diabetes' thing I was now being labeled with was a really big deal, but I was too young to fully grasp the magnitude of its impact on the rest of my life.

Something which really caught my eye though was that whenever we were working with the nurses and doctors, their soothing and comforting demeanors would alchemize the seriousness my parents obviously felt into ease. It didn't matter if we were practicing putting a balanced meal together using plastic pieces of chicken and green peas, or if we were learning how to keep me from passing out into a diabetic coma, and what to do if by chance I did.

I remember being so impressed with these adults whose lives were dedicated to helping other people feel better. They made practicing giving injections into oranges and putting drops of my urine into test tubes as we watched it fizz into a deep blue, things I thought were more fun then buying up houses on Boardwalk and Park Place while playing my favorite game of Monopoly, or proudly cruising around our driveway on my super cool, bright pink, Barbie Big Wheel.

Although I was just seven years old, I was deeply impressed with the thought of helping people feel better as a life's profession, and as a result, it was this very week of my life when the seed of my dream to become a doctor was born.

Day Zero:
Ten Days of Silence

August 2008

Abruptly finding myself in Thailand, jobless and homeless, I decided to embrace the gift of my freedom to do absolutely anything I could possibly dream of doing, and enrolled in a ten-day silent Buddhist meditation retreat - something a recent patient of mine had done and said had profoundly changed her life.

After what seemed like hours on a bus ride to nowhere, I had arrived at a little town that stretched all of about two blocks long, nestled in by trees and rolling hills. The instructions I'd received on the website for the mediation center were to wait at the gas station for pick up at 2 p.m. Luckily it was 1:45 p.m. so I didn't have to wait long. I got off the bus and headed down the barren street to the gas station, found a bench on the sidewalk and took a seat, slowly swinging my legs as I looked around at the deserted town.

I had one of those deeply introspective moments that come every now and then in life. There I was by myself, sitting on a bench in some small town tucked away in the hills of northern Thailand, not a soul in sight. Not a single friend or family member even knew where I was, nor did I for that matter. I had nowhere to be and nothing I had to do. After 35 years of striving, achieving, socializing, traveling, studying, and going non-stop, I found myself just sitting on a bench, wondering how the hell I ended up there.

Part of me felt proud of the sheer tenacity it took for me to graduate from medical school and then move half way around the world, single at the age of 35, to work in a foreign culture. Another part of me felt lost and alone, wondering why I wasn't happily living in Seattle, married to a loving husband and being fulfilled by raising children like all my friends back at home. Regardless of the spinning thoughts in my head and the flashing pictures through my mind of where I thought I 'should' be, I decided not to waste energy judging my present situation as 'right' or 'wrong.' I chose to simply embrace my reality as it was in that moment…that I was sitting there, on a bench, by myself

3

in Thailand.

A van suddenly approached. It stopped directly in front of me and the driver stepped out to greet me. He was a short, elderly Thai man whose green eyes sparkled like diamonds and whose smile beamed like the sunshine. He bowed his head and then put my bag in the back of the van as he motioned for me to get into the front seat.

Without a word spoken, we drove along a windy dirt road, passing through barren, rolling hills, for about 20 minutes until we reached our destination. We pulled up to a modest looking building with small cabins surrounding it. The driver grabbed my bag and walked me to one of the cabins. With his brilliant smile, he motioned me inside. There were two bunk beds already occupied with others' belongings, except for one of the top bunks which I assumed was mine. I put my things on the bed and then followed him back outside, along the dirt trail to the humble main building.

It was a single, large open space. On one side were lines of meditation cushions on the floor and on the other was a kitchen area with picnic tables and benches. Sitting in silence were three Thai women, two elderly and one in her teens; two Thai men, both middle aged; two Caucasian men, probably around my age; and two Caucasian women, likely a mom and daughter. My driver handed me some paperwork, in English luckily, and then motioned for me to have a seat while he brought me some tea.

The paperwork lined out the daily schedule as follows:

6:30 – 8:00 Meditation
8:00 – 9:30 Breakfast/shower
9:30 – 11:00 Meditation
11:00 – 11:15 Break
11:15 – 12:30 Meditation
12:30 – 1:30 Lunch
1:30 – 2:30 Break
2:30 – 4:00 Meditation
4:00 – 4:15 Break
4:15 – 5:30 Meditation
5:30 – 6:30 Dinner
6:30 – 8:00 Meditation
8:00 – 8:15 Break
8:15 – 9:00 Buddhist teachings
9:30 Lights out

I was experiencing a mix of emotions, to say the least. The novelty of the experience of what I was about to embark on actually, in part, excited me…ten days of sitting silently with myself. My patient who told me about her experience said it was life transforming for her, and that intrigued me.

My constant hunger for peace brought me there. I love challenges, and this one was of an entirely new sort. Instead of striving to accomplish something, I was going to be faced with the challenge of literally doing nothing for ten days, except sitting still with myself. This fact also scared me. Furthermore, as I read through the paperwork, in bold letters across the top of each page were the words:

TO ENHANCE YOUR EXPERIENCE OF GOING DEEPLY WITHIN YOURSELF OVER THESE TEN DAYS, THERE WILL BE NO TALKING, NO EYE CONTACT, NO COMMUNICATION OF ANY SORT

Although I had already read about that rule on the website, after reading it in black and white, I took a deep breath and had a moment of total dread which sent my mind spinning…

"Oh my God Jody! You are crazy! Why do you do insane things like this? Do you really think this is going to be fun?! You can't be quiet for a minute, let alone ten days! Nor can you even sit still, ever! You've just signed yourself up for HELL!"

My extroverted, bubbly self was already practically foaming at the mouth to restrain myself from striking up a conversation with one of my fellow, silent tea drinkers around me, not knowing or caring if any of them spoke English anyway. I took a deep breath to calm my stormy mind and had a sip of tea. And then took another breath and another sip of tea, and did that again, and again, and again, for probably three hours…just sitting there breathing and drinking tea.

It was an amazing experience, to be so still, to have nowhere to go, and nothing to do. My mind kept jumping here and there, as if desperately looking for what the next activity was going to be, even though there was literally *nothing* I had to do. The juxtaposition of how still my body was versus how busy my mind was almost made me laugh out loud at one point. The analogy I came up with to describe what I was experiencing (this gave my mind something to do at least) was that my mind was a freight train whose engine had been turned off (equivalent to my body now sitting still), yet the cars were still careening full speed ahead (equivalent to my racing thoughts which had yet to slow down).

Throughout my hours sitting there, breathing and drinking tea, a few others had arrived and joined us in our 'activity' of silent, tea drinking, until there were about 15 of us. At 6 p.m., a metal screen in the wall opened up to reveal our dinner. One by one, each of us grabbed a plate and served ourselves from the bowls of rice and various vegetable dishes displayed before us. My mind was exhilarated that it had a new activity to engage in, and the part of me feeling anxious about this whole, outrageous undertaking was relieved to be able to enjoy the comfort of my lifelong friend, food.

As we sat there silently, it was awkward to not know where to look. So I spent my dinner enthralled by the taste of each bite, closing my eyes and practicing gratitude for every morsel.

6

After dinner, it had already become dark so I figured it was time to head to bed. There was a very basic bathroom adjacent to my cabin, which I discovered I shared with the likely mother-daughter pair, plus one of the elderly Thai women. As I snuggled myself into my sleeping bag on my upper bunk, I went to bed, feeling excited while at the same time full of trepidation for the awesome challenge which lay ahead of me…spending my next ten days in total silence.

Chapter 1:
The Windy Path of Following a Dream
1990's - 2007

Life is full of hungers…We all start out crying because we are hungry for milk. Then, we are hungry for a nap. Then it's toys. Or to have our friends come over to play. Then it's to be good at sports, or school, or to be liked by our peers. To have a boyfriend or girlfriend. To look a certain way. To get into college or get a job. To find a mate and live happily ever after.

We can spend our lives chasing the elusive satisfaction we believe we will find once we satiate our hungers. I know this all too well.

Somewhere along the way, if we are lucky, our hungers shift away from outside desires and more towards internal states of mind. Towards living in peace and contentment, no matter what we are doing, how much money we have, what job we have, what our body looks like, or who we are married to, or not married to.

But then there are dreams, which are not to be confused with hungers. Hungers can come and go, and some seem impossible to fully satiate. Dreams, however, when we think about them, light us up. They make our eyes sparkle and get us excited. The thought of a dream coming true makes us feel enthusiastic…which comes from the latin root word '*en-theos*,' and means, 'inspired by God.' When we are doing things that make us feel '*en-theos*-iastic,' I believe we are in alignment with what we are meant to do with our lives.

Dreams float in and out of our minds throughout our lifetime. When we are young, most of us start with big dreams…of being a fireman, or a musician, a professional athlete, a world traveler, a business tycoon, an inventor, a scientist, a doctor… Or we could simply have honorable dreams such as to be a good hearted person, to be happy, to be healthy… But life circumstances often seem to suppress dreams and replace them with a way of life deemed as more 'realistic.'

Yet, studies show that those who pursue their dreams are not only happier people, but healthier as well. Following ones' dream then is not so much a luxury as a prescription for optimal health.

Dreams that stem from one's ego or hunger for fame or glory however, will not bring the feeling of satisfaction one expects. However, dreams that come from the heart are undoubtedly worth pursuing. If not, the failed potential can be devastating to one's life and would be a shame to never fulfill. Regardless of the challenges faced along the way, I am a huge proponent of following the dreams that simmer in our heart.

As anyone who actually pursues a childhood dream realizes however, the journey of following it certainly isn't all roses. The doubts, the regrets, the fears, the investment of money and the countless hours spent along the way...these aren't exactly part of the pristine vision of a 'dream,' but they are definitely part of the reality encountered along the path.

***

Having seen doctors throughout my life for diabetes, I've had a lot of experience being a patient. Yet one of the key factors which kept me from pursuing my dream for so many years of becoming one of these people, who helped others *feel better*, was that often I left my doctor's appointments *feeling worse*.

Given the complexity of living with childhood diabetes...just one example being never knowing if and when I was going to fall from having a low blood sugar level into a diabetic coma...I always arrived with a long list of questions to discuss with my doctor, yet I was lucky if I could get even five minutes to ask them. The doctor would usually go through some impersonal checklist of questions, tell me I was doing great, and then send me on my way. I always left wondering what the point of even going to the darn appointment was in the first place. I already knew my blood sugar levels were great but I had so much more going on, such as how my emotions seemed to follow along the up and down course of my blood sugar levels, and how painfully left out I felt at birthday parties, with the measured square of sugar-free Jell-O I was given instead of enjoying cake with everyone else. It seemed there was never enough time, or perhaps interest, to ever look beyond my lab results. I always wished I could find a doctor that looked at me

9

as a whole person, not just as someone with the label, 'diabetic.'

Consequently, as so commonly and unfortunately happens with childhood dreams, I did my best to ignore mine for several years. Throughout my twenties I literally traveled the globe earnestly searching for a career path that would satisfy the deep hunger in my heart to make a positive impact on others' lives, while avoiding the arduous path of going to medical school. In my pursuit, I attended four different colleges, earned a business degree (I did start with a pre-med degree, but never stayed in one place long enough to fulfill the lengthy requirements), lived in Italy twice (Florence and Siena…amazing), back-packed around Australia and New Zealand (phenomenal…I highly recommend it), and even endured a job as a pharmaceutical sales rep, selling the anti-depressant Prozac (which, funny enough, happened to be one of the most depressing times of my life).

But after all those years of searching, nothing could squelch my dream of becoming a doctor. The vision of dedicating my life and career to helping others feel better constantly flashed in the back of my mind. To reduce the ironically life-sucking years it would take to become a doctor…someone who actually helps others improve and *extend* their life…I thought about being a physical therapist or a nurse, but I knew I'd never be satisfied. I had a strong sense that eventually I would find myself in medical school.

So while my usual bright and sunny disposition became more and more dimmed during the years I was pushing Prozac, (…day after day I had to paste a big smile on my face in dire hopes of getting the doctors' attention, and yet whenever they saw me approaching, my smile would drop into a frown when they immediately turned and walked the other way…), I finally decided to go back to school part time to complete my pre-med prerequisite classes. I wasn't sure what medical school program I would attend or when, but I knew I would eventually need these classes to finally one day follow my dream.

Then one auspicious afternoon, as I was sitting in a coffee shop after completing my sales calls for the day and was studying for an anatomy quiz, I overheard someone talking about a medical school with the equivalent science curriculum to that of a regular, western medical school, yet where the

10

treatments were based entirely on holistic therapies, such as nutrition, herbs, counseling, homeopathy, and body work. My heart skipped a beat with excitement. I leaned in and listened closely as I heard the name, *'Bastyr University.'*

I immediately looked it up on the internet. Within moments I learned there are only four medical schools in the U.S. with this type of curriculum, and unbelievably, one was located just a mere 30 minutes outside of Seattle! I couldn't believe it took me 30 years to learn about this holistic medical school located practically right in my backyard...the answer to my lifelong hunger of becoming a heart-centered doctor. I immediately called the school and asked what I needed for acceptance into the program, and sure enough, it was the standard list of pre-medical school pre-requisite classes I had never finished during my undergrad years.

I spent the next few years preparing myself for acceptance to Bastyr University, taking one pre-med class per year to complete all the necessary prerequisite classes (while my depression continued to spiral as I endured one self-esteem crushing day after another, selling Prozac).

But in March of 2000, with just one more science class to go, I received a job offer to sell diabetic insulin pumps. Being that I wore one myself, I took the job in a heartbeat. The respect I received was welcome nourishment for my weary soul. Instead of physicians constantly turning the other way when they saw me, now I was sitting down with them, educating their staff and patients about the ins and outs of life with an insulin pump.

I enjoyed this new position so much that I postponed my last prerequisite class in hopes I had actually found a job I loved, while avoiding enduring the rigors of medical school. In the face of all the doctors who had only read about diabetes from a textbook, I was now the expert.

My heart wasn't going to be tricked though. My mind constantly reminded me I was still a saleswoman and that, *'Jody, a saleswoman is not a doctor.'* After taking a year off from my science classes in hopes of avoiding the path of medical school, my hungry heart lead me to indeed register for that final science class....and in September of 2002, just weeks before my thirtieth birthday, I quit my *almost* totally satisfying, six-figure income generating, insulin-pump sales job, applied for student loans that would reach into the six-figure range by the time I had completed the five-year curriculum, and eagerly, (albeit not without trepidation), started my life as a full-time medical school student at Bastyr University.

✳✳✳

After my decade of wandering, I had at last taken the plunge. I was a medical student and finally engaged in a life in alignment with what my heart had hungered for since I was seven. Yet, although I was attending a holistic, heart centered medical school, the curriculum was as militantly demanding as classic western medical school. In just a single quarter, my class schedule included botanical medicine, physical exam skills, massage, homeopathy, pediatrics, geriatrics, and cardiology. The amount of discipline, focus, and determination required for successful completion of the rigorous curriculum could only be possessed by those that confidently knew this path was what they were meant to pursue in life.

So, enduring endless amounts of studying for five years, day after day, night after night, social-life crushing weekend after social-life crushing weekend was something I could have accomplished only if the driving force was truly coming from my heart's desire, not from something I just thought I 'should' do.

The challenges one inevitably encounters while pursuing the path of one's dreams may perhaps be 'harder' than those encountered on an easier path, but in actuality will be endured with more ease. The energizing force that exists when someone is in alignment with what their heart truly desires will allow this to be true, as opposed to when one chooses the 'easier' path or perhaps the 'should do' path, but yet not the one truly hungered for.

Another aspect which made the challenges easier to endure was the fact that I was surrounded by wonderful colleagues. After not having had any coworkers for the previous five years while in sales and having drifted away from my college friends, my soul was desperate to be nourished by the love of new friends! There were 140 of us at the start of the first year,

12

(but come graduation, there were fewer than 100 of us still remaining). The community of individuals drawn to become Naturopathic Physicians consists of some of the most openhearted, loving people I have ever met. After all the ups and downs we had shared over those five years, we became like family, some being closer to each other than others, but inevitably, all connected by the bond of enduring such an intense journey together.

Clearly, to go through such an experience, heart centered or not, one must have certain nourishing elements present in their life to help sustain them. My dear cat, Jennifur, was mine. I've always been a cat lover. There wasn't a single year of my childhood in which our house wasn't inhabited by at least one cat. Fat Cat was my all time favorite because no matter what position my energetic little self managed to hold him in, he would without fail always peacefully close his eyes and immediately fall into an earth-shaking purr of bliss. (And yes, he was fat; very fat, which made cuddling with him all the more wonderful.)

During my first year in pharmaceutical sales in 1997, I bought a home in Seattle and before I even had a thought about decorating the place, I was on a mission to find a feline companion, and that is when I found Jen.

Jennifur had the softest and silkiest fur of any cat in the world. Her hair was lusciously long and brilliantly black, and she 'wore' little white socks on each of her feet, and had a single patch of white displaying itself as an adorable little splotch on the center of her nose.

Each day as I pulled up in front of my house over those ten years when I was depressed from pushing Prozac, fulfilled from selling insulin pumps, or cramming more medical information into my brain than I thought I even had the capacity to contain, Jennifur would always be lovingly waiting for me in the front window. She had been eagerly awaiting my arrival for who knows how many hours, sitting perched up on the back of the couch, peering out the window. As soon as I opened the front door, she would greet me like a dog would, meowing as if to say, *"I have been missing you all day! I'm soooo glad you are finally home!!"* She would persist in tripping me as she danced around between my feet, only to cease once I finally picked her up, gave

13

her some double-armed cuddles and many behind-the-ear scratches.

Once this daily, five-minute display of mutual love was complete, her dog-like characteristics continued as she proceeded to follow me from room to room, wherever I went, and proudly plopped herself down right in the middle of the textbook I was trying to read, or pranced over my keyboard as I attempted to work on my computer. She loved to literally sit directly on top of the dial-pad of my phone, intuitively aware whenever I wanted to make a phone call as if to say, *"Wouldn't you rather be talking to me?"* No matter the bother of these mannerisms, her minute-by-minute, hour-by-hour, day-by-day, unconditional love and devotion was astounding to me, and my heart and soul soaked in every ounce of it.

I had wonderful humans in my life as well. My mom and dad both proudly supported me in my quest for following my childhood dream, and although the majority of my childhood friends had to find a babysitter before finding time to have dinner with me, I was always supported by their love as well. I was so committed to becoming a doctor that the thought of raising a family had never entered my mind. Thus, I was baffled and frankly a bit surprised once all my friends started having children. It was a challenging adjustment for me, to say the least.

Yet, one of the most significant relationships in my life during those demanding years in medical school was my dear aunt Mary. We hadn't always been close though. While my mom pursued a career in law, her sister Mary opted for the more eccentric path of massage and spirituality. Since I grew up with both of my parents being attorneys and I had my own vision of being a doctor, Mary's life, with her vegetarianism and meditation beads, was a stark contrast to anything I had ever experienced. Yet, my view of her being odd and different dramatically alchemized during my five years at Bastyr.

As luck would have it, her home and office happened to be located even closer to campus than my own house. After all the rejection I endured during my sales career, my self-esteem was at an all time low during that first year of medical school. As a result, I was drawn to join Mary's Monday night spiritual group in hopes of finding some nourishing connection and support.

The conversations I experienced during those Monday

14

nights surrounded by people exposing the truth of their emotions at a level of honesty which I found wonderfully refreshing. The realization that I wasn't alone with all my fears and insecurities in life was a welcomed relief. Every week, Mary infused the group with her contagious inspiration and authentic joy. Her message always communicated some sort of beautifully inspired direction about tender ways to navigate through any of life's inevitable challenges. The core message revolved around the message that, 'Life is trustable. All of it...the 'good' and the 'bad,' the joy, the tears, diabetes, and all.'

She would always say, *"Fertilizer is necessary for growth...and fertilizer is made of crap."*

The divinely inspired fact that I wasn't just a client of Mary's, but also her blood-sharing niece, led to the cultivation of the most beautiful and loving, mentor-mentee relationship I could have ever imagined. I stopped going to the Monday night group because Mary and I soon committed to spending one heart-nourishing night per week together just by ourselves, which we maintained throughout the entirety of my years at Bastyr. (And, which we have almost seamlessly continued to do even today, in person or on the phone, depending where in the world I happen to be.)

Given the magnitude of emotions expressed by my personality, on some nights I would arrive at Mary's full of bounding enthusiasm and excitement for life. Yet, on other days, I would arrive sobbing, in a despondent pile of tears, (sometimes fueled simply by an elevated blood sugar level...which often causes me to believe my mental health is worthy of being committed to a mental institution). On these occasions, I would poke my head inside her front door to notify her of my arrival and then immediately go for a run around the block to lower my blood sugar level. (I am never capable of having an inspiring or even intelligent conversation until my sugar level has returned to normal.)

However, no matter what the flavor of my mood for the day was, Mary could always miraculously shift me away from my fears and back into feeling that everything in my life was not only okay, but that it was trustable. Whether I was feeling exhausted from endless hours of studying or tired of being single and feeling so lonely, or sick of dealing with the challenges of diabetes, she would remind me how challenges always bring growth.

"A tree must lose its leaves every autumn and stand naked through the winter in order to allow the beautiful blossoms of springtime to flourish."

After living with my intense character since the day I was born plus having a natural tendency toward the belief I must fight hard to achieve whatever it is I want in life, I found Mary's approach wonderfully refreshing. It allowed me to let go of thinking I had to constantly muster up enough strength to 'fix' the areas of my life I deemed as unacceptable and also allowed me to no longer view my life through the lens of anything being 'bad' or 'broken.'

Mary would always say, *"It's Okay. It's all Okay."*

Every time I would hear her say this phrase, the rebellious voice in my head firmly rejected it. It would scream about how messed up many areas of my life were and how I obviously wasn't working hard enough to fix them or make them go away. Yet simply, with her loving smile, she would gently remind me, *"It's Okay. It's all Okay. You can let go of the struggle."* Mary was and still is a godsend to me.

After enduring five years of the intensity of medical school, albeit following my heart's desire, coupled with the companionship of my colleagues, my dear cat Jennifur, and my beloved aunt Mary, on June 15, 2007, I triumphantly achieved my childhood dream and was pronounced: Dr. Jody Stanislaw.

Day 1:
Don't Believe Everything You Think
August 2008

When I woke up, I looked at the clock and it was 9 a.m. Whoops! I guess I missed the 6 a.m. bell. I've always been a deep sleeper. Apparently following the daily schedule at this retreat is entirely up to me, which makes sense given the 'no communication' rule. I kind of felt bad but was equally happy to have had such a nice, deep sleep. Furthermore, given that my typical activities of working, exercising, talking on the phone, doing errands, spending hours on the internet, texting, and everything else I generally fill my days with were not options, the only activity really left was to listen to my thoughts and observe how my mind reacted to the various stimuli of the day.

"I am not my mind."

This is a key teaching of Buddhism. I was excited to practice it over those ten days...to become aware of the mind as a separate entity from who I was at my core and to see it as just that, a thing which constantly churns out thoughts all day long. Buddhists say peace and freedom are found when one can step away from the game of identifying oneself by the thoughts in one's mind.

I was excited for the stillness I would have in order to truly experience this truth...that most thoughts are simply a result of ingrained, habitual thought patterns, likely established in childhood, and much less of a response to what is actually going on. A bumper sticker I've always loved, which basically teaches this message says, *"You don't have to believe everything you think."*

So there I was on the first morning, already deep into this practice. I was aware of the achievement-junkie side of me wanting to berate myself for sleeping in. Yet I chose not to feed that old pattern of only praising myself for perfection. Instead, I chose to 'feed' the loving thoughts of being pleased that I was able to sleep so deeply. My room was empty, which was nice because I had the bathroom to myself. I took a quick shower and headed to breakfast.

17

The mess hall was packed with all the silent eaters, enjoying oatmeal and stewed fruit. Everyone was either staring straight down at their food, at the walls, or out the windows. I took a seat and chose the option of closing my eyes to focus on thoroughly enjoying each bite. The 9:30 a.m. meditation session was approaching so I quickly finished my meal and headed over to find a cushion on the far side of the room.

There were all sorts of props available to make sitting on a square cushion in the middle of the floor for hours at a time as comfortable as possible. I grabbed a few small pillows for my knees and a blanket to put over my shoulders. I tried sitting with my legs crossed but then worried my feet would fall asleep. So then I tried sitting on my heels but couldn't because my knees hurt. So I shifted back to sitting on my butt with my legs crossed and I used my little knee pillows to prop them up. As I squirmed about I noticed how still all the other meditators were which gave my ever-judging mind something to have a fit about…

"Geez Jody! Look at how still everyone is while you squirm about! You suck at this. Why are you even here? These ten days are going to kill you. Good luck sucker!"

I reminded myself of one of the main reasons why I was there…to practice simply observing my thoughts and strengthening my ability to not believe them.

"Jody, you are not your mind."

Buddhism teaches that when you can detach from the constant stream of habitual thoughts originating from your mind, it allows you to live from the peace which eternally flows from your heart.

I consciously shifted my attention away from my stream of negative thinking as I closed my eyes in preparation for the first meditation session. The starting bell rang. It was official. It was time to begin meditating. I put my attention on my breath as I spoke a mantra silently to myself to help keep my mind still.

"Breathe in. Breathe out. Breathe in. Breathe out. Breathe in. Breathe out…"

We had received instructions the night before to keep the entirety of our attention for the first four days of meditating solely on the breath moving in and out of our nose. But not

18

more than ten seconds had passed before my judging mind
peeped in and a discussion in my head ensued.

"Jody, you are doing great!"

*"Hey there mind, meditating is not about judging if I am 'doing
great' or not. It's about just observing what is...so get back to keeping 100
percent of your focus on breathing, please....Breathe in. Breathe out. Breathe
in. Breathe out..."*

Over and over, my thoughts kept wandering in, as I
again and again, refocused my attention on my breath. At times I
felt like I was involved in a wrestling match, watching breath
versus thoughts.

There is an analogy I love which compares the ability to
continually direct one's mind on a single focus to a muscle which
must be trained. Expecting I could keep my attention entirely on
my breath, without any interruption from thoughts, was as
unrealistic as if I were to expect I could train with a 100-pound
weight without ever starting with a 20-pound one.

Before arriving at the retreat, I had heard this particular
ten-day experience referred to as a 'meditation boot camp.' That
description certainly made sense to me now! Although several
times throughout the day I had a voice whining about what a
stupid idea it was for me to be there and enduring ten days of
hell, a voice from my heart smiled at my dedication and tenacity
to engage in such a valiant undertaking.

After dinner, it was time for our first Buddhist teaching.
I had no idea what to expect, but after eight hours of sitting
silently, eyes shut, observing the breath moving in and out of my
nose, I would have been excited to watch anything; an
infomercial selling Tupperware would have been exhilarating.

Sitting perched on my meditation cushion in the middle
of the floor, I immediately became enthralled in the training
video of two people who were sitting on the floor, with the
backdrop of nothing more than a white wall behind them. An
elderly Burmese man was speaking in English (with Thai
subtitles), while his devoted wife, devoid of emotion on her face,
sat next to him.

The man told a story about how in the 1970s he was a
very wealthy businessman. But in the prime of his lucrative
career, he was struck with debilitating migraines. He spent
thousands of dollars traveling the globe, going to the best

19

doctors in the world, desperately seeking relief from his painful migraines. After a year of searching, to no avail, he came back to Burma downtrodden and hopeless; feeling like his life was over.

A friend of his suggested a ten-day silent, Buddhist meditation retreat in India. At first he laughed at what a fruitless idea he thought it was, but realized he was desperate and had nothing to lose. After ten days of meditating, not only did he experience more relief from his migraines than he had ever found before, but his level of happiness soared.

He became so impassioned about his experience; he couldn't help but tell everyone he knew. He decided to leave behind his lucrative business career and instead, committed his life to creating meditation centers all over the world. Forty years later, there are now hundreds of 'Vipassana' meditation centers around the globe.

After finishing his story, the man explained that the Buddha himself discovered this Vipassana meditation technique, back in 500 B.C. The term 'Vipassana' means to 'see things as they really are." The Buddha taught it as a universal remedy to cure all ails. The man in the video, named S.N. Goenka, then recounted the life of Buddha and how he discovered this technique, explaining that he never taught these Vipassana principles as a religion, nor did he purport to be a God desiring to be worshiped. His teachings were simply meant to be used as guiding principles for how to enjoy a peaceful life.

Siddhartha, the given name of The Buddha, was born within the walls of a palace. He was blessed with all the material pleasures of a prince and was slated to become a king. As a young man, he felt unsatisfied with his opulent way of life and hungered to explore life outside the walls of his palace in hopes of finding peace. To the dismay of his family, one day he escaped from his family's compound, leaving behind his wife and child as well as all of his material possessions, in order to embark on a mission to discover how the rest of the world lived, with hopes of finding joy somewhere other than the life he knew.

As he explored the neighboring towns, he was shocked and agonized by the impoverished conditions of the commoners. Given his privileged upbringing, he had never seen or even imagined such human suffering. The peace he had

20

hoped to find somewhere besides the life he knew was nowhere to be found. He also became acutely aware of the vanity and instability of all objects of desire, as well as the inevitable impermanence of life itself.

This realization set him on an even deeper quest to find peace. He traveled the world looking for answers. He became a monk and studied several forms of meditation, but after several years of seeking, he still failed to find the peace he hungered for. I was enthralled by this part of the story, given how much I could relate to his insatiable quest for peace, from a man who lived thousands of years ago.

Feeling dejected, he sat motionless in meditation beneath a sacred Bodhi tree, purported to be the tree of wisdom. He swore to remain there until his death unless he discovered the wisdom of how to find peace. Local leaders fearful of his potential power to influence the commoners sent beautiful women to visit him, to distract him from his quest. When that tactic failed, others were sent with this same intention of pulling him away from his pursuit, yet all to no avail. Siddhartha remained there, motionless under the tree, eyes closed in a deep trance, hungrily seeking peace.

In meditating on human pain, finally one night Siddhartha was enlightened about both its genesis and the means to destroy it. It was through this newfound knowledge he acquired the title Buddha, which means 'awakened one.' Core to his discovery for finding peace was this process of Vipassana meditation, which I would be learning more about each night of the retreat through Goenka's teaching videos.

As the video came to an end, I was inspired by what I had learned thus far and was eager to learn more over the next nine days about this life-changing process the Buddha had discovered to be the pathway to peace.

Chapter 2:
The Courage to Search
June 2007 – January 2008

After almost 30 years since that original seed of desire had been planted, I had finally earned the title, Dr. Jody Stanislaw. I had reached the culmination of my life long dream. Extraordinary! Incredible! Triumphant! Right? Well, yeah, kind of.

Now I had to get a job and pay back my mammoth loans, which had reached the six-figure level. *"Darn! I thought the tough part was supposed to just be the rigorous studying. Now, I have to make all these big, life-molding decisions like figuring out what kind of practice to have and where I want to live."*

"Where should I go? Where will I be happy? What kind of life am I hungry for?" These questions endlessly spun around in my head, and the answers were nowhere in sight.

Though, one answer I knew for sure was that I was ready to live in the sunshine! After spending 35 years in Seattle, I had no interest in enduring another never-ending winter full of relentless darkness, where the sky is blanketed in heavy clouds excreting dreary raindrops slithering down from above all day long. If I did, I knew I would end up back on Prozac, and I did *not* want to ever do that again.

After living for five years within the confines of constant rigorous studies, I was hungry to be rejuvenated from the fresh perspective that comes with travel. A few weeks after graduation, I packed my bags and hit the open road in search of where I was going to spend the next phase of my life.

My insatiable hunger for the outdoors led me to explore five northwest states: Idaho (to answer the question of whether I should move to my favorite ski town of Sun Valley); Nevada (not actually for exploring the state though....but for a quick side trip to experience the world famous Burning Man festival... OMG!!... 50,000 people coming together for the most spectacular display of art, creativity, generosity, music, and dancing that probably exists anywhere in the world...I highly recommend it); Oregon (the town of Bend I hear has got it all right at its fingertips: skiing, hiking, biking, river rafting, rock climbing...); Montana (stunning nature, beautiful mountains, breath taking skies, and my good friend Ike just moved there); and Northern California (sunshine to the likes unheard of in Seattle...need I say more?). I was on a mission to figure out where the next city I was going to call home would be.

Before I hit the road and left Seattle behind me though, just for fun I went to an astrologist to see where 'the stars' said I should go. Steve Dahmas came highly recommended to me by one of my professors at school so I called him up to make an appointment...and I was blown away.

The three hours he spent analyzing my life, via this circular chart full of esoteric symbols and figures, proved to be astoundingly accurate. Just a few of the remarkable facts that Steve, this man I'd never met before and who knew nothing about me at the beginning of our appointment, presented to me were as follows: *You have a natural gift in helping others, which will be the mainstay of your career path; your self-fulfillment will not come via focusing on appearance nor material things, but only from living out the vision which resides within your heart; your own physical ailments teach you compassion and create a drive within you to heal others; your path of self-actualization will begin with a wavering path but will assuredly ensue via a slow and gradual unfolding; your sensitivity to the opinions of other's creates insecurity yet concurrently, you possess strong, internal confidence; a satisfying relationship will come later in your life due to your soul's desire to allow you to develop your own sense of self and independence first; you want and need a clear feeling of belonging socially yet remain mobile and travel often; you have a strong desire to be a part of foreign cultures...* Every single one of these statements was shockingly accurate.

But the number one question I came to him for was to learn his advice as to where I should move. Here was his answer: *"Jody, Asia looks like a good place for you to live."* I couldn't help but laugh. *"Well, that's nice Steve, but moving that far away wasn't exactly what I had in mind. My question was more about if I should stay in Seattle, or otherwise try Oregon, California, Idaho, or Montana. If the opportunity presented itself to live in Asia, I suppose I'd take it, but I'm certainly not going to pack my bags and move half way across the world..."*

We wrapped up the appointment, and although blown away by the unbelievably, accurate analysis of my life, it didn't leave me any closer to discovering the answer of where the next place to call home should be.

23

Two main criteria I hungered for were more sunshine and less traffic. (The traffic in Seattle is horrendous...I think we've even won the award multiple times, 'City with the Worst Traffic in America.') Other items on my 'ideal list' included working within a community focused on health and wellness, and being near the ocean, but that seemed like a lot to ask...

My travels around the various northwest states were going along smoothly (which was an easy task to achieve ...anything was better than having my head buried in yet another medical textbook). Though no firm decision as to where I should end up next in my life was becoming clear. Then one day as I was driving through California, I made a quick stop to check my email, and there it was, a potential answer to my searching right in my inbox. The subject line read, *"Looking for holistic physicians to work at an exclusive, international health resort on the beach in Thailand."*

Are you kidding?! Is this for real?! It sounded too good to be true. Sunshine? Check. No major city traffic? Check. Near the water? Check! Within a community focused on health and wellness? Check! Check! Check! Although I was excited, I couldn't help but be a bit skeptical. I immediately took a look at the website and my mouth dropped. *"Exclusive, luxurious, destination health spa....catering to the rich and famous...in a quaint vacation town three hours outside of Bangkok...on a long and beautiful beach... with a delicious menu of pampering services, fitness and physical therapy offerings, holistic health practitioners...delectable organic healthy cuisine...."* What was the catch?!

The posting requested a resume and a photo. I figured I had nothing to lose so I sent them in immediately. A mere seven days later, I was scheduled for an hour-long phone interview with the health manager of the resort. After answering all of her questions and expressing my sheer enthusiasm for the position, she replied, "Fantastic! I am so glad I finally found someone who wants to work here!"

Hmm, that wasn't exactly a statement that boosted my confidence in this being a fantastic idea, but I chose to ignore it because the opportunity sounded too extraordinary. At the end of the interview, she asked, "When can you start?"

After a second phone interview the following week, I suddenly found myself making plans to sell almost everything I

24

owned, turning my home into a rental property, and saying good-bye to every person I knew in Seattle, including my loyal companion for the past eight years, my beloved Jennifur...

With all of the giving away of my once treasured material things, and the good-byes to my chummy med school colleagues, my dear childhood friends, and my beloved family members, finding a new home for Jennifur was, by far, the toughest part. Having been in my life for eight loving years, she was the closest thing I'd ever had to a long-term relationship. The pain I experienced in separating from her made me wonder how people ever make it through a real break up from a long-term, human relationship.

I tried to find her a home with a friend or family member, starting with my mom and her husband Chris, but they had Montgomery, an overly-friendly golden retriever that Jen unfortunately perceived as a very evil being deserving of constant hissing at and swatting. The one-week trial period was swiftly concluded after Jen saturated their bed with urine. I knew in my heart Jen would only find peace in a home absent of any other four-legged friends.

I sent out a mass alert email to everyone I knew desperate to find her a new home, but to no avail. I eventually found her a new home with a woman who happened to be in the class below me at medical school. Amy was a self-proclaimed cat lover who had recently been tragically separated from her previous cat. This fact gave me a bit of relief, feeling that giving away Jen was in part an act of benevolence. I asked her if she wouldn't mind if I could be considered a grandmother who lives out of town, and thus could stay in touch over email just to hear how Jen was doing now and then. My heartache was mitigated when she agreed.

As for the separation from everyone else in my life, my community-loving spirit was hungry to find some way in which to still feel connected to them, and them to me. So I made a commitment to everyone I would write a blog capturing my life in Thailand (which by the way is where the idea for this book originally evolved).

Given my insatiable hunger for learning about various ways to achieve wellness, a part of living in Thailand I was excited to experience and write about in my blog were the principles of Buddhism. (I have always been drawn to its teachings because it's not so much a religion as it is guidance for finding peace…something I've always hungered for.) Furthermore, I was looking forward to adopting a simpler way of life. I wasn't going to have a car, so I would walk everywhere. No cell phone. My meals would be prepared for me three times a day. My commute to work would be a five-minute walk from my apartment to the resort. It sounded like heaven to me!

Serendipitously, two of my colleagues from medical school had also been hired at the resort and had arrived two weeks prior to my arrival date. Over those five years of enduring the intensity of our program, a strong sense of family formed among my classmates, so to have Dave and Monica there to share my adventures in Thailand with was a welcomed treat. We weren't best friends at school, but we had often enjoyed chatting with each other at one of Dave's famous raw food dinner parties, or at one of Monica's infamous dance parties, or just simply hanging out in the cafeteria over lunch. Monica and I had even joked one day during our last year about how cool it would be if we were to land our first job at a ritzy health resort on a beach somewhere in the tropics. (Indeed, a good reminder of the power of your words and to be careful what you wish for!)

Dave was an easy-going, guitar-playing, laid-back, beach-loving guy, originally from the East Coast. Monica grew up in a small town in New Mexico and had arrived at Bastyr after spending the previous five years in biomedical research for the Human Genome Project in Seattle. Her warm-hearted, nurturing spirit gave her an exceptional bedside manner with her patients, and not to mention, she soon became a very treasured friend of mine. Her parents are both of Mexican-American descent so when she arrived in Thailand, no one could figure out if she was Hawaiian, Filipino, Italian, Indian, or even Thai.

Monica had sent me an email a few days after she first arrived and before my own departure date. I was eager to hear how everything was going. But I didn't get much information from her. All she basically said was they were being kept very busy with training and adjusting well to their new life. I was concerned her email wasn't glowing with how fabulous everything was, but they weren't warning me to cancel everything and stay home, either. So I kept my hopes high and continued to forge ahead with my plans of leaving Seattle behind, and starting my new life in Thailand.

In my last days of preparation, I kept myself crazy busy until the very last minute. The time sped by like a freight train without any brakes. And on January 3, 2008, with the totality of information I had about the resort being derived from two brief phone calls, checking out the website, Monica's email, and a few delayed emails from the management (my future boss eventually apologized for the delay in getting back to me, explaining it was because he had been busy 'putting out some fires' around the resort…again, another potentially deterring detail I chose to ignore), I boarded that big jet plane all by myself, and headed to embark on my new life.

As I relaxed back into my seat, I smiled with excitement thinking about the life-changing adventure ahead of me, albeit, not without trepidation. But in that very moment, I felt bliss. Just sitting there doing nothing felt fantastic. One thing I love about flying is how I'm physically forced to literally do nothing (which is a rare thing for my highly motivated self to ever really 'do'). I decided to watch one of the in-flight movies, and serendipitously, at the end it concluded with the following line:

"When one immerses oneself into a foreign culture, it is a great teacher of one's own culture, one's own life, and one's own self."

Hearing this immediately dissipated my feelings of trepidation. It felt like a message directly from God telling me all was going to be fine. I smiled as I took a deep breath, let my eyes close and my body fall into a deep sleep.

Chapter 3:
Embarking on a New Life
January 2008

My flight from Seattle to Korea was 11 hours, the layover was four, and the flight to Bangkok was six. The final leg of my halfway-across-the-globe journey was a three-hour drive to the city of Hua Hin, my new hometown, totaling the longest journey I'd ever taken in my life, equaling a full 24 hours. I rode in the back of a taxi with my face anxiously pressed against the window attempting to take in the scenery. I had arrived in the middle of the night though, so I couldn't see much of anything. I felt numb – not nervous, but not excited either.

Suddenly, the taxi driver rapidly decelerated from the loud and busy highway and made a sharp left turn down a narrow alleyway. He then came to a halt in front of a four-story, non-descript, white apartment building, with an exact replica located immediately next to it. Along the north side of the alley was a towering, black granite wall. (I presumed this to be the outer boundary of the resort). The wall stretched all the way from the highway down to what I hoped must be the beach.

Feeling a bit apprehensive about the absence of the stunning, swaying flowers and exquisite Buddhist statues I was expecting to see upon arrival, I took a deep breath and thought, _"You can do this Jody!"_ and got out of the car. It was 4 a.m. so the surroundings were empty except for the uniformed, security guard who opened my door. Although he didn't seem to speak any English, he surprised me by greeting me by name. As the taxi driver placed my bags on the curb, I did my best to hopefully pronounce the Thai word for thank you, "Kop khun ka!"

There was nothing warm or inviting about the area in which I was standing. The long granite wall was on one side of me and the two stark buildings plus a parking lot for motorbikes were on the other (motorbikes being the preferred mode of transportation in Thailand). The now smiling security guard helped lighten my load, both literally and figuratively, as he picked up my bags and motioned for me to follow him. We entered into a tiny, shall I say 'mature' looking elevator. After what seemed like a longer journey than that of a ride up to my dad's office on the 44th floor in Seattle, we arrived on the fourth floor and proceeded down a cold, barren hallway. Whoever designed this plain, white apartment building apparently loved the starkness of the outer façade so much they thought extending it to the inner corridors would be a lovely idea. Living in such a lifeless building wasn't exactly what I had envisioned for my new life, at a ritzy health spa on the beach in Thailand.

The security guard opened the door to a room located midway down the barren hallway and smiled as he handed me the key and headed back down to his post. The childlike, whiny voice in my head was begging my adult self to ask my new friend if he wanted to hang around for a while just to keep me company, but my adult self walked inside and shut the door.

"Welcome home Jody!" I said to myself, in an attempt to invite some warmth into my present moment. I looked around...my room was comparable to a two star hotel room. There was a queen size bed, made up with only two white sheets; a wooden four-drawer dresser with a TV on top; a decent sized closet with wooden doors and a small bathroom. I looked at the bare white walls and did my best to think positively. *"Well hey, it's better than an ugly room, I guess."*

Suddenly, my heart skipped a beat as I heard a knock at my door. I opened it and before me stood a Caucasian man in his mid-forties.

"Hi Jody! I'm Victor, your manager. Welcome!"

I stood back, shocked. "How nice to meet you Victor. But, what are you doing awake at 4 a.m.?"

"I wanted to make sure you received a proper welcome as soon as you arrived!"

Thrilled, I shook his hand, "Wow. How very kind of you. Thank you!"

"Well, I'm sure you are tired so I don't want to disturb you any longer. I just wanted to say hello. We will have plenty of time to get caught up later on. Welcome and have a nice sleep."

"Thank you very much Victor! I look forward to getting caught up with you soon!"

I was incredibly touched by his efforts to extend such an unexpected, personal welcome in the middle of the night. I scratched my head feeling a bit overwhelmed with emotions, exhausted from my long journey (having no idea what time clock I should be paying heed to) and wondering if I should start unpacking or just go to bed. I took a deep breath, relaxed, and smiled as I decided to let go of all the dizzying thoughts in my head, flopped myself onto the bed and simply let my head hit the pillow and my body fall into a well deserved, deep sleep.

***

It was Saturday, January 5, 2008. I woke up on the first day of my new life to a knock at the door. I rubbed my eyes, having no idea what time it was, and arose to my feet. Suddenly standing before me was dear Monica, with her beaming smile and loving, wide-open arms. I poured myself into her hug.

"Mooooonnnnnniicaaaaaa!! Hello my dear! What a treat to see your shining face!"

"Hi honey!! Welcome!! Sooooo great to see you too!"

I stood back and surveyed her face, "How is everything going here?!"

"Great. Busy. I have to be at work in five minutes so I can't stay. I wanted to just stop by to give you a big, warm welcome hug. So I will see you later!"

And with that she was gone, as fast as she had appeared. I was happy and sad at the same time. I felt extreme gratitude to start my first day in this foreign country with a familiar face from home though. Apparently, I was lucky to have arrived on a Friday, which gave me the weekend to adjust to the time difference, get settled in, and explore my new hometown. Monica and Dave had arrived on a Wednesday and had been scheduled for meetings first thing Thursday morning. That struck me as a bit of a merciless management decision, so I felt lucky to have the next two days free to settle in.

Given my love for frolicking in the ocean and my sheer exhilaration to be living near a tropical beach, I immediately dug my bathing suit out of my suitcase, got dressed in my summery shorts and a t-shirt, (in January!! I love it!) and headed down the narrow alleyway, straight to the beach.

Ahh! The brilliant sunshine! The glistening water! The balmy breezes! I immediately dove into the ocean and was in heaven. I jumped up and down in the waves with the exuberance of a child. I did back flips, cartwheels, and swam around like a giddy dolphin for an hour or more.

It wasn't until my skin had become deeply wrinkled and prune-like that I decided to get out of the water. I flopped myself down in the sand and became enthralled by the view of the sparkling, sapphire ocean and the cerulean sky before me. I shook my head in disbelief. Given all those years I spent living under the dark skies of Seattle, living on a beach had seemed like an impossible dream....yet there I was, with the magnificence of the ocean now as my backyard, sitting on a beach and living half way around the world in Thailand....Something I would've never imagined for my life!

After my senses were satiated with the glorious sights in front of me, I turned and realized my first glimpse of the resort had been patiently waiting behind me the whole time. I walked up to the towering rock wall and peaked over. I saw a tranquil lap pool with lotus flowers floating along its edge and a balmy, beachside restaurant surrounded by palm trees. Pure elegance to say the least...much better than my plain Jane apartment building, that was for sure! Now this was more like what I had imagined! I couldn't see much else though. The security was so tight at this exclusive resort that I wasn't even allowed on the property until my first day on the job. So this sneak peek certainly whet my appetite to see the rest of the grounds during my official tour, which I was told would be on Monday.

The beach stretched for miles in both directions so after a moment of looking down to the left and right, I just chose a direction and started walking. For as far as I could see, the beach was lined with hotels, fancy resorts, not-so-fancy resorts, elegant private accommodations, not-so-elegant private accommodations, and curious buildings with signs that said 'private property.' Parts of the beach were empty while others were packed with people of all ages, vacationing from around the world. Numerous little food and beverage huts were located all along the beach, with hard-working locals running back and forth, catering to all the vacationing sun worshippers baking themselves on their cushy beach chairs.

The most culturally unique aspect of the beach (and my favorite discovery thus far!) was the many Thai massage stands located about every 50 yards all along the beach. A one-hour massage on a nice little table in the sand was the equivalent of less than ten dollars! My eyes widened with excitement as I walked up to two eager-for-business looking women standing next to their massage tables, shaded by oversized beach umbrellas. One of the women flashed me her innocent smile as she patted her burly hand down on the table. Given her robust arms, I was not sure if I was signing myself up to be pummeled like a piece of meat or delightfully loosened up into a rubber band. Given my adventurous spirit, I fearlessly laid down on the table, excited and ready to experience either option. But thankfully, I enjoyed a blissful hour of having my muscles transformed into supple rubber bands, all the while listening to the symphony of the rolling, ocean waves and my body being cooled by the balmy, tropical breezes.

After my hour of heavenly bliss came to an end, I gave my new best friend a big hug, paid her 250 Thai Baht plus a 100 Baht tip (which in total is the equivalent of a whopping $10... certainly not something I'd ever find at home – and outside on a glorious beach to boot!).

Laying there for an hour in bliss was apparently so physically taxing that the rumbles in my belly loudly informed me it was time to get some food. I continued onward down the beach and stumbled across a whole string of glorious fruit stands! Fresh pineapple, mango, papaya and watermelon were everywhere. The rumbles intensified as if to say, *"Yes! Yes! Get some of each!"* But as I walked along, I soon discovered I had even more options than just fruit. An adorable woman, no more than five-fee tall, had situated herself under her colorful beach umbrella, with a little beach barbecue, and was busy grilling up divinely sweet smelling corn-on-the-cob. A few feet away from her a frail looking older man carried a straw basket. It was overflowing with fresh roasted peanuts. It was so enormous it must have weighed more than he did. Another man carried a long piece of bamboo over his shoulders with a big basket hanging down from each end selling hard boiled eggs...not exactly a snack I expected to find on the beach, but hey, they travel nicely.

I didn't buy any eggs though, and instead exercised what I felt was exceptional restraint and just chose one piece of delicious watermelon, a beautiful mango, and a perfectly grilled corn-on-the-cob. I flopped down in the sand, eager to satiate my hunger…I was in heaven.

As I was happily munching away on my superb snacks in the midst of the hoards of beach-going tourists, I felt like I was at Disneyland (albeit the seaside version). No beach town would be complete without the full menu of water sports equipment for rent, and this town was no exception. There were windsurfers darting here and there; kite boarders proudly demonstrating their mid-air back flips; ridiculous, inflatable, giant hot-dog rides filled with screaming kids being pulled by some tiny boat with an ear-piercing, screechy engine; jet skiers buzzing back and forth; and… pony rides (akin to the out of place hard-boiled egg beach snacks I suppose).

I later learned the jet skiing is actually, officially, not allowed. The very revered King of Thailand lives in this town and does not approve of the noise pollution they create. Quite apparently however, the rule was not enforced that day.

I finished my snacks and continued on. I stumbled upon the Hilton, the tallest hotel on the beach so far. I was intrigued by the idea of checking out the view of the town from the restaurant I noticed on the roof. I passed by the dolphin shaped swimming pool, with its energized sport fans sitting in between the mini dolphin waterfall statues along its edge, yelling out their cheers of encouragement and praise to their friends playing an intense game of water-volleyball, and continued to the hotel's entrance.

The lobby was stunningly beautiful. The setting was elegant and spacious, adorned with Asian style seating areas brimming with cushy red silk pillows, colorful flowers bursting out of porcelain vases, and a tropical fish pond which stretched all the way from inside the lobby, underneath the entirely glass, eastern wall and then transformed itself into a waterfall outside. I headed toward the elevators and was treated to a ride in one I could gleefully describe using a vast array of pleasing adjectives, other than 'mature looking,' and headed up to the roof.

Wow! This 'little beach town' was much bigger than I had expected! Development stretched from the beach in every direction, and then out for miles until butting up against the foothills of lush, green mountains. Mountains?! I didn't expect this town would be near mountains and I certainly didn't expect I would be able to go hiking in a beach town! I joyfully thought to myself, *"I've got it all! Ocean and mountains!"*

I headed back down to the main lobby and asked the concierge for a map of the hiking trails. The gracious local behind the desk smiled at me as he kindly explained hiking is not part of Thai culture. The temperature outside is usually so hot that most people choose to stay inside, or at least in the shade whenever possible. I learned most Thais would never go on a vigorous hike simply for amusement's sake, be it day or night. Those that live in the rural areas of Thailand are largely engaged in farming. The luxury of time, or even the interest in hiking does not exist there. Alternatively, those that live in the metropolis of Bangkok and have adopted the fast-paced, western way of life, find their likely form of exercise in your typical gym, heavily air-conditioned, of course.

Being from rainy and gray Seattle, the thought of deliberately staying *inside* when the sun was shining brightly *outside* was a thought that had never before crossed my mind. After digesting my disappointment in the lack of hiking trails among the gorgeous, lush green hills, I made a meager attempt to smile at this nice man for my first, mini lesson in Thai culture, and headed back outside, into the sunshine.

Although the Hilton marked the location of the center of town, my hunger for exploration had already been fully satiated so I decided to save that adventure for tomorrow. I headed back to the beach and enjoyed my journey back home, indulging my bare feet being tickled by the rolling ocean waves and my toes being massaged by the fine grains of sand.

Upon returning to my new home, there was a note taped to my door from Dave and Monica informing me they had gone out to dinner with our boss and were sorry to have missed me. I hated missing the opportunity to get caught up with them and to connect face to face with my boss beyond the 4 a.m. introduction we had the night before. There was also a 'P.S.' urging me to get a cell phone when I went to town tomorrow so on future occasions they could contact me. (Before leaving Seattle, I was exhilarated by the thought of living my life without one…I guess I was going to have to rethink that idea.) Still adjusting to the jet lag, I was feeling pretty wiped out, so I

34

decided to just head straight to bed.

***

Sunday, January 6, 2008. Day two of my new life in Thailand. After sleeping in and spending the rest of my morning unpacking and getting settled, I set out to venture into the sprawling town, which I had only seen from the rooftop of the Hilton the day before. Even though it was Sunday, Dave and Monica were still busy with another day of their three weeks of training. The resort life takes no note of weekends since everyday of the week is full of guests needing attention, most notably on Saturdays and Sundays. They told me it would actually be difficult for us to have much time to spend together outside of work since each of us would have a different day off.

Having a sense of community around me is essential wherever I live, but establishing a new one there in Hua Hin was going to prove to be a challenging endeavor, to say the least. For starters, not speaking Thai certainly wasn't going to help with making friends among the locals. As for other foreigners in town, at least from what I had noticed during my adventuring along the beach the day before, most seemed to be only short-term tourists.

I exited the apartment building and headed to town. When I was back home in Seattle, I had envisioned the journey from this 'World-Renown, Exclusive, Luxury Resort for the Rich and Famous' to the center of town to be along a quaint little road that meandered through a beautiful setting of swaying palm trees and lush, green vegetation. Well, as I approached the main road, my nice little idyllic vision was swiftly replaced with its antithetical reality, as I concurrently realized why the towering black granite wall encircling the resort was so exceedingly high.

As the narrow alleyway from my apartment building jutted me out onto the main road, I suddenly found myself walking along the edge of a frenzied freeway. There were two lanes of traffic traveling in each direction absolutely packed with swarms of buzzing motorbikes, racing automobiles, space-age looking trucks full of dirt and construction material (there seemed to be as many new hotels going up along that road as there were existing ones), and the most gaudy looking monster-sized, two-story tour buses, painted in a dizzying depiction of cartoon characters and all lit up with neon lights, you could ever imagine.

The only saving grace of the next 30 minutes I spent walking into town was my love for exercise, and thank goodness I have good knees. As I carefully navigated my way along the sidewalk, I wished I had put on my hiking boots instead of mere flip-flops. The drop off to the curb in some places was about a foot high, and the fractured pieces of cement and the resulting crevices along its surface required my full attention to circumvent falling into one of the holes, exposing the ground below. In the moments along the smoother sections, I was able to look up and notice my surroundings, which were basically the facades of all the apartment buildings and hotels I had seen from the beach the day before.

Once I reached the center of this new hometown of mine, nothing had changed. The unpleasant ambience of the frenzied freeway was interrupted only by the stoplights located at each end of town. As for the scenery, the chain of apartments and hotels had morphed into a seemingly endless chain of restaurants and shops. Suddenly before me appeared the fingerprints of Americans living right there in this little, Asian city of Hua Hin. A huge shopping mall stood massively in front of me with, who do you think proudly owning the grand, front and center location? Starbucks! I couldn't believe it. So much for being exposed to the foreign culture in Thailand. It seems the materialistic ways of the western world have planted their seeds of over-consumption even there in that small beachside town. But, I must admit, I couldn't help myself. Little pangs of homesickness led me straight inside.

I ordered a vanilla latte and held it with two hands (to keep me warm amidst the blasting cold air conditioning…not exactly as if I were in cold and rainy Seattle, but I enjoyed the temporary mental trip back home). EVERYTHING looked exactly as if I were in any other Starbucks in America….the menu, the display case, the tables and chairs. (So if any of you have wanted to travel to Thailand but fear the withdrawals of your Starbucks addiction, fear no more.) I took several photos to

36

email to my sister, Kristin, who happens to work in the international division of Starbucks at its world headquarters in Seattle. I couldn't wait to show her what I had discovered all the way over on the other side of the globe.

I continued meandering through 'the mall.' From a single vantage point I saw a Haagen-Dazs, a Dairy Queen, a Baskin and Robbins, and a Swenson's ice cream shop. The neighboring businesses were good ole' Kentucky Fried Chicken, McDonald's, Burger King, Pizza Hut, and The Sizzler. My homesickness quickly abated and I actually started feeling sick. I was embarrassed and saddened by the gaudy display of what is seen as a corner stone of the American culture....artery clogging, nutrient deficient, health suppressing fast food.

However, one of life's many paradoxes is that when traveling, similarities found among the foreign culture can be a turn off, while at the same time be welcoming. Before leaving home, I feverishly stocked up on my favorite toiletry items (and paid dearly for the extra weight at the airport) and used them as if they were gold, fearing the day when it all ran out. As I continued through the mall, I came across a drug store exactly like those back home. I'm not sure what I was expecting to find in terms of where I would buy my toothpaste, shampoo, soap, body lotion, etc., but regardless, I was pleasantly surprised at this particular familiar sight.

There it all was: Neutrogena lotion, Colgate toothpaste, Oral-B toothbrushes, Tampax...it sounds so silly but I can't tell you what a relief it was to see familiar toiletry brands, albeit not my most favorite natural and organic ones, but comfortingly familiar nonetheless. It also made me realize how vast these companies have spread their wings around the globe, and I was astonished by the incomprehensible thought of how much income they must generate on a daily basis.

I continued on and passed ever more familiar brand names...Adidas, Esprit, Lacoste, Body Glove, Levi, Lee... I came upon a shop where I could buy a cell phone, but my purist aspirations of living as I did just a mere decade ago, free from the dependence on a cell phone, had me walk straight by. I headed up to the top floor. What do you think I discovered up there? A Buddhist meditation room? An authentic Thai silk shop? A hallway bestowed with local art? Nope. I found a food

37

court, a bowling alley, and a Major Cineplex movie theater, boasting seven screens and hoards of movie goers chomping away on extra buttered popcorn and over-sized bags of M&M's. I couldn't help but wonder if all of these culturally rich Thais around me…with their beautifully strong foundation in the importance of family, living in harmony with nature, and enjoyment in a simple way of life…things I've always had a strong desire for…if they were now living a life hungry for this bright and flashy, western way of existence? For the very unhealthy, fast-paced life I was excited to get *away* from? I couldn't help but wonder…are we humans always hungry for what we don't have? Does what our neighbor has always seem more appetizing than what is on our own plate?

I was hungry…for food. I searched until I found a restaurant that had a menu strictly in Thai. I had no idea what I ordered, except I knew it wasn't a greasy American burger and fries…and I savored every bite.

After satisfying my appetite for food, my hunger to continue to explore town led me back outside to see what else was awaiting my discovery. Obviously, Thai food restaurants were ubiquitous, some modest looking and packed with natives, while others were all brightly lit up with flashy decorations and exclusively filled with tourists (and probably charged ten times more for the exact same items that could be found at the local spots). Souvenir shops filled with Buddhas of all sizes were equally ubiquitous, as were Thai massage shops (offering the same remarkable price equivalent to just $10 for an hour massage as I had found on the beach the day before), shops full of Thai silk pillows and scarves, Asian art stores full of paintings of Buddha and beautifully hand carved furniture…as well as tailor shops with eager looking gentleman awaiting outside to take the measurements of any willing passerby, mini versions of the drug store I had found in the mall, more ice cream shops, more fast food restaurants, international restaurants catering to any vacationer from around the world who might happen to be hungry for a familiar flavor from home, clothing stores, banks, foreign currency exchange windows, ATMs…I was just taking it all in. Not exactly the quaint, tropical beach side town I had envisioned, but a mind-enriching experience of foreign culture nonetheless.

As for the type of people whom I saw in town, as I had expected from my experience the day before on the beach, they consisted of all types of tourists, from the backpacker type to the high-class, and representing every corner of the globe. Yet among this diversity stood out a particular type of couple. Everywhere I looked, there were parades of older white men walking hand in hand with beautiful, and usually very young, Thai women. The men apparently came from all over the world. As I walked through the streets, I heard accents from Australia, America, Canada, Germany, England, Sweden, Holland...

At first I became immediately uncomfortable with this whole scene, struggling to digest that this whole prostitution thing (if that's what I could call it) was just a way of life here. I later learned this trend apparently started after the Vietnam War and has exploded ever since. I couldn't help but wonder if the women were treated well. Did they feel trapped? Had they been together for a mere 24 hours? Or did they have a house with two young children at home? Did they consider each other as friends? Were they happy? Or were his lustful desires and her desperation for money the only thing feeding their mutual existence?

The more I thought about it however, (and believe me, my thoughts about it endlessly churned over and over... putting myself in his shoes...trying on her perspective...throughout my entire time in Thailand) I realized he gets to spend his time with an extraordinarily gorgeous woman whom he'd probably never find at home, and she gets to hang out with a relative sugar daddy, who likely dissolves her concerns about money and maybe even gives her some extra cash for her family. When I took this perspective, I was able to accept it as yet another one of the millions of ways we humans choose to satisfy our needs in life. Needless to say, it wasn't exactly the type of community I was hungry to become a part of though.

Chapter 4:
Truly Heavenly Job Training
January 2008

My weekend came to an end and Monday arrived, which was quite a historic day given it was my first day working with my long-awaited official title of Dr. Jody Alison Stanislaw, albeit not at a typical medical clinic by any far stretch of the imagination but nonetheless, with the title I'd dreamed of since I was seven years old. My job at the resort was going to entail administering health intakes for all incoming guests and 'prescribing' a personalized schedule designed to best fit their purpose for coming to the resort, such as to lower their blood pressure or cholesterol, lose weight, de-stress from their crazy non-stop life styles, recover from any array of emotional trauma, or just enjoy a little rest and relaxation. Throughout their stay, I would be checking in with them to give them personalized health advice based on whatever flavor of dis-ease they presented with, which could include a counseling session or two. Some clients would stay for three days, to just get a little taste of what this famous spa was all about. Others would stay for a month or more, perhaps to disappear from whatever it was at home that drove them away in the first place. But the majority stayed for about a week or two.

I arrived at the human resources office at 9 a.m. (located on the third floor of the other stark building adjacent to my 'home') and was welcomed by a kind looking woman from London.

"Hi Jody! I'm Susan, the head of HR. Nice to meet you and welcome!"

I shook her hand, "Thank you Susan. It was quite a long journey to arrive here so I'm very happy to finally be here."

She smiled, "Well, we are happy to have you too. Your department is terribly understaffed, so everyone is excited to have a new team member on board. Victor, your manager, is busy with meetings at the head office in Bangkok for a few days so you won't be meeting him until some time next week, most likely. But we've got a lot to cover in the meantime."

Susan sat me down in her office and presented me with

the 'Welcome New Employee – Here is What You Need to Know' PowerPoint presentation. And this is what I learned: The resort has security guards at every possible entrance. The grounds are strictly closed to the general public. Outside guests are only allowed in with advanced approval. Photos are strictly prohibited. Computers, cell phones, and PDA's are only allowed in the guest rooms and are prohibited in all public areas because, "Our resort is all about embodying the utmost in health, wellness, relaxation, and rejuvenation."

They take health and wellness very seriously …and they should at a price tag of $800-$1500 per day! But hey, that includes a daily massage, three organic meals, group fitness and yoga classes, meditation sessions, and a few extras based on their particular health goal. And if the guests are hungry for any other of the hundreds of treatments on the health and wellness menu? No problem, as long as they dig a bit deeper into their pockets.

The resort houses a full physiotherapy division for those needing help with bad backs, shoulders, knees, recovery from recent surgery, etc., as well as a full fitness staff of personal trainers, yoga instructors, Thai kick boxing masters and more for those coming to improve their fitness. An entire team of holistic healers are at each guest's disposal, such as meditation practitioners, Reiki masters, an EFT therapist (which stands for Emotional Freedom Technique and involves tapping on acupressure points throughout the body to release unhealthy emotional patterns), Chi Nei Tsang therapists (apparently some sort of Asian organ balancing stomach massage), and breathing technique classes for those coming for physical and emotional healing. Finally, being in Thailand, over 30 Thai massage therapists trained in a wide range of heavenly massage techniques are readily available to serve.

On my off hours, I would be allowed to use the gym, attend any of the classes, take a dip in the indoor pool, or relax in the hot tub or steam room. The only activities I would not be allowed to do were to swim in or layout by the outdoor pool nor eat at the guest restaurants. My mind started buzzing with excitement…until I pulled myself back into reality and reminded myself I wasn't there as a guest, but as a staff person. Since my department was understaffed, I was informed I would be working six very full days a week. But I figured all my excitement of living in a foreign culture plus the unique experience of working at a health resort with clients from all over the world would make up for the sacrifice of not having a two-day weekend.

Before arriving, I was optimistic I'd be able to eat the same healthy food that the guests ate. Well, I like to aim high with my visions in life, but in this case my aim was apparently a little too high. When I asked, Susan informed me I would most certainly *not* be dining at the resort. Staff meals were served outside the walls of the resort, in the staff 'canteen' located one floor down from the HR office and next to the modest staff gym. My meals would consist of all the glorious flavors of authentic Thai cuisine...lemongrass soups, coconut curries, spicy hot fried noodles...albeit cafeteria style. Three meals a day was a part of the employment contract of all 400 of the staff at the resort so the food was prepared in pots and pans of sizes suitable for feeding an army and sat under heat lamps for hours...I wasn't exactly thrilled to learn this. Given my status as a health nut, I was relieved to learn there would also be a full fresh salad bar at every meal, as well as at least four different hot food options...thank goodness.

The power point presentation came to an end. Susan stood up and motioned for me to do the same. "Jody, I'm going to take you over to the resort now for a tour because it will be your responsibility over these next three weeks of your training to show up at the appropriate department at the appropriate time."

I bounced up out of my seat like a child who was just told it was time for recess, "Wonderful! I've been dreaming about what the inside of the resort looks like ever since I received that first initial job posting over email, which seems like ages ago! I am so excited to finally be able to see this place in its real-life, full-color glory!"

We exited the building, walked down the alleyway, along the outside of the granite wall which encircled the entire resort, only momentarily walked along the edge of the frenzied freeway, quickly took a right turn past the security gate, and at last, arrived at the grand entrance. After visualizing for months what this world-famous hideaway for the rich and famous would look like, I was at last treated to my first visual taste of this tremendously posh resort. In a word...Amazing!

My first vista was filled with stunning arrangements of tropical flowers, bursting with color in a beautiful outdoor lobby, surrounded by picturesque, swaying palm tress. The lobby over hung a large pond full of tropical fish whose bright colors were sparkling on the water's surface from the beaming rays of sunshine flooding through the palm fronds. Susan informed me that the entire check-in procedure is carried out while guests relax on luscious lounge chairs, sip on chilled lemongrass tea, and enjoy the picturesque view. Once their butler arrives, they are whisked away in a golf cart and taken to their room, as their visual appetites continue to be fed along the way. Already stunned by the beauty I had seen thus far, I eagerly jumped into a golf cart with Susan and embarked on the rest of the tour.

The path began with a ride along an elegant wooden bridge stretching over the tropical fish pond beaming with its brightly-colored orange and yellow fish. Then as we wound past various private Thai pavilions built in classic Asian style, a 300-year-old banyan tree appeared around the corner which took my breath away with its magnitude and magnificence.

"That is the most stunning tree I have ever seen!"

Susan nodded knowingly, "Let me take you over to it Jody so you can experience its magic when you stand right next to it."

We parked the golf cart and walked right up to the tree – the most colossal I had ever seen in my life. I lightly placed both of my hands on its trunk and felt a rush of energy throughout my body. It made the hair on my arms literally stand on end.

Susan joined me as she placed her hands on the colossal trunk, "Jody, if you are ever having a bad day or just feeling sluggish, all you have to do is come over to this tree and you'll get filled up with enough positive energy to put you right back on track."

I was in awe and totally impressed, to say the least.

We got back into our little golf cart and arrived at the epicenter of the resort, which was the location of the private yoga studio, the state-of-the-art fitness center, the indoor bathing pavilion (with its elegant lap pool, Jacuzzi, steam room, and refreshing cold plunge), the private Thai massage huts, the quaint arts and crafts room, the sparkling cooking class kitchen, and the elegant Thai silk boutique. I had to start telling myself the following mantra in order to keep my feet on the ground, *"I am a staff member. I am a staff member. I am a staff member..."* We parked the cart next to an ancient stone carving of Buddha and continued down the elegant marble staircase into the spa area.

There were so many hallways, with so many treatment rooms, I was glad to be in the seasoned hands of Susan's guidance. Without her by my side, I might have wandered down one of the floral-scent infused hallways, become lost and confused in one of the elegant therapy rooms, and fallen upon one of the cushy massage tables, never to been seen again. But luckily (or not) that did not happen. As Susan guided me along the sparkling hallways, she explained to me that there are 57 treatment rooms, which is also the same number of guest rooms, making it the only spa in the world to have a one to one ratio of treatment rooms to guest rooms. (I couldn't help but wonder if I'd actually ever have clients, or if they would just be receiving massages all day long.)

Susan had to excuse herself to take a phone call so I sat down on one of the elegant, silk cushioned sofas in the spa and opened up the extensive spa menu guide, which was comparable in size to the yellow pages directory of New York city! The list of treatments was endless. Hungry for a massage? Well, you'd have to choose between a classic Thai massage, a hot stone massage, a six hands massage ('six hands' means having three people massage you simultaneously), a deep tissue massage, a lymph drainage massage, a Japanese flotation massage, the luxurious hand and foot massage, and the jet-lag recovery massage...just to name a few. *"I am a staff member. I am a staff member. I am a staff member."*

The guests also have their choice of a long, luxurious list of facials...the oxygenating facial, the rejuvenating facial, the clarifying facial, the rebalancing facial, or the very popular anti-aging facial (or they could choose all of them, spread out one day at a time...and apparently that is a popular choice as well). For those guests looking for a more unique spa experience, they could try the flotation therapy, the jet blitz therapy, the chakra balancing, the sacred crystal healing, the luxurious hand and foot ritual. The list went on and on.

For guests looking for a quick-fix weight loss solution,

their options would be to try the slimming body treatment, the hip and thigh treatment, and/or the accelerated body-shaping machine. (No need for my mantra here. With my medical training, I couldn't imagine I'd ever be able to authentically recommend any of these gimmicky treatments to any of my overweight patients.)

Susan returned. We continued through the elegantly winding pathways of the grand spa area, passed by the dramatic, tropical floral arrangements at the entrance, and continued onward with the tour. As if intuitively aware my senses were approaching overload, Susan gave me a quick walk-by of all of the other various departments... the fitness department, the physiotherapy department, the hydrotherapy department, the dermatology department, the restaurant and kitchen...before leading me to the area in which I would be working, the holistic health and wellness department. We walked into a room overflowing with sunshine beaming in from a huge window, which stretched from floor to ceiling. There was an elegant wooden office table and chair in the center, and a bookshelf decorated with stunning purple orchids against the wall. "And finally Jody, this is your office. Welcome!"

Thoughts of overwhelming gratitude flooded my body as I concurrently juxtaposed the stunning setting before me with a vision of a little cramped and dark office, with a heater on full blast, in some crowded clinic located under the gray skies of Seattle.

I felt as if I had died and gone to heaven.

✳✳✳

Tuesday: day two of job training. I met Susan at her office at 9 a.m. and she handed me my schedule for the next three weeks. "Jody, your clients are going to ask you all sorts of questions, not only about health, but also about everything and anything that goes on here at the resort. They are going to view you not just as their health consultant but also as their 'go-to' person for questions regarding their stay with us. Thus, over the next three weeks, we are going to make sure you have a thorough knowledge of everything that goes on here at the resort."

I examined my schedule, which was designed on a grid filled with different colored blocks for every hour of the day, each color representing time spent in a different department. It was packed full of introductions....to the fitness staff, the physical therapy team, the holistic health practitioners, the spa therapists, the chef and kitchen staff... and then lots of other 'training.'

During the initial health consultation with my clients, upon their arrival, part of my job would be to 'prescribe' to them how to get the most out of their stay, given their desired health goals. So my job training included *personally* experiencing everything the resort had to offer! My 'training schedule' for the next three weeks was thus filled with all sorts of heavenly massages, Classic Asian Reflexology, Chinese Acupuncture, Chi Nei Tsang (the Asian organ balancing stomach massage), Reiki, an array of all the decadent facials, craniosacral (a type of energy/physical rebalancing treatment), and more. And please note, as the guests were paying hundreds of dollars for these treatments, not only would I be receiving them at no cost, but I'd be getting *paid* to receive them!

So hmm, let me describe to you what Tuesday, my first official day of 'training,' entailed....The day started with a scrumptious, super healthy, poolside breakfast buffet, (I of course must experience what the guests will be eating too), consisting of every fresh tropical fruit you could dream of. There were perfect pineapple wedges, proud papaya slices, mouth-watering mango slices, gorgeous guava, delicious dragon fruit (in case you've never heard of this one before, its outer skin is a stunning pink with these dagger-like leaves standing tall at the top pointing out like blazing fire, yet the inside consists of white flesh with tiny black dots, resembling a poppy seed muffin), red rose apples (a humble looking fruit with juicy white flesh), and an array of other stunningly sweet gifts of nature I'd never encountered in my life before that morning.

There was also a delectable raw seed and nut bread accompanied by fresh mango and pineapple spread; a rainbow of healthy cereals with a choice of organic soy milk, almond milk, or regular milk; and at the end of the line, just in case my plate wasn't already full enough, stood a smiling chef awaiting my list of desired ingredients so he could make me a perfect custom-made omelet.

Given my love of food, I had to try a bit of everything (as of course was the prudent thing to do, in order to get the most out of my 'training'). So I smiled warmly and said, "Good morning! Spinach, onions and tomatoes, please."

After breakfast, it was time for some serious work...stretch class, fit ball class, body awareness class... Then a delectable lunch made from vegetables freshly picked from the resort's organic garden, followed by a magical massage, an amazing facial which included a wrinkle smoothing laser treatment (not that I have any wrinkles at the age of 35 though, of course), and lastly, an hour relaxing on a table in the care of the electrifying hands of an energy healer. *"I am a staff member. I am a staff member. I am a staff member..."* It was quite the arduous task to ensure I wasn't getting too attached to the life of my 'training' schedule, but needless to say, I was in heaven and ate up every minute of it!

And what was the reward for my stressful first day of 'job training,' you might ask? Well, let me tell you. It was an absolutely delectable four-course dinner, beachside, of course. I was placed at the communal table, where those who arrive solo are able to mingle with other solo guests. The people who come to this exclusive resort, as you could guess, are rich and famous types. Some I was informed are even kings and queens, or royalty of some other kind. Sitting at my table that evening was a vibrant man from Egypt, a lovely woman from England, this Australian man who radiated peace, a Russian woman beaming with enthusiasm, a high-strung Frenchman, and myself...the intriguing woman from America, of course.

Our meal began with a cleansing liquid elixir of ginger, honey, and lemon juice, followed by the most delicious pumpkin soup I'd ever encountered. Next was a beautiful salad, full of an array of vegetables and edible flowers brightly representing every color of the rainbow. Then the entrée arrived, which was an amazing concoction of freshly caught scallops, prawns, and squid scrumptiously paired with julienned vegetables perfectly matched with the signature Thai flavors of zesty lime, refreshing lemongrass, and spicy hot pepper.

As I ate, I truly did not want to talk for fear of

distracting myself from being fully present to the delicious flavors contained in every bite. So I put my typical talkative self on the back burner, and just enjoyed listening to my companions from around the world. (And thus also succeeded in withholding the fact I was just a measly staff person, not an actual guest. As my smile beamed in between each heavenly bite of the five-star cuisine, I thoroughly enjoyed acting as if.)

The main topic of conversation centered around each person's personal experience at the resort...if it was their first or fifth time; if their goal was to energize their tired body or give themselves a break from the stress of their daily life; if their favorite activity was an intense Thai Kick-boxing session, a relaxing hot stone massage, or a health and nutrition overhaul including a personalized take-home plan (which of course, unbeknownst to my dining companions, would be done by yours truly).

Dessert arrived. I don't know how this was possible but it was the most amazingly decadent 'healthy' chocolate cake I'd ever tasted. I didn't want the night to ever end! I soaked in every minute because that meal was the last 'training' session I had which included dining with the guests. (From then on I'd be eating the Thai food in the staff canteen, albeit cafeteria style, yet prepared for me three times a day without me having to lift a finger...I guess I couldn't feel too bad for myself.)

I hadn't exactly started using my doctoral training yet, but could you blame me?! Once I finally pried myself away from the glorious ambience of the expansive outdoor restaurant...with its colorful floral arrangements on the white-linen covered tables, the fragrant flowers raining down from the surrounding trees, the view overlooking the serene lap pool with its floating lotus flowers, the sights of the glistening ocean, the soothing warm ocean breeze... I trudged my way back to my lifeless stark white apartment room and headed to bed, in preparation for my 6 a.m. yoga class and lots more strenuous 'training' the following day.

✳✳✳

Day two of 'job training' arrived. As I entered the yoga

studio at 5:55 a.m., I looked around at the others whom had arrived before me, already patiently perched on their yoga mats. I greeted them with a smile and some of my typical Jody exuberance, "Good morning!"

I couldn't help but wonder what the story was behind each face. Were they born rich and surrounded by a life of lavish abundance? Or was their childhood so destitute it lit a fire inside of them to create a multimillion-dollar enterprise and resultantly suppressed every memory of their penniless past? Or perhaps, as I was now patiently perched on my own yoga mat, I would be stretching and twisting for the next hour alongside a prince or a princess.

As the class began and we were directed to close our eyes and focus our attention on our breath, I couldn't help but realize the common metaphorical phrase 'to live like a queen' was exactly what I was doing! I was living exactly as queens have actually lived, and in exactly the same place as they have been (for at least a week or two, anyway). As the class went on, I metaphorically put a crown atop my head and smiled as I, Queen Jo-Dee, from the glorious land of Sea-Attle, elongated to the right, twisted to the left, downward and upward dogged, inhaled deeply and exhaled fully.

Afterward, I spent an hour floating weightless in my own private salt-water pool surrounded by floating flower blossoms, glowing candles, and the sounds of soft sensual music. Next, it was 90 minutes with a Chinese medicine expert having my 'chi' adjusted via the placement of ten acupuncture needles around my body, followed by two hours of being stretched and massaged during a sampling of this country's signature Thai massage. *"I am a staff member. I am a staff member. I am a staff member..."*

Next came an hour experiencing Chi Nei Tsang, that Asian organ balancing stomach massage (although awkward at times to have someone poking their fingers into my abdomen, I enjoyed knowing it was intended to improve digestion). Then there was an hour I spent rotating between a relaxing herb infused sauna and a refreshingly cool plunge into a pool covered in rose petals (not exactly something I needed 'training' in, but I appreciated the thoroughness of my schedule). Finally, there was, of course, a much needed 30-minute nap on a hot water bed in the spa's 'relaxation room.'

Now, a relaxation room at a dentist's office, or even next to the coffee break room at one's work would certainly be an apropos location for a 'relaxation room.' But to have a 'relaxation room' at a spa struck me as a bit redundant; akin to if there was perhaps a special 'floral' room at a botanical garden.

Anyway, as another day of 'training' came to an end and I laid my body down upon my bed, I delightfully reminisced about the twists and turns that had occurred throughout my life which somehow lead me to arrive at this moment of my existence. *"Am I really living in Thailand? Is my first job as Dr. Jody Stanislaw really at a ritzy health spa for the rich and famous? Did I really get paid today for having luxurious spa treatments all day?"* I couldn't help but be in awe about the fact that today, it really wasn't a metaphor…today I had truly lived as a QUEEN!

Day 2:
Be Compassionate,
Especially with Yourself

August 2008

I awoke to the 6 a.m. bell and man, did my mind have a thing or two to say about it!

"Shit Jody, you never wake up this early! Today is going to suck! You're going to be fighting to stay awake all day. You'll probably fall asleep right in the middle of meditating and totally start snoring and make a fool of yourself, not to mention, completely bother all the other meditators who are actually serious about being here and probably love getting up this early. You are such a sloth. I can't believe how late you usually sleep. Serves you right to feel like crap this morning given what a lazy ass you normally are."

Without all the typical distractions of daily life, it was disturbing to me to realize how cruel the voice in my head could be. My ability to simply observe and not actually believe my thoughts luckily kicked in. I shifted my attention away from the negative rant in my head and instead toward observing my breath, using my mantra.

*"Breathe in. Breathe out. Breathe in. Breathe out.
Breath in. Breathe out..."*

I stepped down from my bunk and anxiously headed to the bathroom, as a voice in my head was trying to get my attention regarding how annoyed it was to have to wait in line for the toilet.

*"Breathe in. Breathe out. Breathe in. Breathe out.
Breath in. Breathe out..."*

I got dressed and headed to the meditation session as a faint cry to get back in bed was desperately trying to get my attention.

*"Breathe in. Breathe out. Breathe in. Breathe out.
Breath in. Breathe out..."*

51

I sat down and sensed a rant coming on about how long it took me to find a comfortable position for meditating compared to the others around me.

"Breathe in. Breathe out. Breathe in. Breathe out.
Breath in. Breathe out..."

I closed my eyes and shortly thereafter, the 6:30 a.m. bell rang to officially mark the beginning of the day's first mediation session, as my mind was adding up how many hours it would be until I could go back to sleep.

"Breathe in. Breathe out. Breathe in. Breathe out.
Breath in. Breathe out..."

Suddenly, I started crying. It was as if the little girl inside myself couldn't hold back her tears any longer. This overwhelming feeling of sadness came bubbling up and yet I did my best to stay as silent as possible. It felt like a levy had broken inside of me. The energy in my body went from feeling tight and constrained, to flowing and open, in an unexpectedly, pleasant way. I immediately became lost in my thoughts.

"Where did this come from? What is this about? Should I keep crying or force myself to stop? Is this a good thing? Is this a sign I am releasing stuck emotions I've suppressed since who knows when? Or is this just my immature reaction to getting up early?"

I was truly taken aback. In addition to stepping back from one's thoughts and finding peace from observing them instead of believing them, another core teaching of Buddhism, which Goenka touched on in the video from the night before, is to *have compassion for all living things, especially yourself.* A quote I've always loved, which dates back to over 2,000 years ago, acknowledges the importance of this teaching: *"Be kind, for everyone you meet is fighting a hard battle."*

My mind was flustered with this upsurge of emotions yet I luckily tapped into applying this other teaching. I did my best to let go of searching for answers to my whirling questions and instead filled myself with compassion; compassion for the fact that for whatever reason, my body felt the need to cry.

*"Breathe in. Compassion. Breathe out. Compassion. Breathe in.
Compassion. Breathe out. Compassion..."*

This new mantra became my sacred companion for the
rest of the day. Tears continued to roll down my cheeks on and
off as the hours crawled by. I wanted to get lost in an endless
debate about what this bubbling up of sadness was all about.
There was a loud voice wanting to underscore this experience as
proof of what a depressed and lonely person I was. But the
compassionate part of myself decided to simply trust I needed to
let tears out for whatever reason, and allowed myself to do so.

The justification my mind came up with over lunch was
that throughout years of dealing with the major challenges in my
life....the complexities of living with divorced parents; the
immense, daily responsibilities of managing diabetes; my, at
times, tumultuous relationship with food; and the insatiable ache
of loneliness seemingly eternally present in my heart...there were
plenty of times when feeling my sadness about these issues and
letting it out was not possible. Thus, now, given I had nothing
but time to sit with myself, all of these unprocessed emotions
were finally being allowed to be released. Who knows if that was
truly the answer but it was sufficient enough to satiate my mind's
hunger to find 'the answer' for why I was experiencing a
constant stream of tears, and to more or less put an end to the
annoying debate in my head, which had been raging all morning.

*"Breathe in. Compassion. Breathe out. Compassion. Breathe in.
Compassion. Breathe out. Compassion..."*

During our lunch break, I decided to take a walk around
the property. The landscape was rather barren. There were low
growing bushes scattered here and there and a few palm trees,
with some brown rolling hills in the distance. As I wandered
about, I suddenly seemed to only notice things in pairs...two
palm trees swaying next to each other, two birds flying through
the sky, two clouds floating along next to each other...

This experience served to open the floodgates of my
seemingly eternal longing and ache in my heart to find a man to
share my life with. After the short time-out from fighting with
my tears after lunch, I found myself smack back in the middle of

my own personal rainstorm. Sitting on the ground, I curled myself up in a ball and let the tears stream down my face. The ache in my heart had ballooned into a stabbing, sharp pain which radiated throughout my entire chest.

When reading on the retreat's website before arriving, I was informed to be prepared for experiencing deep emotional states which otherwise are suppressed by the activities of everyday life. Well, sure enough, there I was in the middle of experiencing exactly what I had been warned about.

As I sat there with my tears, I practiced not being overtaken by the agonizing emotions behind them and instead, decided to react as a compassionate witness to myself. This was an approach taught to me by my fabulous aunt Mary. I closed my eyes and imagined what she would say to me in that moment if she were sitting right there next to me.

"Only love heals, Jody. Harsh self-judgments and telling yourself to 'get over it' just suppress painful emotions and don't allow them to be released, nor allow full resolution of the initial hurt. Don't fall into the pain and let it overtake you though. Take a step back from your sadness and imagine you are a compassionate observer of yourself. This allows your emotions to be released but without you getting lost within their storm. You can trust they will naturally subside, without seemingly but ineffectively pushing them away. It is not your job to stop them as much as it is to be loving and compassionate to yourself for the pain you are experiencing."

I took a deep breath and did my best to apply my aunt Mary's wisdom...to allow my tears to flow, but to not let my sadness turn into a paralyzing storm of self-pity and anger. I consciously let go of my ingrained habit of getting lost in analyzing and judging myself for what I was experiencing and spent the entire rest of the day practicing being a compassionate observer instead...

"Breathe in. Compassion. Breathe out. Compassion. Breathe in. Compassion. Breathe out. Compassion..."

Chapter 5:
A Lesson in Letting Go
February 2008

There are about 400 staff members employed at the resort, comprised of the upper management team, the human resources staff, the food and beverage team, the holistic health experts (my team), the fitness staff, the spa therapists (over 40 of them), the physical therapists (whom I heard are phenomenal...chronic persistent low back pain often magically disappears after just a session or two), housekeeping, front desk, maintenance and engineering, grounds keepers, security guards, and the laundry people. About 98 percent of my coworkers were Thai. Obviously, those that interact with the guests can speak at least a bit of English (some better than others of course) but often, even when they spoke English, I found it challenging to understand them. So in those cases, I started relying on my charade skills.

Case in point: After returning home from yet another strenuous day of 'job training' sometime during week two or three, I miraculously found the energy within myself to do some laundry. (Impressive, I know.) My pile of dirty clothes had grown way beyond a feasible hand washing size for my tiny bathroom sink. So, I gathered my things and headed down to the laundromat on the ground floor of the staff building. I looked around for the self-serve machines, but none were to be found. My heart dropped when all I saw were countless, gargantuan, commercial sized machines, filled with laundry from seemingly every department throughout the entire resort. I stood there for a few minutes, my arms wrapped tightly around my perfectly white shirts, my precious air-dry only pants, my brand new fun workout gear, my sexy bras and underwear, and all my other favorite articles of clothing I had specifically chosen to pack from home, with the same amount of tenderness and concern as if I were holding a new born baby. I was trying to drum up the apparent necessary willingness to turn, what felt like was a part of myself, over to the laundry people and their white shirt staining, pant-shrinking, underwear-eating, cotton-destroying, scary, monster sized washing and drying machines.

I approached a cheery looking woman and attempted to explain I did not want certain things dried. I made hand motions of hanging my pants up on a drying rack and then pointed to the big, scary dryers shaking my head 'no.' Her smile and nod were not exactly reassuring. So I looked around for someone else to 'talk' to. I walked over to a nice looking fellow, shaking my head 'no' when holding my entire pile of clothes up against one of the big, scary dryers. (I hoped this would make my request simpler and thus more likely to be understood.) Smiling, as if to understand me, he pointed towards the back of the room at where I was hoping I would find the drying racks. I walked to the back of the room, full of optimism, and yet all I found was another row of pant-shrinking, cotton-eating, monster-sized dryers. I approached someone else...who barely even looked up when I tapped her on the shoulder. No one in the laundry department spoke English. So I had to make a choice.

I could waste the next hour or two of my life (and countless additional hours for the rest of my time in Thailand) individually washing every article of my clothing in my tiny bathroom sink, only potentially resulting in clean smelling clothes. Or, I could practice letting go of my attachment to these material things (as is a common Buddhist principle for finding peace) and resultantly, make my life a lot easier and thus embrace a simpler way of life (which I had professed to myself before I had left Seattle was one of the reasons I was excited to live in Thailand in the first place).

I stood there for a moment and looked around at all of the mean looking monster machines and these piles of laundry from every department of the resort stacked up next to them like mini volcanoes, until I finally decided to just let go. I released my grip from my prized items of clothing and placed my little pile...with my perfectly white shirts, my precious air-dry only pants, my brand new fun workout gear, and my sexy bras and underwear...and focused on the fact that whatever would happen would happen and life would go on regardless.

Once I made the shift from grasping and fearing to letting go and releasing control, a surprising wave of ease came over me. I reminded myself clothes are just things and things constantly come and go in our lives anyway. So I might as well not waste my energy swimming up stream, so to speak, grasping on with such a tight grip to things that will eventually float away anyway.

✳✳✳

Philosophy is nice and all, but putting it into practice is an entirely different story however. The turn around time for the laundry was three days. During those days, at times I didn't even think about the fact I had turned the 'care' of my clothing over to the monster machine staff. At other times however, I kicked myself for not at least keeping my non-dryer-friendly pants to hand wash myself.

The three days finally passed and I walked into the laundry room full of trepidation. I anxiously scanned the towering piles of clothes until my eyes finally found my precious little pile. I took a deep breath as I noticed not only had everything been dried, but it seemed half of my items were missing. I had a minor panic moment but instead of embarking on a flailing full-body charade extravaganza of fury, I first took myself back up to my room to double check if some clothes were truly missing. I laid my items out on my bed and confirmed that indeed half were missing.

Back down to the laundry room I went (as a very faint voice inside my head was trying to remind the best version of myself of its desire to live a simpler, less-attachment-to-things way of life...yet concurrently an overpowering internal voice was screaming about how much it loved those precious air-dry only pants). I walked straight up to the first laundry person I saw and asked, "English?" She just smiled and called over a man from the other side of the room. As he was walking over, much to my heart's content, I suddenly recognized a lonely little stack of laundry, tucked way in the back corner of the room, and comprised of the other half of my clothing. Indeed, everything had been machine dried. My anger immediately started to rise, as I imagined not being able to fit into any of my clothes (a nice example of my mind's tendency to over-dramatize things, by the way). But I immediately reminded myself to look on the positive side...at least the big monster machines hadn't eaten everything.

I asked the laundry man standing next to me, whom I

was thrilled could understand English, how I could avoid having some of my things dried on future occasions. He gave me a big smile and simply said, "Just attach a note to your laundry bag next time when you drop it off."

I skeptically asked, "But will anyone be able to read and understand my request?"

"Sure," he boldly replied. "No problem at all!"

He beamed as he spoke his words with such confidence. I wasn't buying it though. I wasn't feeling assured this one man who spoke English in the laundry department would happen to be the one in charge of handling my next bag of laundry. I also recalled being told by a friend of mine who had lived in Asia to be aware that being agreeable is often more highly regarded among Asians than honesty. I just smiled and said, "Thank you."

As I walked away in my disgruntlement, I kindly reminded myself to practice releasing my tight grip of clinging onto material things, which will always eventually float away anyway…the Buddhist principle of non-attachment to things as a pathway to peace.

Regardless, I stomped back up the stairs to my room and laid out my clothes for inspection, but was able to calm myself down after realizing most everything was fine. My white shirts were a bit less white. I could button my favorite air-dry-only pants, even though I'd likely only be able to wear them if I didn't feel like breathing, and yet I was able to let go of being bummed about such a trivial thing.

Buddhism is a central part of Thai culture and I have always looked up to its ideals. Growing up in America, I was raised with the message that acquiring 'stuff' is one of the main goals in life. Yet Buddhist wisdom teaches that anything we have an attachment to will eventually cause us suffering…because everything in life is impermanent. Things and even people will always be coming and going from our lives. Always. So why cling on so tightly? Wouldn't life be more joyful if we could let go of all of our clinging to things, to people, to our stern ideas about the way life 'should' be, and even to our own emotions? Instead, imagine how much more joy we could enjoy by focusing on the inherent beauty which truly is present in every moment of our lives when we are willing to look for it.

Already in that second week of my life in Thailand, my

dirty laundry experience had proven to be a great practice in living out a core Buddhist principle. Lesson learned: I always have a choice. I can waste precious energy clinging to material things throughout my life, resultantly making myself tense and unhappy...or instead, I can choose to lighten up, let go, and fill myself with that same peace I saw emanating from all the alluring smiles of the tranquil statues of Buddha, humbly placed throughout the resort.

Chapter 6:
The Other Side of Heaven
February 2008

My 'training' continued for a total of three weeks, some days filled with heavenly spa treatments, while other days consisted of painfully boring introductions to the operations of each department (where I was rudely awakened to the reminder I was indeed a staff member, not a guest, and every time I looked at the clock on those days, it seemed somehow time had gone in reverse). Dave and Monica were working long hours, and much to my dismay, we kept passing each other like ships in the night.

The hot stone massages, the replenishing facials, the Japanese Watsu water massage...I didn't know this was possible, but I eventually got sick of them! It didn't help that in the midst of receiving the treatments, in addition to being shuffled around for introductions to all of the various departments, still with wrinkles all over my face from having laid face-down on a massage table for an hour, I was learning computer programs, and getting overviews of the details of my job and the piles of necessary (or, as I tend to think, unnecessary) associated paperwork. That exciting feeling of 'newness' quickly began to wear off...and there were a few things about my new life I was not too thrilled about.

First, I need to tell you something about the 'glorious' sunshine of Thailand. The country is located slightly north of the equator, which means the temperature is hot; really hot...every single day. 'Winter' does not exist. There is a rainy season, which simply means the heat turns into humidity...creating sticky beads of sweat which seep out from my pores and drip down every inch of my body all day long. So when buildings are designed in Thailand, they are done in a manner to keep the sun OUT.

The resort was originally built 14 years prior by a Thai man with the intention of attracting wealthy Thais from Bangkok to come down for a weekend getaway. Nowadays, the guests come from all over the world, and yet after weeks being at the resort, I had not met a single Thai guest. Nonetheless, the original structure was built with the Thais in mind. So what I am getting at is when I went to the resort each day, I often did not see the sun at all. I spent the entirety of my days inside rooms blasting with freezing cold air conditioning.

Rated as one of the best spas in the world, when I was letting my imagination go wild with all the pictures in my mind of what my new surroundings were going to look like, I envisioned the resort to be perched out on a big bluff, elegantly laid out among palm trees and majestic bushes bursting with colorful tropical flowers, surrounded by green rolling hills that leisurely stretched down to the ocean. Well…I was wrong.

The grounds are shaped as a long and narrow 7-acre rectangle, with the beach on one end and the frenzied freeway outside the entrance at the other end. The towering black granite walls enclose the entire property. It took me awhile to realize that as guests walk amongst the beauty of the resort, they're in such bliss that none of them seem to ever realize they're actually contained within a man-made, granite compound. Most didn't even set foot on the beach and would only lie out around the pristine pool.

During my time off, I was not allowed to lounge in the beauty of the resort, or even be on the grounds for that matter. The entirety of my 'home' was basically my stark white room in the stark white utilitarian staff apartment building. Not only did it not have a view of any kind, but it didn't even have a window. I'm serious. There was a door to the outside, which opened to a patio barely big enough for a drying rack, and a view of the adjacent ugly apartment building situated so close to the patio I could practically touch it. I eventually pleaded to move to a new room, one that at least had a window! Luckily, my wish was eventually granted.

My new room not only had a window but also sliding glass doors that opened to a balcony, albeit a very narrow one, but at least wide enough for a little plastic chair (which I found amongst the cobwebs in an old storage room up on the roof) and a few extra inches that just barely allowed me to stretch my legs out and rest them on the ledge. The view was through a chain link fence to a dilapidated tennis court; not the ideal vision of a beachside view, but hey, it was better than not having a window at all. The trade though was ants seemed to love my new bathroom, and I could pee with more pressure than what

61

came out of my shower. Susan had told me, if I 'successfully' completed my first four months of being an employee at the resort (whatever that meant), my 'probation' period would end and I would be given the choice to use a housing allowance to live in a place of my own. However, after my experiences of exploring town, I wasn't really sure if I'd even be able to find an area any more enjoyable to live.

As for the food served in the staff cafeteria, I really didn't know what I was eating half the time. Deep fried mystery balls seemed to show up in many of the entrees. Seafood (I think) was often swimming in some sort of greasy green sauce. 'Vegetable' dishes often made finding the vegetables a feat in itself. Noodles were to be easily confused with some sort of white stringy goo that perhaps had melted from being under the heat lamps for hours. The salad bar was nice, as long as the veggies hadn't turned sour since they were put out as soon as breakfast was over (around 9 a.m.). None of it was kept on ice and it sat out among the ants and flies for the entire day. The filtered water was good. As for other beverages, it was all just sugar water of various colors.

As for having a day off, I was lucky to even get one. My position as a holistic health expert was historically filled by naturopaths from Australia, and the turnover rate in the last year had been almost 100 percent. The one woman who had chosen to stick around for over a year had fallen in love with a Thai and had plans to soon marry him. All the others had quit after just months on the job. Apparently they were forced to work so much overtime everyone had burned out, got fed up with 'living in paradise,' and quit.

Given the appalling turnover rate, the new manager of my position, Victor (and beside the periodic hallway greeting of, *"Hello! Busy! Gotta' go,"* I still hadn't had a proper meeting with) was acutely aware he didn't want that to happen again. He was an American who had spent the previous ten years working in Hong Kong and seemed like a great guy for as much as I could tell thus far. During my second phone interview back when I was still in the states, he was very transparent with the issues of the past and promised they wouldn't be repeated. The first policy he initiated toward that pledge was instead of working a full six-day workweek (as was the norm at the resort and in the

Thai culture in general), we would finish at noon the day before our day off, have one full day off, and then return to work at noon following our day off. Given the other 99 percent of employees at the resort worked six full days a week, he said he had decided on this schedule as a fair compromise; my colleagues and I would still work six days a week, yet in a sense have two days off.

Not creating resentment towards us from the Thais about this 'special treatment' was indeed challenging though. Yet, this policy was justified by Victor given the obvious turnover rate problem, the lifetime of adjusting to a six-day workweek among the Thais versus a five-day workweek among us westerners, and the fact we had been uprooted from our own culture, we had a much bigger challenge feeling 'at home' and thus the extra free time could hopefully mitigate that.

Making friends in town proved not to be an easy undertaking. The two people I felt most at home with were of course my colleagues, Monica and Dave. I also was getting to know Olivia, (the Australian woman who had survived the past year of backbreaking overtime), since she was the one showing me the ropes of my new job, as well as two other naturopaths recently hired, Katrina and Nadine. But the issue was we each had a different day off. So when my 'Friday' arrived, I was the only one in a celebratory mood. To everyone else, it was just another day of the week. And then on my actual day off, everyone was at work…a major bummer to my gregarious spirit!

Well, another major bummer was that I was not allowed to call myself the title I had dreamed about since I was seven years old…the title I had been working so intensely to achieve for all those years. I was not allowed to call myself 'doctor.' My title was 'Health Advisor.' Since the position was historically held by naturopaths, (natural health experts whom did not go to the level of schooling needed to earn the 'doctor' title) they wanted to unify our roles into one coherent team in which everyone shared the same title. Furthermore, they were concerned if one guest saw a 'doctor' while another saw a 'naturopath' for a similar appointment, the client would complain and feel they got gypped.

So, besides spending my days *shivering* in air conditioned rooms, entrapped by the walls of a towering granite compound;

besides living in a room *without* a window or in one with a view of a dilapidated tennis court through a chain-linked fence; besides taking a shower with pressure similar to what it would feel like if I were being urinated on, and then drying off among *hoards* of ants parading up and down the walls of my bathroom; besides dining on deep fried mystery balls, seafood swimming in greasy green sauces, and salads that *might* have tasted fresh had they been set out on ice in the morning; besides feeling *totally* lonely and homesick during my day off in which I didn't have any friends to hang out with; besides dreaming of becoming a doctor for my *entire* life and now with my first job having finally earned that triumphant title and yet being called a measly 'Health Advisor;' everything was GREAT!

Regardless, it was an experience I was keeping myself open too. I trusted I was meant to be there, as I do wherever I am in life, and was excited about the mystery of whatever lay ahead.

Luckily, given how much my soul delighted in regularly connecting with my fabulous aunt Mary during my years in medical school, we decided to seamlessly continue our weekly chats while in I was in Thailand, albeit over Skype. I cannot fully express in words how nourishing it was to be comforted by her pearls of wisdom each week. And with Skype, to be able to see her face made me feel I was sitting right there next to her. (I love Skype!)

Mary continued to get an earful of everything going on in my life on a weekly basis, and I continued to be reminded of her simple and beautiful wisdom for living peacefully...

"Life is trustable, all of it. Every challenge in life is an opportunity to either reject and react to negatively, or to welcome as a teacher for strengthening your ability to respond to life with grace. The more you fight your reality, the more you miss the lessons and miss the joy..."

And my favorite quote of hers, which almost magically and without fail elicits an immediate transformation of my fighting and judging thoughts into soothing feelings of trust and faith...

"It's okay. Everything, it's all okay."

Here is a sample of what was a common internal dialogue of mine in those first weeks:

"I miss Mary! And all of my friends! And my dear Jennifur! I was crazy to leave, wasn't I?!"

Then Mary's wisdom would surface. *"Life is trustable, Jody. It's okay. It's all okay."*

"I'm going to get sick eating in that disgusting, oil-ridden, mystery-food-filled cafeteria everyday. The salad bar isn't even kept chilled! I have to smell each vegetable before I even feel safe putting it on my plate. It's awful!"

"Life is trustable, Jody. It's okay. It's all okay."

"I haven't met my manager for longer than two minutes yet. So I don't know if I'll even like working for the guy; I can't understand what my coworkers are saying half the time; and I never even get to see Dave and Monica! I am soooo lonely!"

"Life is trustable, Jody. It's okay. It's all okay."

…Something I think is very amusing is how we go to school to absorb endless volumes of information which we proudly embed into our brains to then be called 'intelligent' and 'smart.' Then others say, *"Wow! You know so much! You are so wise!"* And yet to me, the most noteworthy wisdom in life, above all other pieces of information one could glean throughout their lifetime, consists of simple and basic truths: Life is trustable. Everything in life is a teacher. One can choose to react negatively to life events, or to see everything as an opportunity for strengthening one's ability to live with more grace.

The priceless value of fully embracing such simple wisdom in life often makes me shake my head and laugh when I think of the lofty six-figure school loan I accrued and the endless hours of studying I endured during medical school in hopes of gaining wisdom to help others improve their well-being. Although I will eventually pay off that mammoth loan, I am lovingly forever indebted to my dear aunt Mary.

So as my days continued on, often oscillating between feeling immensely challenged by adjusting to my new life, I regularly reminded myself of the following truism for life: It is up to every individual to find the paradise which is *always* present in life, regardless of physical location or anything else external, because even living in 'paradise'…near a beach with palm trees and sunshine…is no guarantee for living in the state of paradise most humans long for...living in peace within one's mind, body, and soul.

Day 3:
Joy Comes from Within
August 2008

What a difference a day makes! My aunt Mary's wisdom once again proved to be true. By allowing my feelings out the previous day without distracting myself away from feeling them, they had naturally subsided on their own. I woke up with a huge smile on my face and bounced out of bed. I felt like a new woman! I felt light. I felt happy for no apparent reason other than having allowed myself to release a heavy load of sadness the day before. The entire day I was in bliss.

The 6:30 a.m. meditation session was a breeze. I sat motionless on my little cushion on the floor and joyfully focused on my breath for the entire 90 minutes. At breakfast, I felt such love in my heart I had to make a conscious effort to not disobey the rules and accidentally 'communicate' a smile to somebody. During each break throughout the day, never once did I notice all the 'pairs' of trees, which had sent me into a tailspin of sadness the day before. All I saw was beauty...the paint strokes of wispy clouds dancing against the canvas of the blue sky, the tropical birds singing their songs of delight, and the peaceful, rolling hills stretching out to the horizon.

Nothing had changed from the day before. My daily activity of meditating, interspersed with meal breaks was exactly the same. My meals were basically the same. My barren list-to-do was still barren. My communication with others was still non-existent...the only difference was the thoughts in my head. Never in my life had I experienced multiple days in a row where the events of the day were literally exactly the same. In regular life, it's easy to blame external events for being responsible for a good mood or bad. But absolutely nothing had changed from the day before, yet I was miserable all day long the previous day, and now beaming with joy.

This realization fascinated me and deeply underscored the truth that our experience of life comes much more from our own internal environment of thoughts, than from whatever is actually going on around us. At lunch, I pondered other situations which made this truth easy to see...same movie: one person loved it, another hated it. Same party: one person had a blast, another person thought it was a bore. Sunny day: one person loved it, another person hated it because the brightness gave them a migraine.

The joy I felt in the morning extended through the entire afternoon and evening. During each meditation session, I was in bliss as I reveled in the uncanny feeling of deep peace I was experiencing.

Serendipitously, the topic of that night's video touched on the very point I had pondered earlier. Goenka told a story about a very expensive watch breaking. After explaining in detail about its exclusive design, the fact it was hand made, and contained diamonds and pearls, he posed the question, "Does the fact this watch broke make you upset?"

I sat there, wondering why he asked such an inane question but the next question he asked was, "What if this watch belonged to you and was a family heirloom?"

Ah, I got it. A watch breaking is not a tragic event in itself. The terrible feeling only arises depending on my attitude about it. This is also true for opposite emotional states. Feelings of joy do not arise so much from what's going on, as they do from one's attitude about what is going on. His point was, instead of wasting energy trying to orchestrate the events of life to fit one's desires, a much quicker way to joy is to simply change your thoughts and attitude.

This was truly a radical point. All the striving I had done in my life for the goal of becoming a doctor. I had imagined it would bring me great joy, but had it? I was proud of my accomplishment, but was I a happier person because of it? Not really.

The second point he made was how suffering comes from having attachments. If the watch did not belong to me, thus I was not attached to it, and it broke, this event would not bother me. Yet if I felt attached to the watch and it broke, then I would be quite disturbed. He made the point that the only constant in life is change and thus nothing can or will last forever. What is here today must and will eventually be gone. Embracing this law of physics elucidates why being attached to something, which sooner or later will inevitably disappear, die, or be destroyed, sets us up for suffering.

He said as humans, of course we will naturally become attached to our friends and loved ones, as well as certain mementos throughout our lifetime. Yet by being aware of this truth...that attachment leads to eventual suffering once the person or object expires...it will help to lessen our grip on our attachments. By practicing finding the ever-present joy which truly can be found within ourselves at all times, instead of depending on receiving it from our external attachments, we are able to experience greater peace and tranquility.

I went to bed that night gnawing on these two truths...that attachments cause suffering and that happiness originates from my own thoughts and perceptions, not from the events of life themselves. I imagined letting go of connecting the amount of happiness I've always assumed I will feel once I finally meet my adoring husband and was actually able to experience a similar level of happiness, simply lying there as I fell asleep in my bed...by myself.

Chapter 7:
The Four Pillars of Health for All
February 2008

'Job training' came to an abrupt halt and before I knew it, had suddenly become a faded memory of the past. I had to briskly wake myself up out of my reverie of living the life of a queen at a five star luxury heath resort, and get to work. Although excited to finally start my new job as a physician, I reluctantly said 'good-bye' to my coveted silk robe and slippers. I tried with all my might to cheerfully welcome my green, polyester shirt and matching skirt…my daily attire for the next several months, or year, or for however long my life in Thailand were to carry on.

It was my 'Monday.' After having a heart-pumping and spirit-cleansing sweat on the elliptical machine in the staff gym; showering and feeling as stylish as I could in my green polyester uniform (it had gold threads embedded throughout and gold edges along the sleeves which I guess you could say made it look sort of regal); choosing two hard boiled eggs for breakfast (the most recognizable and safest option of what was on display under the heat lamps); I headed out the door and embarked on my walking commute down the narrow alleyway to my office, with _an umbrella_ in hand (as I saw all the other local women doing).

Being a Seattle native, I never imagined I would do such a thing…_carry an umbrella to shade me from the sun!_ But given my desire to stay youthful looking and protect my skin, I did some math one day to estimate how many minutes I would be exposed to the sun during my commute over a year. I guessed it would take about three minutes to walk from my apartment, down the alley, and into the secret staff entrance of the resort. So multiplying three minutes by four commutes a day (at the start and end of the day, plus at lunchtime) equals 12 minutes. 12 minutes x 6 days a week x 52 weeks in a year = 3744 minutes. That equals 62.4 hours of sun exposure from my mere three-minute commute in a year! And of course, that didn't even take into account all the other times I'd be exposed to the sun during my day off. So the umbrella suddenly didn't sound like such a silly idea anymore!

So instead of exiting my apartment building to the left, in the direction of the frenzied freeway and the main resort entrance, I turned right towards the beach. Yet about 50 yards prior to reaching the sand and immediately after passing the relatively well-contained stench of the resort dumpsters (not exactly an idyllic setting for arriving at work but with the entirety of my commute being a three-minute walk, I realize I don't have grounds for any complaining), I turned left through a wide gap in the tall fortress comprising the staff entrance. Next, I journeyed through a maze of industrial looking, stark white, and clearly staff-only hallways (I think whomever designed these secret, underground, staff-only hallways must have done so borrowing ideas from the layout of Italian fortress cities, making sure the design was so confusing that if one's enemy ever entered the city, they would surely never find their way to the center of town)...up a flight of stairs so narrow only one person could ascend or descend at a time (which I thought was an annoying design, until I realized that if two people of the typical, petite, Asian frame were trying to pass each other, it would probably suffice)... through a secret door reminiscent of what I imagined it would be like walking into Alice's closet and exiting out the backside into Wonderland... suddenly arriving in the front entrance of the elegant spa area, adorned in its breathtaking tropical floral arrangements.

I would then give a quick wave to the spa front desk staff who'd usually be inundated with guests kindly requesting (or fervently demanding as it so happened at times) to make changes to their daily schedule, as I continued onward, down a short, non-descript hallway, and finally arriving (even though in entirety, it took me less than four minutes) in the first-time-ever office of Dr. Jody Stanislaw! (Oh whoops, I mean 'Health Advisor' Jody Stanislaw...boohiss.)

Dave and Monica suddenly appeared in my office to welcome me to my first real day on the job. Monica, in her loving exuberance, hugged me as she asked, "How does it feel Jody?!"

Taking a deep breath, I replied, "A bit of everything I must admit!"

Dave's smile beamed. "Can you guys believe it?! After

71

studying like mad dogs for five years, here we are, all together working at a ritzy health spa on the beach in Thailand?! It's crazy! I love it!"

Given the resort had yet to drop in occupancy since the peak of the holiday season, our morning team-bonding circle was brief, as we each felt the call of emails awaiting our attention prior to the arrival of our morning clients. However, we didn't have to venture far. Much to my heart's delight, our respective offices were all wonderfully located immediately adjacent to each other, as were the offices of the naturopaths from Australia, Katrina, Nadine, and Olivia. I delighted in being part of such a cohesive team of loving individuals, each involved in a career dedicated to improving the well being of others.

From the knowledge I had gleaned during the 'I am a staff member' portion of my training, I then obediently sat down at my computer and checked the schedule of patients I would be seeing that day. I opened up my schedule and took in the following:

9 a.m. Ann* from Germany
10 a.m. Ron from China
11 a.m. Rolf* from Austria
12 p.m. Lunch Break
1 p.m. Rajesh* from Dubai
2 p.m. Susan* from Australia
3 p.m. Abida from Malaysia
4 p.m. Sabah* from Iran
5 p.m. Francois from France

I took a deep breath and thought, *"Well, I certainly won't be bored today!"* I took a moment to calm those infamous first-day-of-work butterflies and headed to the back office. The asterisks indicated the client was a returning guest (or RG as was the coined term) and thus I needed to pull their archived file to familiarize myself with their medical chart and any other details regarding their prior visit. I took the stack of old charts back to my office, yet before even perusing my 9 a.m. client's file, my phone rang.

"Jody, you guest please." (Being able to pronounce the English 'r' sound is not a common skill found among many Asians.)

I replied, "Khop Khun Ka, Sak," which means, "Thank you, Sak." Sak was one of the adorable receptionists who made my heart smile on a daily basis each time I walked by the front desk and simply saw his smiley face.

I anxiously and excitedly walked down the hall to the reception area to greet, unbeknownst to her, my very first client. I noticed a woman sitting patiently on the sofa who was elegantly dressed in a white linen shirt and pants, adorned in matching emerald green ruby earrings and bracelets. Her makeup was of light earth tones and her silver hair was neatly pinned up in a tight bun. Sak and I made brief eye contact as he gave me the confirmatory head nod indicating that yes, she was the correct guest for me to approach.

One thing I quickly learned about why this resort holds such worldwide accolades is simply from the impeccable care almost every single staff member gives to ensuring all guests are greeted by name. It is the responsibility of each department to know in advance who will be arriving and thus, greet them by name upon arrival. Thus everywhere the guests went, they had the experience of feeling like an honored guest. It was soon evident to me how this seemingly trivial act of recognition, regardless of the exalted positions many of the guests held in their daily lives, made an extraordinary impact on how special and loved the guests felt. It was but another one of life's many indications to me of how hungry people are for respect and recognition.

"Hello Ann. Welcome. I'm Dr. Jody and I will be your health advisor during your stay. Please come with me."

"Thank you! I can't tell you how wonderful it is to be back!"

As we walked to my office, Ann immediately started lamenting about how tired she was from her long journey, how she barely slept a wink on the plane due to the obnoxious snoring of the man sitting next to her, how surprisingly delicious her in-flight meal of chicken pasta was, and how she had been dreaming about coming back to the resort ever since the day she left last year.

Ann's tune turned upward. "I LOVE coming here after the holiday season! The holidays take every last bit of energy right out of me. I don't think I could continue on with my life if I didn't have this wonderful vacation every year!" We entered my office, I shut the door, and we both took a seat.

"We are thrilled to see you again, Ann. As you know, there is an endless list of activities available here at the resort focused on enhancing your health and well-being. The purpose of this time with me, as you may recall, is for me to go over your health history, make sure I am aware of any pertinent health needs you may have, and find out what your goals are for your stay. I will then use this information to recommend to you a personalized schedule, taking from all of the most pertinent activities available here, which will be designed to optimize your time during your stay for reaching your goals."

Even with the obvious fatigue evident on her face, her eyes danced with enthusiasm as she replied, "Sounds great!"

I smiled, "Okay, tell me your main goal for your stay?"

"To relax and get healthy! I have been so horribly stressed. To be honest, I can't remember the last time I had a day off from work. I can't sleep at night because my mind is so overcome with anxiety about stupid things I did during the day, and then I start thinking about everything I must accomplish the *next* day to make up for all the time I wasted. Furthermore, I'm getting old, and I absolutely cannot stand all of these wrinkles I have! Look! Look at all of these horrendous wrinkles! I look in the mirror and wonder who the ugly old lady is looking back at me. I am 52 and my boyfriend is only 49 so I am constantly worried he is going to leave me for a younger woman since I am soooooo old. It's awful! I worry about losing him everyday. I would hate to be alone again! I can't stand being by myself! I get so lonely and depressed." Deflated, she looked at me, desperate for answers, "Dr. Jody, what do you think I should do?"

I attentively listened to Ann, this woman who, given her outside appearance, displayed such poise and elegance. I empathized with her struggles, while personally relating to her fears of being single and getting old. I couldn't help but wonder how many millions of other woman were being simultaneously haunted by these very same thoughts around the world.

"Ann, first of all, I want to congratulate you for giving

yourself the gift of this time off, for recognizing your body's need for rest and relaxation. You've certainly come to the perfect place. You are in good hands. Let's start with some simple questions so I can get a feel for your daily health habits. Tell me about your sleeping and eating patterns."

Ann shook her head, eyes pointed down at the floor. "Oh, I am just awful. I can't get myself into bed before 1 a.m. because I'm addicted to surfing the internet. But then I sit there wide-awake for hours haunted by my endlessly racing mind, which makes me think I'm going crazy. Then, once five o'clock hits, I have to drag myself out of bed to get to work by seven. My horrible commute takes over an hour, and that's assuming there isn't some stupid accident backing everything up, making me go even more crazy.

I'll have a pastry at work and then drink about five cups of coffee to get going. I'm usually too busy to stop for lunch so I'll either just skip it or maybe have another pastry. Then for dinner, my boyfriend Franz and I will meet up at some restaurant where I pig out because I am so ravenous by that point. We share at least a couple bottles of wine too. I know, I am just awful!"

I did my best to reassure her. "Well, Ann, I can understand why you have been feeling so stressed. I have plenty of ideas of how I can help you feel better."

"Oh, thank God Dr. Jody!" Ann looked cautiously optimistic.

"No matter what health complaint patients come to me with, I always start with an inventory of what I call 'The Four Pillars of Health.' The Four Pillars are key areas which provide a firm foundation for good health. Just like a table needs four legs to be sturdy, you need these four areas in your life to serve as the most fundamental action steps for improving and optimizing your health. The Four Pillars are as follows: nourishing food, adequate sleep, physical movement, and emotional well-being. If even one pillar is weak, any other treatment recommendation will not have a lasting and significant impact on improving your health."

She seemed to drink in my words. "No wonder why I'm such a mess. I don't have a single pillar in place!"

"That's okay Ann. That is exactly why you've come on

this vacation. You've been feeling out of balance and have listened to how hungry your body is for a healthier way of life.

So let's start by discussing the first pillar: nourishing food. As you know, all of the food here is healthy, so that pillar has already been taken care of for you while you are here. I encourage you to enjoy as many vegetables as you can at each meal. Fruit is an excellent choice too, but three servings a day is enough. Vegetables and fruit are packed with the nutrients your cells need for adequate nourishment and rejuvenation. I also suggest taking deep breaths throughout your meal, focusing on chewing thoroughly, and taking moments to look around you to feel gratitude for the beauty of the ocean and the sky you are surrounded by. Each of these small steps will send a message to your nervous system to relax and greatly improve your body's ability to absorb nutrients from your food."

"I actually love healthy food. I just never have the time to make it for myself." She shook her head and went on, "And it seems that the tastiest food served in restaurants is *always* full of fat."

"Well, not at our restaurant; you won't find any excess fat here. And we only make GREAT tasting healthy food." I smiled, grateful to see her eyes widen with enthusiasm at the idea of eating healthy.

"Okay, pillar number two: adequate sleep. Did you bring your laptop?"

Ann answered strongly. "No!"

"Great. Now realize, however, your habit of having a racing mind every night will not just turn off like a light switch. We are going to have to patiently work on retraining your brain to slow down after dinner. I suggest taking a soothing bath, reading an enjoyable novel, or playing calm music for example. Engage in some sort of soothing activity after dinner, and I suggest being in bed with the lights out by 10 p.m., or 11 p.m. at the latest."

Everything stopped. Ann looked at me incredulously, silent for some time. Finally, she said, "Dr. Jody, are you kidding? I'll be sitting there for hours!"

I could hear the distress in her voice. Obviously this issue was a huge block in her life. "Well, if you were having the same kind of days like you were at home, yes, that would likely happen. But your time here is all about relaxation and *retraining* yourself to adopt healthier, more nourishing habits. Habits don't change overnight, but each little step will contribute toward helping you reduce stress and allow you to feel happier and healthier."

Ann seemed to breathe that statement in for a moment, "Okay, I suppose I'll try that."

"Good. Now pillar number three: regular movement. What your body needs right now is just some gentle movement; nothing too strenuous. What I suggest for you is to take part in the relaxing yoga or stretching classes. Leisurely walks on the beach would be good too. It's important to move your body but with how little sleep you've been getting, I would recommend your focus during your stay be to rejuvenate your body, not on getting fit. Any kind of movement is always a good idea as a regular part of your life, but for now, I suggest you only take part in mild exercise which does not take a lot of effort."

"But isn't running everyday good for me?" Ann asked, shocked at my gentle suggestions.

"Actually no, not right now. You've been pushing yourself hard enough at home. I don't want to see you continuing to do so while you're here. Your priority needs to be relaxation."

Inspiration shined in her eyes, "Wow. Dr. Jody, that makes a lot of sense! I always tell myself I need to work harder. Thanks for telling me it's okay to relax."

I smiled at her. "Of course!" Three pillars were already outlined; one more to go, "Now, pillar number four: emotional well-being."

"I'm hopeless with this one, Dr. Jody."

I thought for a moment before responding. "Well, let's start by choosing a different word than 'hopeless.' Yes, this is a challenging area for you, but that doesn't mean there aren't things you can do here at the resort to nourish your spirit." I paused for emphasis. "For starters, you'll be receiving a massage everyday, which is an excellent time for you to shift your thoughts toward things you feel grateful for in your life."

Ann's face brightened. "Yeah, I guess that is a good point. I have two great kids who I'm really proud of."

"Great! And the longer you spend time thinking about

your gratitude for them, the more you'll be able to fill your mind with other elements in your life which you are grateful for too. Simply focusing on what you are grateful for, in each moment of your day....even if it's just that you have eyes to see or legs to walk...this can be a huge benefit to your emotional health. This pillar does not have to be about taking part in lengthy religious ceremonies or spending hours on a therapist's couch. The littlest steps, those that are easy enough for you to actually *have* the time to do on a daily basis, these are the things which make the biggest impact."

I could see the change in Ann. No longer moving from inspired to deflated, she was brighter and open. "That makes sense and makes me feel better already. If I had one more darned thing to add to my 'to-do' list, I think I'd collapse." She laughed. "Thank you for the simple suggestions, Dr. Jody."

"Great! You're already focused on gratitude. See how easy that was?" For the first time, I heard Ann's contagious laugh and saw her radiant smile.

Moments like these are exactly why I became a physician...to remind people of their humanness, thus bringing kindness to how we treat ourselves, and to inspire people to make their health a priority and thus feel great in their mind, body, and soul.

The rest of my day was packed with more of the same...overly stressed, wealthy people from every corner of the globe, each with a deep hunger to improve their well-being.

Ichiro from China couldn't remember the last time he had a good night's sleep. Rolf from Austria was looking for advice on how to reduce his painful heart burn. Rajesh from Dubai was desperate to lose 50 pounds due to the humiliation he constantly received from his family. Susan from Australia was hungry for relief from her depression. Anita from Malaysia needed motivation to kick start her much needed exercise regime to avoid a heart attack like her mother and sisters had experienced. Sabah from Iran wanted to learn about nutrition so he could pass this knowledge on to his five young boys. Marie from France was hungry for a break from her 80-hour workweek and was desperate for some much needed rest and relaxation she never could find time for at home.

As a naturopathic physician, my first step with every

client is to look at simple shifts around improving their Four Pillars. Unlike the classic western medical model, the last thing I reach for is a pill. Every patient I saw from that day forward enjoyed dramatic improvements in their health, simply from following my simple suggestions for improving their sleep, nutrition, exercise, and/or emotional well-being. Having these four areas strong is absolutely essential for optimal health, for anyone and everybody, no matter the socio-economic status, and no matter what corner of the globe one calls home. A weakness in just one area can, and will, create dis-ease, sooner or later.

I found it absolutely fascinating to work with such a wide variety of nationalities. That day, I became acutely aware that each of us should really put aside all cultural barriers, colors of skin, style of clothing, financial status …. and realize how similar we all are. At some point in life, everyone has a physical issue they are looking to resolve, a stressful family situation they are dealing with, and / or emotional pain they are hungry for relief from. When certain guests arrived in my office, I felt a bit nervous…nervous I would not be able to relate to them or help them in anyway because they seemed too 'foreign' to me…but as the hour went by, it became very clear that the person in front of me was just as human as I, and I could relate to them. It was an awe-inspiring experience. We are truly are one big global community.

I completed my charting for the day and proudly headed home, my first official day on the job a success. After exiting through the secret staff passageway in the wall of the granite compound, I turned down the alley toward the beach. My stomach was growling for dinner but I needed to have a quick taste of the visual nourishment of the glistening ocean, with the shimmering diamonds of sunlight dancing on its surface. This time last year I was probably in some cold, depressing corner of the library at school, cramming to pass another back-breaking exam. Life constantly amazes me….you just never know what's going to show up.

Day 4:
The Transformational Power of Focus
August 2008

Day four, once again, proved to be an entirely different experience than any of the previous days. At the 6:30 a.m. mediation, for some reason, music of Goenka singing was being played…and the sound he was making was absolutely horrendous (at least, my personal impression of it anyway). He sounded more like some sort of animal, moaning and screeching in pain.

I had spent days one through three diligently practicing keeping my focus on my breath, and away from my constant stream of thoughts. Yet during that particular morning session, my mind felt as if it were literally screaming.

"Oh my God! This is HORRENDOUS! Somebody, please make it stop! How the hell am I supposed to sit here calmly when I have to listen to this vile crap?!"

Luckily, I had built enough strength from the previous three days I was able to have a part of myself actually remain calm in the face of the storm raging in my head. I used my mantra to focus on my breath and did my best to not pay heed to my internal hissy fit. Though, I couldn't help but be fascinated by the juxtaposition of experiencing part of myself screaming, while at the same time, I was sitting calmly, meditating.

But as the minutes went by, it was as if my 'muscle' of focus began running out of fuel. Focusing on my breath became more and more scant, as the part of me totally annoyed by the 'singing' was taking over my thoughts.

"Enough! I can't take this anymore! Jody, you've sat through this long enough. Get up and leave!"

An unbelievable test of will ensued. It took all my might to not obey the screaming demands in my head telling me to get up and leave the room. My tenacious self pressed on. I diligently focused on my mantra, adding in a new phrase.

"Breathe in. Compassion. Breathe out. Compassion. This too shall pass. Breathe in. Compassion. Breathe out. Compassion. This too shall pass…"

Then the blessed moment arrived. The 'singing' stopped and the ending bell rang. I opened my eyes in such triumphant joy; I had to keep myself from making a squeal of joy.

Luckily, the 'singing' was not played during any of the other sessions of the day, thank God, so I was able to keep my focus on my breath with ease, more so than any of the previous days. It truly felt like my 'muscle' of focus was becoming stronger. Throughout that day, I didn't experience beaming joy, or feelings of despondency like I had during the previous days. My mood just remained pretty neutral throughout the day.

In the evening video, Goenka talked about basic principles for improving the quality of one's life. To make his point, he used an analogy of how a gardener would improve the quality of her garden. A foolish gardener would exert all of her efforts towards doing more pruning to get rid of dead leaves and wilted flowers...a superficial task. A wise gardener would ensure adequate watering, fertilizer, and nutrient dense soil...thus fixing the problem at its root.

He mentioned all the various efforts people typically make to heal their pain and satisfy their hunger for improving their life, such as ending a relationship or starting a new one, changing jobs, moving to a new city, buying new clothes, getting plastic surgery, taking mood altering drugs and more...and compared these actions to the foolish gardener.

"None of these efforts get at the root cause of unhappiness," Goenka commanded, in his thick Indian accent. *"The actions you make in life stem from your words, and your words stem from your thoughts. Your thoughts are at the root of how you experience life, not from the events themselves."*

But then he went on to reveal how there is something that even lies behind thoughts: sensations. He explained that physical sensations in the body precede all thoughts. Goenka then described the actual technique of Vipassana meditation.

"Each of you has been a diligent student these past four days, allowing time for your busy mind to calm down and to sharpen your ability to keep a continual, razor sharp focus on your breath. Now you are ready to practice the real Vipassana.

In Vipassana mediation, you methodically scan you body, becoming aware of the ever-present micro sensations throughout your body. You may start at your feet and scan upward and then back down, or, if you wish, start at the top of your head and proceed downward, continuing this cycle over and over. As beginners, move your attention extremely slowly, sharpening your ability to feel a sensation in a micro-sized area before moving on. It may take you 30 minutes or more to complete one cycle. Some sensations may feel more pleasurable than others but the most important rule is to stay equanimous to your sensations, neither growing attached to a nice feeling nor averse to an uncomfortable one. Just notice, and then move on.

Becoming skilled in this technique is the secret to a peaceful life. Life events will forever happen, which are analogous to the various sensations in your body, but in learning to become neutral to your physical sensations, you will be able to remain peaceful in the light of any storm. Instead of letting your reactions to the events of life be the determining factor of your moods, the ever present well of peace within you will prevail as the most determining factor of your experience of life."

Sitting there on my little meditation cushion in the middle of the floor, I let his teachings sink into my mind. Growing up in America, I was taught that achieving career success and physical beauty were the source of happiness. Yet at the age of 35, having achieved my dream of becoming a doctor, as well as a level of beauty deemed as attractive by most (never mind all the manipulations with food and exercise I have endured to achieve this...sometimes in healthier ways than others), I had realized the fallacy of this empty promise. Learning about 'an ever present well of peace,' which resides within me, and has nothing to do with external events, was a radical idea.

As I got ready for bed that night, I pondered my experience from that morning of staying calm and peaceful (or at least part of me) in light of listening to Geonka's wailing. By not letting my screaming mind take over (as is a typical reaction in life when things are going on I don't like) I truly had dipped into a deeper, calmer place within myself. I was able to shift my focus away from feeling annoyed, and instead doggedly kept my focus on staying calm.

Peace found not from the outside, but from within...I liked this philosophy.

Chapter 8:
Life on the Inside and Out
February 2008

My days started to fly by and my 'foreign' life begun to not feel so foreign anymore. Rather, it became kind of boring, actually. My daily routine consisted of exercising at the gym, going to work from nine to six, dinner, emailing aunt Mary, mom, my sister and friends, and then going to bed. As for my clients, however, their days were anything but ordinary...

One Thousand Dollars a day. One, zero, zero, zero, point zero, zero. Imagine what your vacation would look like if you spent that much in a single day. Well that's the average amount guests spent *per day* at the resort. Let me paint a picture of what it looks like...

The resort is a private secluded haven. To begin with, there are only 57 rooms in the seven acres of the resort....which means the maximum number of guests at any one time is a mere 114. The spa has over 50 massage rooms with a smorgasbord of indulgences for one's body. There are two fitness studios for all sorts of exercise classes. A gym with the standard equipment. The yoga pavilion. The Thai Chi pavilion. The outdoor private massage pavilions. The outdoor pool. The indoor pool / Jacuzzi / steam room / cold plunge pavilion. The physical therapy rooms. The ocean view restaurant. The poolside / beachside restaurant...So with all of this decadence, you can imagine wherever the guests are, they feel as if they have the place to themselves.

Coming to this resort is not like coming to any other hotel in the world. First of all, there is a security guard at every entrance and only guests staying at the resort are allowed on the property. No kids under 16 are allowed. The guests don't come to see the surrounding town (frankly most don't even set foot on the beach). They don't come to see Thailand either (unless they do so before or after their stay). People fly from all over the world...just to be at this resort.

Guests receive the most personalized treatment imaginable. If your mattress is too hard, they'll bring you a softer one. Want a foam pillow instead of a feather one? They'll bring that too. Have dry skin or hair? There will be bathroom products in your room for dry skin and dry hair, and the contrary if you have oily skin or hair. Guests are sent a preference form before their stay to mark down these details and thus their desires are taken care of before they even arrive.

Most guests chose to wear their bathrobes all day, which was perfectly acceptable anytime and anywhere, except at dinner when the attire was stated as 'elegantly casual.' Of course, if becoming 'elegantly casual' after a day of personalized exercise sessions, energy rebalancing treatments, rejuvenating facials, and a relaxing massage or two was just too much work, they were 'free' to have their meal delivered to their room (albeit not 'free' in the true sense of the word).

The list of awards the resort has won is endless… from the number one Spa in Asia multiple years in a row, to countless other 'Best of's' and 'Top Ten' lists. From a business perspective it's a brilliant idea to build an elegant spa that caters to the uber rich from all over the world, yet in a third-world country…. The general manager at the time was French. My boss was American, as were Dave, Monica, and I, plus the acupuncturist from New York. There were two naturopaths from Australia and two other professionals from England. We few westerners were each paid a wage that probably seemed like winning the lottery to our local counterparts. The other 400 or so employees were pretty much all Thai. I never learned exactly how much they were paid but I wouldn't be surprised if it were close to an equivalent of ten dollars per day or less.

So for $1,000 a day, you could lounge about in your bathrobe all day, enjoy a massage or two, workout with a personal trainer, get stretched out by someone for an hour, have a physical therapist fix your stiff back, be dazzled with how to improve your health from me (well actually, that usually costs extra), and enjoy three delectable organic meals…all while being carried around by your personal golf-cart chauffer, within the confines of this pristine little secret hideaway, surrounded by a towering granite wall, allowing you to forget that any other way of life even exists. Ahhhhh…….

✳✳✳

One night after work, I was hungry for a break from living in my stale apartment building and decided to check out what the nightlife in town had to offer. Generally, I'm not much of a fan of cities though. They're loud and crowded, push a materialistic lifestyle, and encourage people to waste money on stuff they don't need. They generally make me feel tense and annoyed, and this town of Hua Hin was no exception.

Instead of putting my hiking boots on to tackle the sidewalks, I decided to take the bus. The local 'bus' consisted of a pick-up truck with two horizontal benches in the back. They came about every 15 minutes at a stop just minutes from my apartment. I jumped aboard this night and headed down the frenzied freeway…passing by all the dilapidated apartment buildings, crowded hotels, barren plots of land, and 'the mall' with its proud displays of American fast-food: McDonalds, Pizza Hut, etc. (Sigh.) The ride to the center of town took about ten minutes. The buzzing that emanated from the swarms of motorbikes flying by was so loud, I could barely hear myself speak (not that I could ever engage in conversation with the interesting locals of all ages who I sat beside on the bus though…but I must admit, I have been known at times to have discussions out loud with myself so I might have unconsciously engaged in a few of those…).

Anyway, once the bus arrived in the center of town, I pulled the string hanging from the canopy above to announce my desire to depart. I handed a coin (equal to about 25 cents) to the driver through the back window, and stepped off the back. As I had discovered before, the majority of town consisted of a wide variety of restaurants (from a street-side stand with fold up chairs on the sidewalk, all the way to those with elegant settings adorned with orchids and other tropical flowers) and a bunch of shops selling touristy crap. I discovered an intriguing looking night market though which sprawled over about four blocks.

Night markets are common throughout Thailand. Shopping at local markets, day or night, is the standard way of life for the Thais. I appreciated the ubiquity of the 'shop local' concept in the country. Massive stores like Kmart and Walgreens are still generally unheard of (except for at the occasional

85

'shopping malls' found in touristy towns and in the materialistic behemoth of Bangkok).

This night market was packed wall to wall with foreigners and locals alike, snatching up all the local foods and trinkets Thailand had to offer. Vendors were selling all sorts of food, fresh tropical fruits, fresh coconut water served with a straw stuck right through the top of the coconut, as well as a rainbow of silk scarves, carvings of elephants and Buddhas in all shapes and sizes, Hello Kitty trinkets, illegally copied DVDs of the latest Hollywood movies for $5, postcards, sunglasses...

After making my way through the dense crowd of hungry shoppers, I continued meandering through town just to find even more restaurants, shops filled with tourist crap, and bars filled with older, white men holding hands with very young, beautiful Asian women. I was feeling uninspired and I was hungry. My adventurous and gregarious spirit was nowhere to be found at that point, so I sat down for a bowl of rice and vegetables and called it a night.

***

Another day off arrived. Being the environmental lover I am, I was proud to be living without a car. But I must admit, not having the freedom to just jump in my car and go explore was something I greatly missed. That is where FRIENDS WITH WHEELS comes in very handy.

I had met an English man, luckily about my age, a few weeks back while walking on the beach one night after work. Simon was taking a break from his acting career and had decided to relax in Thailand for a few months. He had plenty of free time, and I thoroughly enjoyed his company (in a purely plutonic way, however). And he had a motorcycle! This combination made me very happy, not to mention the simple fact I had a friend! Outside of work! Who spoke English! (Living in a foreign culture certainly has a way of making one appreciate those little things in life which we often take for granted at home.)

Since I had yet to roam anywhere outside of Hua Hin in the weeks since arriving, I was dying to get out of the loud and busy town and explore the countryside. I called up Simon and suggested we just go for a drive and see what we could find. He hadn't explored much outside of town either. So he was game.

He picked me up in front of my lifeless apartment building and instead of taking a right down the frenzied freeway (the way to town), we took a left. Within minutes we found ourselves driving through a quaint little town, kind of like a mini Hua Hin. It had all the same knick-knack shops, restaurants, and little hotels but just less of everything, and on a smaller and less busy street. I liked the energy of it....more mellow and less chaos.

We continued riding through the little town and soon found ourselves on a big four-lane highway. We were curious where it lead so we just kept on driving. The sea remained on our left for the next two hours (by varying degrees...from us being immediately adjacent to it, to it being out of sight). On our right we saw everything from smiling groups of men standing in front of tables proudly selling fresh fruit, little convenient shops run out of garages with kids playing in front, dilapidated buildings, wide plots of undeveloped property, sectioned-off square plots of water with little mechanical things driving around in them to stir up the water (which after much debate we decided must be shrimp farms), rolling lush hills covered in tropical vegetation, stagnant pools of stinky water, shiny temples, and many, many Buddhist shrines.

We eventually came upon a quaint little straw hut on a small beach and decided to take a break from driving. We sat down at the wooden table and smiled, taking in the stunning view bestowed upon us. Anchored along the shore was a fleet of about 20 fishing boats, vibrantly painted in pinks, greens, and blues. Beyond the fleet was the priceless view I love so much of sunlight dancing like diamonds on the ocean's surface, stretching out as far as I could see....I wasn't stuck in my air-conditioned office. I wasn't stuck in my lifeless apartment building, nor some dark depressing office in Seattle. I was in heaven.

Virtually out of nowhere suddenly appeared before us a smiling Thai woman who reached out her tanned hand as she offered us a menu...in English (and my prideful thinking we had gone beyond where most tourists ventured was quickly shot down). How serendipitous to have found this 'restaurant' because we were both more than ready for lunch. After a quick glance at the menu, we ordered some stir-fried veggies, calamari, fried eggs and rice, plus two bottles of water…which, by the way, was all priced at the equivalent of barely even five dollars! (There were many aspects of living in Thailand I was really beginning to enjoy, and a delicious meal on the beach for just a few dollars was certainly one of them!)

We thoroughly enjoyed our tasty meal and once we were 'full' of taking in the stunning ocean view, we jumped back on Simon's motorcycle and continued south. We wound our way through a national park with lush hills on both sides of us. Then passed by flat areas of wild, low growing, vegetation; numerous food stands; and navigated through neighborhoods consisting of dilapidated shacks with joyful children playing while smiling parents relaxed in front.

A quick side note…the level of joy displayed on the smiling faces of the families I saw throughout Thailand was priceless. I never received the impression anyone felt their home was too small, nor had shame about its dilapidated condition. Nobody seemed to be bothered with how manicured or not their front yard was, nor could I imagine anyone worrying about needing updated furniture or how they were going to be able to afford a new roof. As they proudly stood in front of their shack they called 'home,' their beaming grins radiated utter joy and satisfaction.

Furthermore, the Thais seemed to always be surrounded by their loved ones, smiling and enjoying themselves. I've always found it unfortunate how much focus is put on the financial wealth of countries, as if it were some absolute measure of the 'goodness' or even 'well-being' of its people. Imagine if I were to tell these smiling faces that they really should work more to afford a bigger house, to buy a bigger car and better clothes in order to be happy. I would expect them to stare at me in confusion or just laugh at me hysterically, as they should! How wonderful it would be if the high-stressed Western world, myself included, adopted more of this happy-as-is, carefree way of life.

Simon and I continued on and eventually found ourselves meandering through another version of a mini Hua Hin. It only stretched a few blocks until it reached the seashore. The beach stretched for miles and miles in both directions without a soul on it. We jumped off the motorbike, found the only tree on the beach and flopped ourselves down in the sand. We couldn't go for a swim though. It was one of those beaches were you'd have to walk for half a mile or more before the water became any deeper than ankle height. Furthermore, it was apparently a fishing town, and there seemed to be a swarm of hidden nets lurking under the surface. I decided to just stretch out on my towel and soak in the view.

Simon headed out to take a walk along the water's edge. As I relaxed under the tree, away from the ever present noise of Hua Hin, I pondered my new life as a doctor, working at a ritzy world-class resort in Thailand, and thought about everything I had experienced in order to arrive at that moment...How I had been dreaming about becoming a doctor since I was seven years old but for almost a decade, ignored my calling...how I had my mind set on becoming a naturopathic doctor for ten years...how I studied my #^%$! off for five years during medical school...spent months stressing about where the hell I was going to live after graduation in order to finally escape the depressingly, gray Seattle weather (to be fair, July and August are beautiful, during a good year that is)...spent three months selling almost everything I owned in preparation for moving to Thailand...gave away my beloved cat Jennifur (an experience which still causes me pain when I think about it, to this very day)...agreed to let a stranger live in my Seattle home...dried my tears countless times after saying more heart-wrenching good-byes in a span of a few weeks than I'd ever like to do again in my life, including to my 94-year-old grandfather...all in preparation for moving literally half way around the world to start this new life of mine in Thailand.

And after all of that, there I was, simply lying on a towel under a palm tree. I had nothing to do. Nowhere to go. No commitments to fulfill. No 'have-to's' or 'must-do's.' Nothing I was trying to achieve...except to relax and let go of my almost *addictive* thought of, "*Jody, you should be doing...* (fill in the blank)." I took a deep breath and attempted to grasp how monumental that moment truly was for me in my life. After decades of striving and pushing myself towards various achievements I believed would 'prove' I was a worthwhile person, there truly is not a word that can capture the feeling of bliss I experienced in that moment.

Chapter 9:
Addiction and Gratitude
March 2008

Three months had passed. The rush of excitement from the newness of my life in Thailand was completely over. Yet, I was still amazed on a daily basis how I was finally fulfilling my lifelong hunger to be a physician and I had somehow ended up after graduating from medical school working at a world class health resort, halfway around the world, seaside in Thailand. All throughout my years of education, starting practically since the day I was born, I knew where I would be in the following year...in the next grade. Yet after graduating from college, the world was my oyster. That fact of life fascinates me...the fact there really is no guarantee about where you'll end up at the end of each day. There are the plans we have for our life, and then there are the plans life has for us; what lies ahead each day is truly a mystery.

My job was going well. I talked to people from all over the world on a daily basis and thoroughly enjoyed spreading the wisdom of natural medicine to my clients. I love teaching others about how to establish a firm foundation for optimal health by strengthening the Four Pillars of Health, i.e., eating wholesome food, engaging in regular exercise, getting adequate sleep, and achieving emotional well-being. The sun beat through my window all day long, which felt like a miracle given how many dark and dreary days of my life I'd spent in Seattle. But sitting at a desk all day was nothing this high energy woman had ever done before and was something that took adjusting to. To deal, I would often skip my lunch hour so I could break a sweat at the gym and give my ass a break from being sat on.

As for my coworkers, I had countless Thai colleagues but my interactions with them never seemed to go beyond superficial smiles and small talk. Being someone who is constantly hungry for deep connection with good friends, my western colleagues were vitally important to me. I couldn't imagine how I would've coped if they weren't there with me. Dave and Monica, as well as the naturopaths from Australia: Katrina, Nadine, and Olivia...seeing their smiling faces every day made my heart sing, even if we only had time for a friendly wink in between clients.

I was truly amazed and intrigued on a daily basis by the cast of international clients I was blessed to work with. My cultural judgments were being broken down, one by one, with each new person I met, while my realization strengthened that every person on this planet, no matter their cultural background, shares this common thread of experiencing the ups and downs of simply being human. And even more than that, I was becoming even more aware of the universality of addiction…

Soizick from France felt addicted to sugar and yet desperately wanted to be thin. Sabi from Iran was addicted to smoking and felt powerless over his ability to quit. A lovely Swiss woman was depressed from her fourth divorce and felt she was addicted to marrying unavailable men. A Japanese client was in desperate need of breaking free from her addiction to work and was under so much pressure she had been considering suicide. A client from Italy, Antonio, was terrified that if he couldn't find help for his alcoholism, his wife and kids would leave him.

Being someone who has struggled on and off since my teenage years with an overwhelming obsession with finding comfort from food, I could relate to these people, desperate to stop their destructive behaviors, yet feeling hopeless and powerless to do so. It was incredibly eye opening and heart breaking to learn how this phenomenon of addiction truly envelops every corner of our globe.

Buddhism explains that most humans spend their lives constantly in a state of either seeking pleasure or avoiding pain, and yet that this way of life leads to suffering. Addiction is when both states are taken to the extreme; taken to the point where the craving for a particular substance or activity creates havoc in one's life, and yet the craving itself exists in order to mask emotional pain; emotional pain the addict is unable to address, either consciously or subconsciously.

The sugar addict hates themselves for the extra weight they carry and eventually refuses to attend social events in order to 'stay safe' at home. The smoker can't keep a job because of their inability to concentrate due to their constant craving to go outside for yet another smoke break. Relationship addicts are

91

terrified to be single yet feel hopeless in their ability to find a suitable mate and thus, settle for destructive relationships. Work addicts live their lives singly focused on productivity, leaving no room for satisfying relationships, relaxation, or even sleep (which can lead to a heart attack or even suicide). Alcoholism and drug abuse, the most common 'addictions' create havoc in absolutely every aspect of one's life.

In my opinion, it doesn't matter what the object of addiction is because all addicts are the same. Underneath the craving is an insatiable hunger…an insatiable hunger for experiencing peace within, for self-acceptance, for feeling safe and loved exactly as you are. This state is priceless and we humans can spend our entire lives in search of it. Insecurity is a universal human experience and everyone designs their unique way of dealing with it…financial success, physical beauty, a refusal to admit fault…. Some adapt quite well and create lives that protect them from feelings of inadequacy. Yet for addicts, they wear their internal pain of self-rejection on their sleeves and desperately reach to their substance of choice in desperation to find relief from it.

I often wondered, "*What could I, a food addict, offer to these desperately hungry clients?*" I could of course give them the typical tricks for how to manage their addiction….avoid slippery situations, create motivating incentives for staying away from the addiction, call someone for support when a craving hits, etc….but these management tools don't address healing the deeper hunger within, which the addiction is unsuccessfully trying to solve in the first place.

As I pondered these questions and studied my constant flow of clients from all over the world, the lines started to blur between the obvious addicts and those with just your everyday, low level of discontent and dissatisfaction with life, who were just hungry for…something…something to bring more joy into their life.

Since I believe addictive behaviors are a band-aid of sorts for covering up deeper issues, I began to ask probing questions that dug beneath their cries for the exact formula for stopping their addiction. At the beginning of every appointment, I started giving my clients a piece of paper and asked them to write the answers to the following two questions: "What do you love about your life?" and, "What do you love about yourself?"

'Success' in today's world is generally defined by fame, fortune, and/or beauty, and many of my clients had all three. They were CEOs of worldwide financial organizations, stunningly beautiful movie stars, talented musicians, influential political figures, celebrated professional athletes…they were 'successful' in every sense of the word. Yet how did they answer these two simple questions? How many put they loved how much money they had? None. How many put they loved how famous they were? None. How many put how much they loved and appreciated their beauty? None.

As a matter of fact, simply answering either question was extremely difficult for many. One man even shrugged when I gave him the paper and handed it to his assistant to answer for him. Most of them stared at the paper for some time before they started writing, some changing the subject to avoid the exercise all together. Others asked me if they could complete it at the end of the day because they needed time to think about it. This apparent universal struggle to answer these simple questions shocked me. It painfully demonstrated how out of touch many humans are with the very aspects of ourselves and of our lives that give us joy. Regardless of their monumental, external accomplishments, there seemed to simmer inside almost every one of them a hunger for something missing in their 'successful' life.

I couldn't help but make the connection between the struggles with various addictive behaviors (and those with just everyday, low-level discontent) and the apparent inability to answer my simple questions. I decided to start asking my clients to describe to me the happiest moments of their life, in order to help them reconnect with what brought them joy throughout their years. Their answers were beautiful and heartfelt…*the day I met my wife, the times I've spent playing with my kids, the year I spent learning to paint, the time I spent playing in a band, the walks I've taken with friends through the gorgeous scenery of nature, the weekends where I did nothing but relaxed and read a good book, the day I could walk again after being on crutches for months, the time I organized a surprise party for my best friend, all the times I've made dinner for loved ones and enjoyed a meal with them, the times I've practiced generosity and helped others in need, the years I made my health a priority and thus felt great in my body…*

When clients answered these questions, their eyes lit up. They sat taller. They suddenly had more energy and their complaints began to dissipate. As a holistic physician, I have been trained to dispense nutritional advice, herbal medicines, vitamins, homeopathy, etc., to treat various ailments. But I began to realize none of those 'medicines' could alchemize someone's discontent into joy as fast as when I asked them to tell me about the happiest times in their life. My favorite 'prescription' soon became having them spend time pondering what they loved about themselves and about life…and then to come see me afterward to discuss what actions they could make once they returned home to create more joy in their life.

I took this same piece of advice for myself. After working six days in a row each week, my day off was always a treat. Since all of my colleagues and I had different days off, and Simon had his own life to attend to thus wasn't always free, I usually spent my day off by myself with plenty of time to ponder my own answers to what I loved about my life, and what I loved about myself.

* * *

There were many gifts about my day off in Thailand while living at the resort. I had no housework to do, no errands, no car, no to-do lists, and no social obligations. It was just me. And the beach. And the sunshine.

After sleeping in, enjoying usually a solid ten hours of sleep, (a precious luxury to be blessed with, I know) I would open my blinds and the sliding glass doors, close my eyes and then soak in the warmth of the morning sun on my naked body. It was an absolute heavenly way to start the day, which I never took for granted. After many attempts to go for a run on the beach and yet arriving with the tide so high that the beach had disappeared, my standard routine was an energizing workout in the gym on the second floor of my building, a quick bite to eat, and then I'd head out for the day.

Most days, I walked the three-minute path down the

alley as I did everyday to work, but instead of passing by the resort dumpsters and heading left through the secret staff entrance, I continued another few seconds and hit the beach. The sand stretched for at least a mile in both directions. The beach was relatively clean but certainly had a bit of trash here and there. Some areas were barren, while others had an assembly line of lawn chairs 'for rent' for $1/day, associated with a little hut that sold food and drink. Then there were the massage tables where I could get an hour-long massage on the beach for a whooping 250 Baht (about $10... and yes, I did that often!). Finally, there were the private beachfronts associated with the Hilton, the Hyatt, or the Marriott (and if you had white skin, you could get away with lying there all day for free).

So my options were to lay out among the swarms of tourists and get hounded non-stop by locals trying to sell me everything from clothes to bananas to sarongs to silk scarves and dried squid, (I never had the guts to try the later though...they sold the whole darn thing, eye balls, guts, and all) or I could pretend I was a guest at one of the fancy hotels and hang out around the pool....which is generally what I did.

Given that hanging out at the hotels became my habitual day-off undertaking, I consciously avoided wearing anything flashy, always wore a big hat to hide my face (I changed them up each week, of course), and diligently suppressed my natural desire to say hello to all the friendly staff poised at any moment to take a drink order or offer me a new towel, in order to fly under the radar of being recognized...a plan I strategically followed successfully, month after month after month.

I had finally begun to release my grip on my lifelong obsession with my daily to-do list running my life (a habit I'd been living with probably since about the seventh grade). I suppose by watching my high achieving parents work diligently as successful attorneys, I had internalized the inaccurate message that the more I achieved, the more I would be considered a good person and the more I would be loved. I've often wondered if my seemingly endless single status is connected to a subconscious belief that I'm still 'not good enough' for love.

These messages we all receive as children...from how smart or dumb we are told we are, to how athletic or not we are, to how lovable or not we are...it is so sad to me to see the

95

degree to which most people live out these often falsely acquired, demeaning messages, long into their adult lives, if not forever.

Although I never had any real errands, my to-do list would still make occasional appearances. It would contain frivolous items such as particular websites I thought I should look up, unimportant errands (like buying a more comfortable seat cushion for my chair at work to reduce the stress on my poor ass from being sat on all day), finding music I wanted to download... Talk about addiction! I often felt like a 'doing' addict. These were the kind of to-do items which could continually churn through my mind on my day off and seriously make relaxing a challenge for me to achieve. (Funny, there's that word again...achieve...looks like I even think of relaxing as something to achieve).

Anyway, the 'pro' side of my endless mental push to always be accomplishing something is I've been very productive in my life, traveled the world multiple times, fulfilled my dream of becoming a doctor, and more. The 'con' side, however, is it's a frickin' exhausting way to live! The ability to just sit down and relax has never been a skill I've been very good at. The good news though is I was getting much better, and often literally threw away my list and simply headed for the beach, which was a huge victory for me indeed!

After I found a comfy lawn chair, I would either take a nap or read. The warmth of the sunshine, the elegantly swaying palm trees, the sparkling ocean, and the travelers from all over the world strolling about...it was a heavenly way to unwind from my old non-stop, high-stress lifestyle of medical school and my endless hours cramped in my little air conditioned office at the resort. Occasionally though, I'd get sad, lying there by myself, surrounded by these seemingly blissfully happy honeymooners and families enjoying their beachside vacation. Loneliness would hit me like a brick, and I would ruminate about how much I missed my family and friends, and wonder how my beloved Jennifur was doing with her new owner.

But then I would remind myself how my life in Thailand would someday just be a distant memory, and I would eventually wish I was actually right back in that moment, lying there in the sun. So I would diligently refocus my thoughts on feeling gratitude for all the beauty that surrounded me. (Practicing being fully present in the moment…not reminiscing about the past, nor fearing or fantasizing about the future…is a core principle of Buddhism I had learned from one of my Thai colleagues. She told me Buddhists believe peace is found by fully being immersed in the present moment. So I started to enjoy practicing that tenet anytime I could remember to.)

I brought my journal on this particular day off and decided to write down my answers to the questions I had been posing to my clients. Exploring and being clear on what one truly loves about life and about oneself I believe is an absolutely necessary exercise for being able to have a pleasurable life. If one does not discover this information for oneself, the fast moving current of life will likely carry them far away from their true desires. The endless expectations from family and from society in general, to attend college, then to start this or that career, to get married and have 2.3 children…ultimately all of this often leads to tragic divorces and painful mid-life crises. Instead of pursuing a life which truly satiates the unique hunger within one's own heart, most pursue 'the right thing to do,' as one's childhood dreams become smashed and forgotten.

"What do I love about my life?" I sat with my journal, pondering the question for a moment. I began to write. *"I live in the sunshine, on a beach. I work with clients from all over the world. I have a steady paycheck. I have a career where I make a positive impact on other's lives. I have family and friends who love me. I have access to insulin, without which, my life would not be possible. I have fresh water (one in eight humans do not). I have a toilet (2.5 billion humans do not). I have all my limbs. I can walk, run, swim, dance, and more. I can see, hear, taste, smell, and feel. I can speak English. I have been blessed with an education. I am a woman, and I can do anything I wish. I am safe. I am free. I am warm. I have clothes"*…I felt blessed how my list kept going on and on and on.

(By the way, it's amazing what a gratitude list does for one's mental health! Each time I do this exercise, which I have made a nightly habit now for many years, it washes away any discontent that may be stirring in my mind from the day and reminds me how fantastic my life really is. I love this daily practice and I highly recommend it!)

"What do I love about myself?" I continued to write…*"I make my health a priority: I exercise daily, eat a healthy diet, sleep eight*

97

hours regularly. I fulfilled my childhood dream of becoming a doctor. I am passionate about inspiring others to improve their health and to live a life of their dreams. I've made a career out of helping others. I have a radiant smile and an athletic body. I am bold. I am adventurous. I have been to 23 U.S. states and 24 countries. I always call my family or friends on their birthdays. I love sending greeting cards just because. I am responsible with money. I take great care of the environment. I am willing to admit fault and apologize when needed. I love telling others what I appreciate about them, strangers included..."

I felt blessed to have my answers flow so fluently. Furthermore, I was touched by how the very things I loved about my life and myself were a part of my present experience. I closed my journal, inhaled a breath of gratitude for my surroundings, and exhaled into a deep slumber, right there on my elegant lawn chair, on the beautiful grass, under a swaying palm tree, in the sunshine...beachside in Thailand.

✳✳✳

The beach faced east so the sun disappeared by 4 p.m. and the slight chill awakened me. But I continued to lie there until dark, which was around 7 p.m. because, well, why not?! I certainly didn't have anything I should do or anywhere else to go! The only impetus to eventually get me up from my state of relaxed bliss was hunger. (This was the downside of lying on the hotel property versus on the beach. If I were on the beach, I would've been swarmed by the locals, hungry in their own right, to sell me their wares.) So I eventually packed up my things, became incognito by donning my big straw hat, and headed out barefoot along the beach in search of food.

I strolled along for only about five minutes until discovering a swanky, touristy restaurant all lit up in sparkling lights. I checked out the menu...no local Thai prices here! In town, I could enjoy dinner for the equivalent of two to three American Dollars. But at this place, I might as well have been at some hip restaurant in downtown anywhere, USA.

As I walked in the smiling hostess asked, "Two for

dinner?"

I confidently replied, "No, just me."

In addition to my big straw hat, I was also wearing a loud, striped skirt. So there I was, this boldly dressed woman, dining alone…not a common occurrence in Thailand to say the least. The charming hostess sat me at a large table in the middle of the dining room, and then flashed an awkward glance my way as she brought me a magazine. I was not sure if this was customary or if she just didn't know what else to do, since I was a woman eating alone in their dining room.

I ordered a tropical papaya-pineapple drink and a delicious grilled zucchini appetizer to start. My entrée was a divine seafood dish, artistically placed in a coconut shell. Sitting there glancing around at the tables full of vacationing families and love-struck honeymooners, I started fantasizing I was there as an actress, staring in a Hollywood movie. I felt compelled to keep my big straw hat on throughout my entire meal. In order to see anyone, I literally had to tilt my head back a bit and look up from underneath its wide brim. Throughout the evening, I just lounged there smiling and enjoying my scrumptious meal, fully embracing my self-proclaimed role as the mysterious movie star, hidden under her big straw hat, eating alone in the dining room.

Day 5:
Learn to Play With The Curve Balls of Life
August 2008

I woke up on day five, and was greeted by thoughts of dread. _"Oh my God! I already feel like I've been here for a year yet I'm not even half way done with this treacherous retreat!"_

The thought of sitting with myself and diligently focusing on being neutral to my bodily sensations, hour after hour, while attempting to find a comfortable position on my little meditation cushion on the floor, sounded like absolute hell to me that morning. I took a deep breath and reminded myself of the lesson from the night before.

"Jody, you do not have to pay heed to your negative thoughts. Shift your focus to find that eternal well of peace within you." As I rolled my eyes, my over-achieving self stepped up and donned the hat of 'obedient student.'

During the first session of the day however, I had an experience unlike anything I had encountered during the previous days. It effectively dissipated my thoughts of dread, as its oddity fully captured my attention. As I was sitting motionless, scanning my body for sensations and remaining neutral to them, my body started to jerk. It wasn't consistent jerking, like having a seizure, but my body would jolt about every minute or so. Preceding the jolt, I would feel a surge of energy tightening, usually somewhere in my back, and then suddenly, POW! My whole body would flail causing the original tight feeling to dissipate.

I was fascinated by this odd occurrence, which continued on and on…sitting there as I was calmly meditating, then JOLT, calmly meditating, then JOLT…all day long. I was a bit disturbed and confused about this when it first started happening. I opened my eyes in hopes of seeing others experiencing the same thing, but no luck.

My mind was spinning, hungry for an explanation. I came up with a theory at lunchtime that I must just be releasing knots of physical tension I'd been carrying around for who knows how many years. I didn't have any other ideas of how to explain it, so this theory luckily satiated my curious mind for the time being.

After lunch, I decided to go on a leisurely stroll around the property. The jolting did not occur as I walked, as it did during the subsequent meditation sessions that day. This strange and unexpected phenomenon made me think about how life is inevitably always full of surprises. I certainly could never have dreamed my first job after medical school would be at an international, health resort for the rich and famous in Thailand. Nor did I imagine I would still be single at the age of 35.

I smiled at this truth that inevitable surprises and unexpected detours are inherent in life. No matter how well thought out my plans may be, life will continue to pitch countless curve balls my way, some explainable and some not; some enjoyable, some not. I related this truth to the lesson about how peace comes from practicing non-attachment... not only to material things but to ideas and plans as well. No matter how predictable life may seem, it is impossible to accurately predict what will unfold each day.

Thinking about the depth of uncertainty inherent in life and the fact how the only things I really have full control over are my thoughts and attitudes, my motivation to strengthen my ability to connect with my supposed eternal spring of peace within me suddenly soared.

For the rest of the day I did my best to continue with the instructed methodology of how to meditate. But one minute I would be calmly noticing the warmth in my toes, and then the next, JOLT! My body would suddenly contort. I almost laughed out loud at one point, just at the mere peculiarity of what I was experiencing. In my mind, I diligently kept tabs on the fact that, even though sitting still as I was instructed to do was proving to be impossible, it was entirely up to me to choose my attitude about it...as is true with absolutely every situation in life.

Chapter 10:
The Inevitable Ebb and Flow of Life
April 2008

Life constantly ebbs and flows…the waves roll in and out, the sun comes up and goes down, the clouds rumble in and float away, I laugh and I cry, there is beauty and pain….and in Thailand there is an interesting mix of both wealth and poverty. For example, as I drove through town (or I should say…as I rode on the back of a motor bike taxi or sat on 'the bus'), I would often pass by luxury resorts, built next to makeshift homes made from metal and wood scraps. I'd see stunning homes with spectacular views built high on a cliff top, built next to shanty towns for laborers who were building yet another ritzy resort on the beach.

One of the many beautiful parts of the Thai culture is how kind and gentle the people are. Men and women of all ages always smiled at me. I never saw anyone upset or angry. The nurses I worked with were always laughing (but usually spoke in Thai so I felt a bit awkward, not ever knowing what was so funny). The men at the cafeteria during our lunch hour would commonly be engaged in an impassioned game of chess or checkers.

As I listened to the BBC news on my television every morning while I got ready for work, the most common words I heard were, 'the economy,' 'the markets,' 'the recession,' 'the mortgage crisis,' 'money, money, money…' I would think to myself, _'Something is missing here.'_ It was becoming very evident from working with many of my clients that money certainly does not create fulfillment, nor guarantee happiness. And yet, isn't exactly that ultimately what everybody is _truly_ hungry for in life…a true sense of happiness and fulfillment?

The 'poor' people who lived near the resort were almost always smiling and laughing with their friends. Juxtapose that to the rich executives who would walk into my office, overweight, stressed, and seemingly minutes away from having a heart attack. This was an enlightening observation. I realized a vast array of possibilities indeed exist for how to create a fulfilling and 'rich' life, which go far beyond simply having financial 'security'.

Because I spent most of my days off by myself, I had plenty of time to ponder life's truths. I realized beauty always exists right in front of me, yet the choice to see it or not is totally up to me. It just depends on how I choose to define it. Were the smiling Thai families 'richer' than my stressed out wealthy clients? I think so. An 'enjoyable' life is purely a matter of perspective and attitude.

Furthermore, I realized that viewing life's ups and downs, the ebb and flow of life if you will, as both necessary and purposeful is a much more joyful way to live, as opposed to constantly judging our experiences as good or bad, right or wrong. The sun cannot come up if it never goes down. The tide cannot come in if it never goes out. The Eastern principle of yin and yang states opposites must and do co-exist in nature in order to create balance. How could we explain 'hot' if we did not experience 'cold?' Without contrast, we experience nothingness. Everything in the world exists as either yin or yang: male and female, stillness and movement, stone and water, joy and pain...and yet each opposite is intricately connected to the other, thus always containing a bit of the other within itself. It is impossible for a one-sided coin to exist. Men have a female aspect to their personalities and women have a male aspect. One cannot exist without the other for life to sustain itself. A key principle in Buddhism is to embrace this concept of the necessity of balance between yin and yang.

So for myself, instead of judging my successes as 'good' and my failures as 'bad,' I choose to now see both as necessary and valuable parts of my journey through life.

One evening, hungry for a massage after sitting inside my office all day, I exited through the secret staff entrance in the granite fortress and took a walk on the beach, watching the sun fall low in the sky. My options were limited because most of the massages huts had already been broken down and closed up for the day. But I got lucky and found one place still open for business. I walked up with a smile and gleefully laid down on one of the tables in the sand. None of the women in the hut seemed to speak English, but they clearly knew my desire.

As I lay there receiving my heavenly, beachside massage, I was captivated by the music of crashing waves and the beauty of deep orange and red hues of the night sky. I felt so lucky. To

103

my right was a group of local kids playing soccer, laughing and having a great time. In terms of yin and yang, they would represent the yang side of life. Yang is represented by the characteristics of fire, wind and movement (versus 'yin' characteristics, which are heavy, slow, and dark).

Then I turned my head and looked down the beach to my left. I noticed a dog. Swarms of homeless dogs were often on the beach, as well as running around in town. They ran around all day long hungrily looking for food. Well to my left, was a dog, but the dog was dead. Children joyfully playing soccer to my right (yang) and a dead dog to my left (yin)…a perfect depiction of two necessary and inevitable extremes in life.

Death to me is not something 'bad' – in fact, it acts as a powerful reminder that life indeed will end and it serves as a motivator to savor every day we are blessed to have. Don Juan, an elder from the Yaqui Indian tribe and teacher of the famous author Carlos Castenada said, *"Always keep death at your left shoulder."* The lesson of this quote is that by keeping death on the forefront of our mind, it acts as a daily reminder that everything in life is constantly changing and will inevitably come to an end. And as the Buddhist teach, why bother tightly clinging to or resisting anything, since it will eventual fall away anyway?

Life for everybody will indeed come to an end one day. By remembering this truth, the present moment and the many gifts it holds are far less likely to be taken for granted. We focus on living in the now, and realize the futility of holding onto past regrets, or fearing the future. We allow more joy to flow to us as we relax into accepting the present moment exactly as it is, letting go of resistance.

Yet living fully in the present moment is incredibly challenging for most adults. Children, on the other hand, do it effortlessly and thus usually live with much more joy than grown-ups. Why is this? First, we have been taught that thinking and analyzing, which keep up us wrapped up in our thoughts, are powerful and effective means for achieving success. Secondly, many of us fear looking deeply within. We fear seeing our own truth of how far we are from living the kind of life we truly desire, and/or we fear fully accepting life as it is and letting go of the way we think it should be.

I often think of the many stories of cancer patients who

are given three months to live and then go on living for years. This 'death sentence' makes them realize the futility of their fears and worries, and allows them to live an unabashedly, authentic life. The resulting shift in their energy actually has a healing effect on their body and can result in experiencing the happiest years of their life, as well as living years beyond their given prognosis.

So how would I describe my overall experience that evening on the beach...heavenly massage plus dead dog? It was perfect; perfectly imperfect. The luxuriousness of receiving a massage at dusk on the beach contrasted by lying next to a dead dog, with its reminder to me to focus on the profound beauty present in each fleeting moment of my life. If it were not for the painful experiences of life, no one would be able to experience and more importantly, appreciate, the opposite state of joy. Learning to embrace the light, as well as the dark side of life, without judging one as good or bad, as well as focusing on the gifts always alive in each present moment is where I believe true peace lies. This was a core piece of wisdom I was certainly learning to embrace during my life in Thailand.

*** *** ***

I used to love doing handstands in the shallow ocean water as a little girl during our annual trip to Maui with my sister and wonderful grandparents. My prudent and loving Granddad (who's upcoming 95th birthday party in Seattle I would be missing) would always have to be sure to catch me as soon as we arrived at the beach to lather on the sunscreen and have me put on my white t-shirt before I ran off to play in the waves for hours on end.

One of my days off was reminiscent of these past memories...I was playing in the waves, doing handstands in the water with the exuberance of my childlike self in full radiance. Two young Thai girls were attracted to my zest and floated over to me on their inner tube. We communicated using the only language we shared, smiles and body language. Much to my heart's content, they motioned for me to join them. Within seconds after I climbed aboard, we got pummeled by a wave, which flipped our inner tube upside down and sent us spinning into the rumbling white water breaking up on the shore. We burst out laughing as we each tried to find our balance and come to our feet.

Quickly, we dashed back on the inner tube just in time to be pummeled again by the next incoming wave. With every wave crashing on top of us and flipping us over, we laughed harder and harder. I hadn't laughed this much since I'd moved to Thailand. It felt phenomenal. Eventually though, my adult self was ready to lounge on the beach. I smiled and hugged my newfound friends as I walked out from the water and joyfully took a seat on the sand.

Relaxing for not more than a few seconds, I suddenly noticed a young boy about ten yards ahead of me building a colossal sculpture in the sand. I absolutely loved making sand castles with my sprightly grandfather during our annual trip to Maui. I immediately let go of any notion of how a 35-year-old woman in a bikini is 'supposed' to act and ran over to help him. He smiled as he signaled to me thumbs up. I was thrilled.

He was digging up sand from one area and putting it into a huge pile so I followed suit to help him. As I continued to dig and dump, his facial expression became very focused as he began morphing our pile into some sort of creature. His artistic passion came out as he started directing the angles of four legs, perfecting the shape of the back, and sculpting a spine. I just kept digging and dumping sand for him to sculpt, digging and dumping, digging and dumping.

Soon a small crowd gathered around us. There were two blond kids, (whom I'm guessing were Swedish…lots of Swedes spend their winter there; there is even a small Swedish elementary school in town), four white-skinned adults from who knows where, and a couple of local Thai kids. They all just stood there, admiring this mass of sand the young boy was bringing to life, moment by moment with every creative detail he added.

The boy stood back and accessed his stunning creation, then leaned in to make a few adjustments to the 'bones' of the spine and the size of the feet. He then pulled out a handful of shells from his pocket and with them made two eyes, a pair of ears, a long nose and a full mouth of teeth. He took a step back to assess his creation, smiling with a look of great pride. He seemed thoroughly satisfied with his accomplishment of transforming this previously nebulous pile of sand into a beautifully sculpted, incredibly life-like dinosaur.

Suddenly, a group of stray dogs noticed the 'dinosaur' and began madly barking at it! They were about 30 feet away and seemed reluctant to come any closer. The whole crowd of us just stood there, half in awe and half laughing out loud. I imagined their thought process as they looked at one another quizzically, and back again at the 'dinosaur' to be something like, *"What the %$#! is that?!"* This went on for almost five minutes...more barking, attempts at coming closer, then running back, tilting their heads as they exchanged perplexed looks with one another, and more barking.

My stomach ached from laughing so hard. It was absolutely one of the most hilarious experiences of my life.

✳✳✳

Four months had passed. Things at work were going pretty well. I was feeling extremely fulfilled by the positive impact I was having working with my patients. For example, one day I had a 59-year-old, very proper German woman break down in tears in my office about an unresolved issue she had with her mother, who had passed away years ago. Throughout her childhood, her father was very sick and needed to be cared for around the clock. She told me she was never a very good helper to her mom during their struggles caring for her father.

Through her tears, I heard her mutter, "I was a horrible daughter."

She quickly tried to suppress her tears and belittle the level of impact this lifelong belief was having on her present day life.

I spoke to her gently, leaning forward as if sharing a precious secret, "Just ignoring it does not make the pain go away."

As the tears streamed down her face, I sensed it was the first time in her life she'd ever let herself feel her pain around this issue. She continued to tell me however that her mother actually never verbalized this belief to her. In fact, she often told her what wonderful a daughter she was. Yet, as children often do, she had come up with her own distorted version of reality, and sadly had been carrying the guilt of being a 'bad daughter' her entire lifetime. For whatever reason during her appointment that day she was finally ready, to let go of her false belief and accept she had done the best she could.

After her tears had ceased, she looked at me with a newfound glow of peace. She stood up tall and thanked me for allowing her to feel so safe and hugged me before walking out.

The following day she stopped by my office and I almost didn't recognize her. She had a lighter air about her and looked dramatically younger. Her husband came in to thank me too. He was glowing, as was I. It felt fantastic to be interacting with people on such a profound, healing level.

Another client of mine was a self-professed, life-long alcoholic. He was convinced because he had been sober, exercising, and feeling better than ever for a mere six days at the resort, his drinking life was forever behind him and he was confident he'd never touch the stuff again. Although it was wonderful to see him feeling so great, I had to teach him about the 'pink cloud' phenomenon.

"There is a term for the initial joy and exhilaration one feels after finally being free from any sort of habitual, destructive behavior. It's called, 'riding on a pink cloud.' It feels wonderfully freeing, but the reality is this period does not last forever. When the elation comes to its inevitable end, it is vital to have a strategy in place for avoiding cravings when they arise, because they inevitably will again. Establishing a plan for continued help once you return home is essential." Unfortunately, I don't think he absorbed much of what I said, but at least I had planted a seed.

It was incredibly fulfilling to be having such a positive impact on others' lives. It brought to mind all the wonderful help my family and I received 30 years prior during the week I was at the hospital learning to live with diabetes. Now I was the one giving back to others. If I hadn't become diabetic, perhaps I would not have pursued such a satisfying career. To me this is a great example of the balancing forces between yin and yang...the weight of living with my chronic condition served to create my drive to pursue a career of helping others. Yet, although I do my best at accepting this laborious challenge of living with diabetes on a daily basis, the dream of being cured, someday, has always simmered in the back of my mind.

Speaking of diabetes, a quick side note…no matter where in the world I go, there is no such thing as taking a 'vacation' from managing Type 1 Diabetes (which is a very different condition than the pandemic in America of Type 2 Diabetes, by the way). It doesn't matter if I'm living in America or Thailand, I must always be diligent about taking care of my condition, as I have been everyday since I was seven. Before every single meal in the past 30 years, I have poked my finger in order to test my blood sugar level and then have given myself an injection of insulin. The only other event in my adventurous life which has occurred with more steadfast consistency is the beating of my heart. When in the company of others who witness me milking my finger to get a drop of blood or who see me giving myself a shot before a meal, a common response voiced is, *"Are you a diabetic? Oh, I'm so sorry. That must be awful."*

If you are ever in the company of a diabetic (or, I think it's safe for me to speak for anyone living with a lifelong, physical condition, for that matter), let me just take a moment to request to please *never* say that. Yes, living with a chronic disease is challenging, but a key way in which I have chosen to surmount this fact is by focusing on how living with diabetes has *strengthened* my life, and certainly not by subscribing to the belief that my life is 'awful.' However, of course there are days when my thoughts get sucked down into that black hole of negativity. Thus when others echo that sentiment back to me, it fuels that line of pessimistic and pitiful thinking, which I'm trying with all my might *not* to pay heed to.

Also, by uttering that statement, it makes me acutely aware the person truly has no idea what the real challenges of living with diabetes actually are. If all I had to do was poke my finger and give myself a shot before each meal, frankly, I would be elated! That part for me is the easiest part of living with this disease. What people *don't* see behind my smiley face are the endless calculations that churn through my mind (which literally at times can make me feel like I'm going crazy, or can make those I am eating my meal with think I've mentally disappeared from the table) as I try to figure out how much insulin I need at each meal to keep my blood sugar level balanced.

I must calculate the amount of carbohydrates I eat at every meal and snack, and then figure out the corresponding correct dose of insulin to keep my blood sugar level in the normal range. As I sit there and try to enjoy my food, I can second-guess myself throughout the entire meal, wondering if the salad dressing is so sweet that maybe I need another unit of insulin. Or if I order chicken (which does not contain carbohydrates, only protein) but it comes with an unexpected pile of rice, I need more insulin to cover the carbohydrates if I decide to eat the rice. So as I'm calculating the dose I need for each meal, I also need to know in advance if I'll be having dessert. If I will, then I need to account for that when I give myself my shot. But then suppose for whatever reason, dessert doesn't happen. Well, I'll still have to drink some juice or eat some other carbohydrate to keep my blood sugar level from dropping due to the insulin I gave myself in expectation of dessert.

But relatively speaking, deciding on the correct dose of insulin is still a somewhat easy part of my challenge. What taxes me more than anything is when I don't accurately match the amount of carbohydrate (which is not just 'sugar' in the dessert or candy sense but includes rice, bread, fruit, corn, potatoes…) with the appropriate dose of insulin, what ensues is an exhausting (and that is a gross understatement) emotional and/or energy roller coaster. For example, when my blood sugar level drops too low, I get weak and extremely tired. If I don't ingest some sugar quickly, I will fall into a diabetic coma (induced by the lack of fuel to my brain…yet luckily in all of my years living with this disease, I have been fortunate to never experience this, knock on wood). A low blood sugar is something that can be reconciled in minutes (assuming I have had the foresight to carry sugar with me…which does not always happen).

Alternatively, if my blood sugar level soars too high, it can take an hour or more before it is restored to a healthy level. Being 'high,' as I refer to it, is when depression, foggy thinking, and exhaustion tend to rear their ugly heads. If I am lucky, I'll figure out the true cause behind my sudden dark turn in mood and energy, and immediately head outside for a run around the block for 10 or 20 minutes to restore my sugar level to normal (given I am not stuck in some meeting, attempting to focus my energy on a brain draining medical exam, or am trying to enjoy the elegance of a fancy dinner, for example). However, the thought that I am once again having another bad day often trumps my ability to make the wiser choice.

Lets say I happen to hit the bulls-eye and actually choose the exact dose of insulin I need to perfectly balance my blood sugar level given the amount of carbohydrate in my snack or meal. Well, there is another element that must also be present to allow my blood sugar level to remain stable. Just because I inject the insulin into my body does not mean it takes immediate effect. If I am, let's say, just sitting and chatting at the table after I take my shot, it can take up to an hour for the insulin to start working. Alternatively, if I am moving around at all, let's say, in the kitchen cooking, it works faster. Furthermore, just because I am chewing and swallowing my food, does not mean the carbohydrates immediately enter my blood stream. Thus another key element, after matching the amount of insulin I need with the amount of carbohydrate in my meal, is to also somehow time the peaking of my insulin with the digestion of my food into my blood stream. (Are you tired yet?) AND, another element I must consider before deciding on my insulin dose is the level of exercise that I may have undertaken before my meal or will undertake after my meal.

High blood sugar levels over time damage arteries and thus are the cause behind the potential long-term side effects of diabetes, such as heart attacks, strokes, kidney failure, blindness, and losing toes or even feet to gangrene. Having revealed those horrific truths, I actually feel confident that, given the regularity with which good nutrition, regular exercise, adequate sleep, and a generally positive attitude (indeed, I diligently follow my own advice of keeping a strong Four Pillars of Health) have been a part of my life, I will live a much longer and healthier life than many of the "normal" people in American culture today, who damage their lungs and arteries with smoking, fast food, sedentary lives, and the like. But of course, I still dream about the day I will be cured...

Chapter 11:
The Promise of a Cure for Diabetes
April 2008

So one day as I was walking through town on my day off, I strolled by two Caucasian men and just so happened to hear one of them say the word, 'diabetes.' My gregarious and curious self had to stop and say hello.

"Hi, my name is Jody. I couldn't help but overhear you talking about diabetes. I have had Type 1 for 30 years."

(When you are in a foreign country, just the fact that someone standing next to you is speaking your language is enough of a reason in itself to say hello and start a friendly conversation...well, at least I think so.)

Tom, the taller of the two, was the CEO of a stem cell research company. They were talking about a procedure his company was having success with in curing diabetes, and then said, *"including Type 1."*

Type 1 Diabetes is an autoimmune disease where the immune system attacks and kills the insulin producing cells. At this point in history, Type 1 is considered entirely incurable (as opposed to the good potential for reversal in the more prevalent condition of Type 2 Diabetes, given the person adopts a healthy lifestyle).

Having been promised a cure 'within five years' since I was ten years old, (I still have the original newspaper article my dad cut out for me, dated June 13, 1983 professing this prediction, as well as a treasure chest of other empty promises about a cure), my initial reaction to his audacious statement was one of doubt and skepticism. Yet, within seconds of listening to his scientific explanation of the procedure his company had developed, my doubt alchemized into child-like hope and excitement. I started crying, standing right there in front of him on the street, drinking in with unbridled hope his every word.

Our conversation unfortunately came to an abrupt halt as he looked at his watch and informed me he had to get back to his office in Bangkok by 4 p.m. He said he would be happy to discuss the procedure further and asked if I could make it to Bangkok sometime.

Knowing I would do anything in my power to get myself there on my next day off, I asked, "How about exactly a week from today?"

"Sounds good. Call me to set up a time." He handed his card to me as he and the other gentleman rushed away.

I stood there in disbelief and shock, yet I decided to suppress any glimmer of hope until I found out more. I've ridden the roller coaster of exhilaration and disappointment about being cured so many times in my life that I decided to put it out of my mind until then. And that is what I did for the next week.

✳✳✳

Some random day, early 1970s: A young boy, by the name of Bill Gates is sitting at a table with his friend, Steve, and few others. They are discussing this 'thingy' they want to create...

Bill: Its like a typewriter but bigger, faster.

Always-negative friend: Why would you want something bigger than a typewriter?

Bill: It can hold lots of info, maybe even more than an entire volume of an encyclopedia. You could use it to write a book, to write a letter, to save any written document you could ever dream of wanting to save...all in this one 'thingy.' It will even be able to do math if you want it to.

One of much doubt: If it's like all other machines, it will break down and the math won't be accurate.

Bill: It will be able to double-check itself. It will even be able to tell you if you spelled something rong.

Skeptical voice: Operating it will be incredibly complicated. Nobody would be able to handle it.

Steve: Anyone will be able to use it. All ages. Students will need it. Retirees will want to play with it. And everyone else, everyone will have one.

Naysayer friend: Well then, even if that is true, which it's not, you certainly wouldn't be able to produce enough to keep up with the demand.

Steve: That won't be an issue. Production will take care of itself...because we will be using 'it' to run everything. Businesses will be able to organize all of their operations with it...they will eventually not be able to survive without one.

Naysayer friend: Don't be ridiculous. That's thinking a bit too big, don't you think?

Bill: Nope. It's going to be huge.... change the world. And anything you naysayers have to say, go ahead. Just watch me...

One of much doubt: rolls his eyes... *"Lunch, anyone?"*

...This dialogue is the perfect introduction for what I was about to learn the following week in Bangkok. After my meeting with Tom, I felt as if I had been introduced to the 'Microsoft of medical advancements!'...

When Tom invited me to see him in Bangkok to learn more about his company's procedure to potentially cure diabetes, I really wasn't expecting much more than a quick meeting. During our brief interaction on the sidewalk, Tom had mentioned that his sister died at a young age of cardiac complications due to diabetes, so I knew he had a soft spot for helping other diabetics and figured he just wanted to share the good news about this potential cure with me. I assumed we'd just be having coffee or lunch, maybe 30 or 60 minutes at the most. Regardless, it was a great excuse for me to get out of Hua Hin and check out the thriving metropolis of Bangkok, which I had yet to even explore. (When I flew in, I was whisked away in a town car in the middle of the night so I didn't get to see the city at all. The only thing I've ever had to relate to Bangkok thus far in my life is that 80's song, *"One night in Bangkok, and the world's your oyster…"* So I was ready to finally be able to experience, first hand, what it felt like to have the 'world be my oyster'…)

The week crawled by and finally my day off arrived. I jumped on a bus to Bangkok in eager anticipation. Tom and I met in the lobby of one of Bangkok's many high-rise office buildings at noon. I reached out, shaking his hand, "Hi Tom! Thank you very much for taking the time to meet with me today. I greatly appreciate it!"

We headed down a hallway and then entered into an elegant boardroom…not exactly the coffee shop or lunch spot I was expecting! I hoped the shock I felt didn't show on my face. Not only were we meeting in an elegant boardroom, but there were three men already sitting at the table wearing suits and ties. I shifted from foot to foot, uncomfortable in my laid-back-Jody attire, a t-shirt and baseball hat, thinking, *"Okay, just be yourself. It's not a big deal."*

"Hi Jody. My name is John Eker and I am a biomedical scientist."

I shook his hand, "Nice to meet you John."

"Hello. I am Robert." That was all I got. No title or company name. But after my initial confusion to his role in this esoteric meeting, I later figured out he was an investor. They continued around the table, introducing themselves, one by one.

"I am Terrence, from Scientific Marketing Agency."

"It is very nice to meet all of you. I cannot thank you enough for your time today." I was experiencing a mix of emotions, to say the least. Why these men were taking their time to meet with me was a bit of a mystery, but I wasn't going to question it; I was too excited to hear what they had to say. After the introductions and some small talk, they pulled down a movie screen and for the next TWO hours, we had a discussion about this new process called, 'Autologous Adipose Tissue Stem Cell Transplantation.'

We went through over 50 slides. Knowing I was a physician, John gave me in-depth detail of the biology and physiology behind the procedure. But before explaining what I learned, a little biology lesson is needed first…

The human body is made up of trillions of cells. In every moment of one's lifetime, cells are dying and new ones are being born. This phenomenon only comes to a halt once ultimate death arrives. In fact, even 'solid' bone tissue continually undergoes this process. So it makes sense that stem cells exist all throughout our bodies. How does a broken bone heal? Stem cells become activated and new bone is made. After skin is cut, stem cells housed in the skin are activated to heal it. Anytime there is damage in the body, the damaged cells send out chemical messengers to activate stem cells to arrive on the scene and create new cells.

Embryonic stem cells have been a topic of great debate because they are almost totally 'undifferentiated,' which means they have the potential to turn into almost any cell in the body. Once cells mature, their potential becomes narrower and narrower as to the range of what cell type they can turn into. (Yet new sources of stem cells are being discovered in the body continually, so hopefully the fiery debate around stem cells will soon be a thing of the past.) Bone marrow is a rich source of stem cells, and scientists from around the world have been dabbling in experiments using another plentiful source: adipose tissue, or more commonly known as, FAT.

I was blown away by what I learned that day (as I sheepishly sat there in my t-shirt and baseball hat with these well-dressed men in that elegant boardroom in Bangkok). I felt as if I were one of Bill Gates friends, sitting with him as he was sharing his ideas on this 'thingy' he wanted to invent...

The procedure they presented was simple. Fat is removed via liposuction, using local anesthetic. The fat is dissolved and the stem cells are purified out, which only takes about an hour. Protein peptides are then added to the mix to turn the dormant stem cells into 'activated' cells. (Takes about another hour). The activated cells are then put back into the body using a simple IV drip. The activated stem cells are then drawn to wherever damage exists in the body (because damaged cells actually secrete chemical messengers which say to the body, *"come help me please"*).

They had data from almost 200 people over the past two years....three with MS, one with cerebral palsy, one with Parkinson's, thirty-seven with Type 2 Diabetes, and (drum roll please) three with Type 1 Diabetics. The thirty-seven Type 2

Diabetics had all experienced significant drops in their blood sugar levels, as was true for the Type 1's.

Two big questions arose for me. The first was, having had diabetes for almost 30 years, it is theorized my insulin secreting cells are all dead and gone, and have been for years. But was that really true? I wanted to know if there would be an adequate amount of chemical messengers still being secreted from my damaged pancreas to even direct the activated stem cells to make new insulin producing cells. The second was, the reason I have diabetes in the first place is because my immune system, for some unknown reason, erroneously killed my insulin producing cells...so what would keep my body from doing that again?

John, the biomedical scientist, answered my first inquiry, confidently replying that yes indeed my pancreas would still be secreting the needed chemical messengers. I wasn't sure I believed him though. As for my second question, he explained the immune system can be retrained to welcome the new cells and not attack them. I accepted this answer with cautious optimism.

However, even if my immune system eventually killed my new insulin producing cells, receiving two injections a year of new stem cells (or whatever the necessary frequency would be for keeping enough insulin producing cells constantly alive inside of me) would surely beat my present daily ritual of ten shots per day, plus all the other headaches I incur living with diabetes, literally and figuratively!

Towards the end of our meeting, the mystery of why they were taking so much time with me was finally solved. Their company was based in the Philippines. Being that Thailand was fast becoming *the* hot spot in the world for medical tourism, they had come to Bangkok for a few days to seek out opportunities to expand their work there. They informed me that when relatively healthy people have this procedure, results seen include dramatic weight loss, improved energy, decreased blood pressure, improved skin tone, re-growth of hair for men, increased sex drive, and more. Ah-ha! I figured out their motive. The most lucrative market for this procedure is not diabetics, but wealthy people looking for the fountain of youth.

When first meeting Tom on the sidewalk the week before, I had casually mentioned the name of the spa where I worked...which happened to be one of the main targets on their list to meet with while in Thailand. So when Tom learned I was an employee there, he apparently was as overjoyed to meet me, as I was to meet him. (A great win-win you could say!)

Our meeting came to an end. Tom handed me the email addresses of the three Type 1's who had received the procedure and in return, I promised I'd talk to my boss about setting up an appointment to meet with him. I walked away, grinning from ear to ear, envisioning my boss agreeing to have the procedure available at the resort and me being the first client! My excitement though was mixed with the desire to suppress it, in order to keep me from experiencing yet again another failed promise of a cure. But nonetheless, I mostly let my imagination go wild and enjoyed the fantasy of it all working out perfectly, and finally being cured of this lifelong disease.

I walked outside to the bustling metropolis of Bangkok. Yet my desire for exploration was nowhere in sight. I headed straight into a Starbucks (which I happened to notice that morning next door to my hotel) to use their free WiFi to email the three diabetics who had experienced this procedure. Were they really cured?! Was their pancreas really making insulin again?! Nothing I could see or do that afternoon in Bangkok...this famous international city, rich with its long history and sparkling temples, which I had yet to even explore since arriving in Thailand months prior...mattered to me more than reaching the three diabetics and hearing about their experience.

I anxiously sent the three emails, full of my spinning questions, and then had to take a deep breath as a reminder of the virtue of practicing patience. I decided to head straight to the bus station to embark on my three-hour ride back home. I needed to use the time to mentally prepare myself to somehow be fully present for the needs of my clients the next day.

***

Much to my heart's delight, when checking my email the very next morning before work, I had already received a reply.

Philip was 23, and he'd had diabetes for seven years. His uncle was the surgeon who performed the procedure in the Philippines. He received it three months ago, and as a result, his insulin needs had been gradually dropping and were continuing to do so. He had thus far cut his total insulin dose by half. He had nothing but positive things to say about his experience. The procedure went smoothly and he felt safe with every aspect of it. And although the question of whether he will reach the point where he no longer needs insulin had yet to be answered, he seemed to be thrilled with his results thus far. I finished reading his email, not so much with excitement though as with disbelief and skepticism.

I was ten years old when my dad handed me the article stating there would be a cure in five years. I held onto that article with brimming anticipation as I became more and more excited each year as the date drew nearer. When the five year mark came and went, my optimistic self just smiled and knew it would be, 'any day now!' But as the years continued to pass, with no announcement of 'The Cure,' somewhere along the way my muscle of optimism and faith became too weary to be sustained any longer, and sadness and disappointment took over. I built a wall of protection around my heart to make sure I'd never again become excited about any news touting the promise of a cure.

But this situation felt more real to me than anything I'd ever read before. Philip had actually experienced the procedure and his insulin needs had consequently dropped dramatically. It didn't feel like an empty promise. Those were real life results. The skeptical voice in my head though would remind me of the endless empty promises of the past and shake its finger at my excitement to protect me from being disappointed again.

But then my thoughts would swing back to eager anticipation and joy. At some point during medical school, I started having a deep sense I would indeed experience life without diabetes, someday, just as I had for the first seven years of my life. I couldn't help but think perhaps my time had come! *"Hi, my name is Dr. Jody Stanislaw. I USED to have Type 1 Diabetes."* That astounding dream kept dancing around in my head. I started having visions of talking to Oprah about my miraculous transformation, while giving inspiration to the world about never giving up on believing anything is possible. I was ready to be living proof.

Day 6:
Patience and Persistence Bring Success
August 2008

Day six had arrived. I had made it over the hump. Yes!
But I still had five days to go. To entertain myself as I was
brushing my teeth that morning...standing next to the others in
the bathroom doing the same, yet with each of us looking off in
different directions to avoid 'eye communication' and, heaven
forbid, perhaps an accidental smile...I added up how many
hours I had meditated thus far.

I had missed the early morning session of day one
(admittedly, on two other days as well), as well as skipped out on
a few other sessions to keep from going stir crazy and having my
butt fall asleep from sitting hour after hour on my little cushion
on the wood floor. The total time scheduled each day was eight
and a half hours, but I figured I missed at least an hour and a
half each day, so the total I came up with was 35 hours. As my
electric toothbrush was whizzing away, I almost choked on it
after having made this realization (which was a bit awkward of
course with the other women having to avoid staring at me).

In addition to watching Goenka on the evening video
each night, for a few minutes at the start and end of each
meditation session, an audio played of him reminding us of the
rules of the technique (in English and then in a Thai translation),
and it always ended with him chanting this same phrase:

_"By practicing patiently and persistently you are BOUND to be
successful. BOUND to be successful. With patience and persistence...you
are BOUND to be successful."_

I had grown to love that mantra. Every time I had
doubtful thoughts creep into my mind about what a waste this
whole ten days of silent hell was, and how it would likely not
make a hoot worth of difference in my life, I just repeated the
mantra.

_"By practicing patience and persistence, I am bound to be successful,
bound to be successful."_

As I lassoed the little girl inside of me that morning who wanted to go run outside and play and sing and dance and talk up a storm with the others, my mature self calmly took a seat on my little cushion. I closed my eyes and silently chanted the mantra.

"By practicing patience and persistence, I am bound to be successful, bound to be successful."

Because it felt like a task I was already totally burnt out on continuing, even though I was only half way through the retreat, I wasn't ready to start focusing on my bodily sensations yet. So I just kept repeating the mantra for several minutes before I started scanning my body.

"By practicing patience and persistence, I am bound to be successful, bound to be successful."

Once I finally found the motivation to start scanning my bodily sensations, my left leg started to cramp. In the previous night's lesson, we were encouraged to practice sitting absolutely motionless during at least three of the sessions that day. Goenka acknowledged that when sitting for long periods of time, it is common to experience cramping or knee pain. He challenged us to see this as just another bodily sensation to notice but not react to. He made an analogy to how by not letting physical pain bother you, we are training our minds to not let other types of pain be bothersome either.

But my pain was *intense*. There was a huge knot of heat simmering right above my left knee. Every cell in my body started to get uncomfortable as well. I wanted to stand up, to shake it out, yet my determined self was committed to remain motionless through the pain. The cramping intensified…then the warmth turned into fiery heat…then shooting pain began moving up my thigh…and then more cramping.

"Breathe in. Compassion. Breathe out. Compassion. This too shall pass. Breathe in. Compassion. Breathe out. Compassion. This too shall pass…"

Comparing this to when I sat through being practically traumatized while listening to Goenka's horrendous 'singing,' this new experience made that seem like a piece of cake, so to speak.

It took all of my might not to move. Calmly scanning my bodily sensations was not even an option. One hundred percent of my focus went toward my breathing and somehow on remaining still.

"Breathe in. Compassion. Breathe out. Compassion. This too shall pass. Breathe in. Compassion. Breathe out. Compassion. This too shall pass..."

The throbbing eventually took over my entire body. Although I had never given birth, I felt like I was experiencing a similar level of pain. I became so hot, I felt as if I had a fever. Focusing on just one second at a time, I hung all my hopes on that last phrase of the mantra and just kept breathing.

But then something happened that actually had the power to distract me from the pain. I hesitate to even describe this, given how crazy it sounds, but I literally started having visions of evil spirits flying out from the top of my head. It is hard to put into words what I was really experiencing, but all I know is that it felt as if demonic energy was being expulsed from my body.

"Breathe in. Compassion. Breathe out. Compassion. This too shall pass. Breathe in. Compassion. Breathe out. Compassion. This too shall pass..."

I had truly never experienced anything like it. Sitting motionless through intense pain, coupled with a tenacious determination not to flinch, while at the same time feeling as if evil energy was being extricated from my body. I miraculous continued sitting there motionless...for the next 90 minutes.

"Breathe in. Compassion. Breathe out. Compassion. This too shall pass. Breathe in. Compassion. Breathe out. Compassion. This too shall pass..."

Then the blessed moment finally arrived, and the ending bell rang. I opened my eyes and almost cried tears of triumphant joy. I slowly picked up my legs as the blood rushed back in. The resulting tingling was almost worse then the cramping. I slowly shook my leg in hopes of making the transition to standing less painful. I finally made it to my feet and headed outside.

With the sun beaming on my face, I felt an unbelievable feeling of lightness. As I continued to walk, with every step I felt as free as a bird. My entire body felt light. I felt as if I had lost ten pounds. I'd always read that negative emotions literally can make you feel 'heavy,' thus why that word is used to describe challenging emotional states. But in that moment, it wasn't just a theory. I was actually having the physical experience to prove it.

Then, as if what I've just explained is not mesmerizing enough, I had another seemingly miraculous experience happen. I had a vision of a butterfly emerge from the top of my head and then blissfully fly away. This stunned me. I have always loved the symbolism of the butterfly...It starts its life as a destructive caterpillar. Then it loses itself into a tiny cocoon where it entirely leaves behind the body it once knew. Next it transforms itself into a colorful, winged creature now able to flit and fly about, as it pollinates and spreads life to beautiful flowers.

Having a vision of a butterfly emerge from my head made me beam with joy. I felt it was a sign of my own transformation and a validation for what I had just sat through.

Amazingly that night, Goenka touched on this very point. The lesson was when we are willing to sit with our pain, instead of running from it or distracting ourselves from feeling it, only then can it be released and we finally become free of it. Indeed, I felt free.

Chapter 12:
Adventures in Bangkok

April 2008

My love affair with the vision of being cured of diabetes endlessly danced around in my head for days to come. I had to make a diligent effort at work to turn off my internal movie screen in order to focus on the needs of my clients. Luckily, I had some entertaining folks that week.

Angelique was a 40-year-old redhead from Ireland with a wonderfully laid back personality who loved to laugh. We clicked immediately, and after her official health evaluation with me on her first day, she would swing by my office at least once a day to say hello and have a chat. During one of our talks, in which I was lamenting being single, she exuberantly informed me about her 35-year-old Canadian friend who lived in Bangkok, "...who you absolutely must meet! His name is Tyler and he runs his own Thailand tour guide company so he knows all the best spots in town! I'm headed up there this weekend and will be meeting him for dinner at some amazing place at 7 p.m. on Friday. Come with me!"

My smile beamed like the sunshine. "I would LOVE to! Count me in!"

Dreams of being cured of diabetes, and now a date! I had yet to meet the rich and famous, dreamy man of my dreams I'd fantasized I'd meet while working at the resort so this invitation made me overjoyed. I was as exhilarated as if it were my birthday and New Year's Eve all at once! I was walking on air the entire week in anticipation of it. Regardless of if Tyler and I hit it off, so to speak, frankly I was just thrilled to have the usual absolute romantic void in my life be filled with a flicker of hope.

I had to do some finagling at work to make spending the full weekend in Bangkok possible though. The standard schedule of finishing at 6 p.m. on Friday, working from 8 a.m. to noon Saturday, have Sunday off, and then back at noon on Monday would just not suffice this particular weekend. (The six-day workweek practiced in Thailand was a huge drain on my adventuresome spirit! Having only one day off never felt like

125

enough time to really relax; it was as if the each week just endlessly ran together. Urghhhhh.)

Serendipitously my schedule that Friday was clear after 4 p.m. and I only had one client scheduled for Saturday morning, which I was thankfully able to give to Monica in return for taking one of her clients on a later day.

Getting to Bangkok from Hua Hin was no easy task. After leaving work at 4 p.m., I still had to pack my bag, make myself look sexy for my date, get on a motorbike taxi to the mini-van station, wait for the mini-van to become full with passengers (no schedule; departure was determined by when enough people filled the van), and then endure the more than three hour drive to Bangkok, as it dropped off and picked up a bazillion passengers along the way. Needless to say, I was going to be late for dinner.

I was also traveling on April 13. Mid-April is the annual Songkran festival in Thailand, which is a time of vacation for the entire country and when huge parades happen in practically every city. April is also the hottest month of the year and a significant part of this week-long festival consists of people of all ages, in every city around the country and literally on every city block, throwing water at anyone and everyone who happens to be walking by or driving on a motorbike, locals and tourists alike…most especially a young, white, female dressed for a blind date in Bangkok.

Yes, it's true. On my way to the mini-van station, I was attacked by an entire truck full of teenagers, armed with buckets of water and plastic water guns, eager to ensure there was not an inch of my body left dry…and they were very successful. Luckily while waiting for the mini-van to fill up with passengers, the heat of the day dried me off a bit, but not entirely. You can imagine my three-hour ride, in a heavily air-conditioned van, wearing wet clothes, was not part of my idyllic vision of this joyful afternoon preceding my blind date in Bangkok.

But eventually, I made it. I arrived at the restaurant, a bit tattered looking, but presentable enough I didn't think I looked too bad. The décor was stunning. It was one of those 'best kept secrets' you'd never find unless you were at the hands of a very 'in the know' tour guide, like Tyler. This humble gem of a spot was nestled away from the chaos on the streets of Bangkok.

From the quiet alley on which it was located, it was barely noticeable. The entrance was covered in lush vegetation, giving me the feel of walking into a jungle. The path curved up a wooden staircase leading to the front desk, also barely recognizable due to the jungle-like décor enveloping it. The hostess who greeted me was one of those elegant, porcelain-skinned, Asian beauties. She knew what party I was with without even having to ask me. As I followed her to my table, we passed elegant wooden art sculptures tucked away in little nooks, covered with more jungle-like foliage. The restaurant had multiple cozy rooms situated on different levels, each containing only about five tables, yet allowing guests a peak into all the other rooms, and each had their own flare and flavor.

My long and wet journey was over and I arrived at the table. "Helloooo Angelique!"

Angelique stood up, hugging me. "Hello Jody! So glad you finally made it! This is my friend Tyler; Tyler, meet Jody."

Tyler reached out his hand to shake mine, "Hi Jody. Nice to meet you. I've heard a lot of great things about you."

After the awkward introduction was over, (because when is meeting a blind date ever not awkward) I took a seat. Tyler was handsome, good smile, seemed nice...but I didn't experience a strong spark, nor did I sense he did for me at our initial introduction.

I arrived so late they had basically finished eating dinner but luckily they had ordered Asian style (a variety of dishes meant to be shared) and so there were plenty of nibbles left for me to enjoy. The conversation ebbed and flowed as it typically does at a dinner table with three incredibly interesting, international people. I wasn't getting much from Tyler though. No flirty energy. Not much eye contact. No direct questions shared between us with the intent of learning more about the other. A bit disappointed, after a certain point I realized I'd just go with the flow and see if anything came of it later on.

One thing I've painfully learned over the past two decades is that being a strong and powerful, go-after-what-I-want-with-gusto kind of woman has failed me miserably in the dating world. Still single at the age of 35, I had finally decided to adopt a toned-down approach and did my best to practice just seeing what could naturally unfold…indeed a novel approach for me, but I did my best to let go of expectations.

I savored every scrap of food left on the plates and practically licked each one clean because everything tasted so amazingly delicious. (Given my love for food, the thought did cross my mind though, but have no fear, I was able to restrain myself from actually doing that.) The barren plates were cleared and Tyler ordered dessert. This unbelievable array of bite-sized sweets designed like a piece of artwork suddenly appeared. Little fluffy pastries. Bites of chocolate decadence. Mini berry pies. I experienced that same feeling of anxiety as when opening a box of chocolates, wanting to try all of them yet needing to limit myself to just one. To lessen the weight of the very big decision I was being faced with, I let the others go first and then gleefully picked up the remaining decadent chocolate square, and fully savored its divine taste on my tongue.

Dinner came to a close but when dining with a famous tour guide, there was certainly more on our agenda. Our next locale was Tyler's favorite bar in Bangkok, Scirroco. Scirroco is an incredibly swanky, open-air bar on the rooftop of a 64-story skyscraper. After the elevator ride up, which seemed to last at least a minute, the doors opened and I then experienced my first ever bird's eye view of Bangkok. Wow! Imagine San Francisco with no water or mountains inhibiting its sprawl in any direction, thus allowing it to be as wide as it was long and stretching in every direction as far as the eye could see. Well, welcome to Bangkok and its ten *million* inhabitants!

Even with the 360-degree view availed by this swanky, rooftop bar, there was no perceivable end to the city in sight, in any direction. The lights just went on and on and on. Trying to wrap my head around its enormity was a challenge. Bangkok makes Manhattan look like a tiny island by comparison.

The rooftop bar was split into three levels. The lowest level containing a scrumptious dinner buffet with elegantly set white-tablecloth-covered tables full with sharply dressed folks enjoying their meals. The upper level was a music stage where a woman wearing a red dress blowing elegantly in the wind was gracing the crowd with her musical talents. And the mid level held the swanky bar, which was glowing in a constant changing of colors.

I drifted away from the others and just kept walking from one edge of the rooftop to another, my mouth open in awe.

Once I had digested all the view I could handle, I headed to the bar to meet up with the others who had already finished their first round of drinks. Unfortunately though, it was getting late and it seemed everyone's energy had taken a sharp dive. Our conversations turned flat, and the flirtatious energy between Tyler and I had still never flourished. They asked for the check and we decided to call it a night.

Angelique headed to her room at the famous Oriental Hotel (which was way, way, waaaay out of my price range), and Tyler used his tourist guide connections to get me a room at a somewhat less but still fabulous hotel for half price. So after our goodnights and see-you-in-the-mornings, I headed down the road to The Majestic Grand Hotel. I was a bit disappointed about the lack of spark between Tyler and me, but it was a great night nonetheless.

After a short five-minute walk and checking in at the front desk, I opened the door to my elegant room. Beautiful, but nothing over the top. Yet compared to my stale and lifeless apartment, spending a night in this room was an absolute luxury for me. I flopped myself on the bed and threw my arms open wide. I couldn't help but smile …There I was, a single woman from Seattle, living on my own, halfway around the world, having just spent an evening with a cast of international people whom I'd just met, in one of the largest cities in the world! "Wow. How cool is my life?!"

With a smile on my face, I headed to bed to get a good night's sleep, in preparation for the following day of more adventures with Tyler and Angelique, exploring one of the most electrifying cities in the world.

***

Our plan for Saturday was to convene in the lobby of the Oriental Hotel at 9am. Tyler and I arrived first. We took a seat on the elegant, silk lounge chairs and were thoroughly entertained by observing the various guests from around the world coming and going through the lobby until Angelique arrived.

After a few exchanges of how great we all had slept and appreciation given to Tyler for the events of our previous night and for what we knew was going to be a fabulous day ahead, we headed out. Because the Songkran festival was still on, we passed many eager Thais poised with their loaded water guns and buckets. Luckily, my fate was better than the day before and we somehow walked by unscathed. After just a minute or two of walking, we arrived at one of the city's many water-taxi stations and joined the rush of people climbing aboard one of the big passenger shuttles. The boat was jam-packed with locals, but there were a few other light-skinned folks too, toting cameras around their neck with their faces buried in a map.

Bangkok possesses an extensive grid of waterways throughout the city, and Tyler informed us the river we were on, the Chao Phraya, is about 400 meters wide and winds all the way through downtown, with major public transport stops all along its edge. An endless maze of smaller canals extends from the main river source, creating waterways in every direction, much like regular streets. Our boat was packed with people holding on to handles hanging from above, similar to a morning rush hour scene on a subway, with mobs of people exiting and entering at each stop. Eventually, we joined the ranks of the exiting mobs and jumped off.

We arrived at our first stop of the morning. The Grand Palace was built in 1782 under King Rama I. All 218,000 square meters are walled in by a towering white cement fortress. Within the compound lies government administration halls, the residence quarters for the royal family, and most spectacularly, numerous temples, including the renown Temple of the Emerald Buddha. This site is one of the most revered sites in Thailand where Thais can pay respect to the Lord Buddha and His Teachings. Because of the Songkran festival, the temple was packed to the brim with Thais paying their respects. Before taking our place in line, we removed our shoes and placed them on one of the many shoe racks outside the entrance to the temple, as is the custom before entering any Buddhist temple.

Thais consider the foot to be the dirtiest and lowliest part of the body, while the head is the most respected part. This influences how Thais sit when on the ground, most especially when praying in a temple. Their feet will always be pointing towards the back of the temple, away from revered sites, tucked to the side or behind them. Pointing at or touching something with the feet is considered rude, but so is touching one's head due to its sacredness.

After shuffling along in the packed line for a few minutes, we arrived inside. The Emerald Buddha sat high up on an ornately decorated throne, only about one-foot tall, carved from a block of green jade. It was first discovered in 1434. Even though this one-foot-tall Emerald Buddha is way above the rank of us ordinary people, he is apparently a bit fashion conscious. He is only found wearing one of three outfits: one for summer, one for the rainy season, and one for winter. Apparently, on the three days each year in which He changes His attire, there is quite an ornate ceremony. (Luckily, that particular day was not one of them. I couldn't imagine the enormity of the crowd on one of those days. It was already packed enough!)

After paying our respects, we headed to our next destination, the very revered sight of Wat Pho, also known as The Temple of the Reclining Buddha. Due to his repeat visits as a tour guide, Tyler had befriended one of the official tour guides. Nakorn was a slightly overweight, bubbly and jovial man – a teddy bear type that could make you laugh all day long. Humor seemed to be his antidote for the fact that he'd likely given the exact same tour thousands of times throughout his lifetime. He had grown up living at that very site in one of the servant quarters and my guess was he had probably never left. He provided us with a wealth of knowledge about the temple, to say the least!

The Wat, meaning 'temple,' was the largest temple in Bangkok and was also technically the oldest, having been originally built about 200 years before Bangkok even became Thailand's capital. Given the previous statue I had just seen of Buddha being a mere one-foot tall, my mouth dropped open when I laid my eyes on this 46-meter-long, gold-plated statue of The Buddha laying on his side! Imagine a statue which stretched the length of half a football field. That's how long he was!

131

His reclining position was designed to illustrate the last few moments of His life before passing into nirvana. The entrance was at His head so the first detail we saw were His majestic eyes made out of sparkling white, mother-of-pearl. They perfectly captured the look of someone experiencing a joyful moment of bliss. As we walked along the length of His body, I was doing my best to keep my mouth closed as I was simply trying to digest the enormity of this stunning sculpture. Once we reached the feet and turned the corner, the souls of His feet came into view. On them were carvings of 108 different depictions of the most auspicious events in the life of Buddha. To better imagine it, picture an impressive mural intricately carved with details expressing stories about the various ups and downs of life…birth, death, celebrations, famines, triumphs, mountain tops, ocean sides…through images alone.

Given my ignorance of Buddhism, I actually started to feel a bit embarrassed and ashamed to be there. The significance of this 46-meter-long, gold-plated Buddha was completely beyond my comprehension. The temple was packed with hundreds of Thais, likely from all over the country, bowing and paying their respects to one of their most revered relics in the history of Buddhism…and there I was, just standing in ignorant awe.

We turned the corner again and walked along His backside. Along the edge of the entire corridor leading back to His head were 108 bronze vases. It was customary for visitors to buy a bag of coins and drop one in each vase while saying a prayer. I was so moved by the energy of reverence vibrating throughout the temple, I decided to take part. For just a few Thai baht, each of us purchased a bag of 108 coins and joined in the massive line, as we slowly dropped a coin into each vase, and silently said our prayers. Having been away from those I love back at home for over four months at that point, I said a prayer and wished them all well … mom, dad, my sister, aunt Mary, my dear Jennifur and her new owners, all my other friends and family…as well as prayers for my own dreams and aspirations for the future.

By the end of the line, I was so full of emotion, tears dripped down my cheeks. Given my love for the significance of numbers, I was even more moved by the fact that when I reached the 108th vase, I had exactly one coin left. (The norm was to be a bit over or a bit short on coins by the end of the line.) I took a deep breath in gratitude for every amazing blessing in my life as I dropped my last coin into the very last vase.

After the tour, we said good-bye to Nakorn. We generously thanked him for sharing his knowledge with us and headed back to the taxi boat station. On our way there, right in the middle of this loud and busy city, we came across a very intriguing, little, narrow walkway. Looking down its length, there seemed to be a market with goods for sale at its end. We decided to take a quick detour and check it out.

Its width demanded we walk in single file. But suddenly we realized it wasn't a path at all. We were walking through somebody's home. To our right was a cement wall with little makeshift tables and cupboards built into it. To our left was a line of little, square shacks with living quarters set up inside. Amazingly, in addition to little pillows on the floor and mini tables with plenty of food on them, many were sporting flat screen televisions and major sound systems. The people inhabiting them, from young children to elderly, certainly seemed happy, with their faces full of smiles. Luckily, Tyler was fluent in Thai. So after realizing we weren't on a public pathway, he kindly made friends with these people and apologized to them for our intrusion. After a short exchange of words, everyone started laughing. I had no idea what they were saying, but the rest of us just smiled as we turned around and headed back out the main street.

This experience sent my mind spinning. My deeply held beliefs about how to live life 'the right way' and the very purpose of life itself came crumbling down in the face of these happy, smiling people living in their ramshackle boxes. As an American, the obsession with the accumulation of wealth and material goods can become the entire defining purpose of one's life. Yet this material obsession rarely brings the lasting happiness I believe we humans are truly hungry for. My experience with the clients at the resort proved the fact that being rich was certainly no guarantee for health and happiness. It has always seemed funny to me how rich people, just because they have a lot of money, are deemed 'successful,' while people with little money or material goods are described by the adjective 'poor,' which is

133

defined as, 'less than adequate.'

The glow of peace and joy emanating from the eyes of the elderly woman in that alley certainly did not contain any hint of self-pity or lack. Nor did her beaming smile communicate she believed there was anything 'less than adequate' about being surrounded by her joyful family in their humble abode. There she was, living in a box on the street, yet full of more joy than I generally witness in the eyes of most 'successful' Americans, who proudly drive their fancy cars and live in over-sized homes. To me, Americans are hungry for peace, yet only look for it through what they can buy or achieve.

I walked away in gratitude for this eye-opening experience. As a constant over-achiever myself, who seems to be on a never-ending quest for peace in my life, it highlighted to me that what I'm truly hungry for is to emanate peace from within myself; that peace does not have to, nor is likely to be found from striving for and achieving anything on the outside (especially given how everything on the outside is impermanent anyway).

Having just met Tyler and Angelique, I figured I'd keep my deep thoughts to myself. As I followed along in silence, we headed back to the river. This time we didn't squeeze into one of the crowded boat taxis and instead stepped aboard a private canal tour boat, which we had to ourselves. It reminded me of the gondolas in Venice, but instead of being propelled by the ore stroke of a handsome Italian, it was powered by a very unromantically loud, roaring engine.

We spent the next two hours winding our way through the impressive, massive grid of Bangkok's tiny, out-lying waterways. Along the banks were mostly homes where the main source of transportation for the homeowners were little wooden boats which without close inspection could almost appear as scraps of floating wood. Each neighborhood we passed through had its own unique feel, from those with neatly manicured yards to homes so run down, I wondered if anyone truly inhabited them. There were a few odd homes here and there, built up tall with new construction and an elegantly designed fence around the perimeter, but they were certainly the exception to the rule. In Western standards, even the 'nice' neighborhoods would be deemed dilapidated, yet this did not seem to be the opinion of the owners themselves. The faces of the people living in these homes beamed with joy as they waved to us when we floated by.

As for the water, the color was as you would expect for a river in the middle of a huge, over-populated city: jet black. It was so intensely black you wouldn't even be able to see a hand if it were just one inch below the surface. (That is, if someone was brave enough to put their hand in the water in the first place.) I would certainly never dream of swimming in it, for fear it would make me sick. Yet, the human body is incredibly adaptable...as was apparent by all the smiling and laughing children we passed playing in the water. One group of children was bellowing out the most beautiful heartfelt laughter, as they were doing cannon balls off a dock. From the joy apparent in their eyes, these children certainly were not experiencing any fear of getting sick.

We continued to wind our way through the narrow canals and came across a group of monks motioning us to come over to the riverbank. They were eagerly waving bags of bread at us. We decided to give in and buy a few loaves. Via the hand gestures of our boat driver, we figured out we were meant to break the bread up into pieces and throw it into the river, so we did. Suddenly, the entire surface of the water transformed into a dense blanket of big, fat, gray fish. The water prior to their arrival was as calm as glass. But as soon as the first piece of bread hit the surface, masses of them appeared all around us. My mouth dropped wide open in disbelief, *"How does such disgustingly polluted water actually support life?!"* I wondered.

After we had thrown our last crumb into the water, we smiled and waved to the monks in gratitude for the very unexpected and entertaining sideshow and then decided to move on. The lasting impression I had from that experience was I would certainly second-guess ordering fish for the rest of the trip!

Our private tour came to an end, and we emerged out from the tiny canals and entered back into the bustling, main thoroughfare of the river. Instead of fighting for space to depart on at one of the public ports, our driver dropped us off at the serene, private dock located in front of the elegant Oriental Hotel. Tyler exchanged a few words in Thai with the driver as he tipped him generously, and Angelique and I waved good-bye. We took just a few steps before deciding to sit down at a quaint, little table on the hotel's patio restaurant and enjoy a beverage and a snack, because we were all quite hungry at that point...but certainly not for fish.

After a full day of hanging out with Tyler, it seemed neither of us were 'the catch' the other was looking for. No sparks ever ignited; no flirty energy shared. We decided to quench our other desires instead and order some drinks and a few nibbles to enjoy, as we watched the ever-bustling river continue to serve as the main thoroughfare for a countless number of various sized boats coming and going, some chock-full of people, others transporting goods. It was rush hour on the river. The scene was so engaging we ended up sitting there for quite some time before we finally decided to wrap up the day and say our good-byes. Angelique and I expressed our deep gratitude to Tyler for our spectacular day of adventures. I exchanged contact info with them both and pledged to keep in touch as I bid them farewell.

I shook my head. What an amazing day. I felt so lucky to have been invited. I jumped in a taxi and headed back to my hotel for a luxurious, long night's rest.

***

The next morning was pure luxury. I reveled in the elegance of my king bed until sometime after 9am and then headed downstairs for a quick workout at the hotel's gym. The row of cardio machines looked out over the river and made my typical half-hour workout seem like it was over in five minutes. Afterward, I showered and headed to the hotel's restaurant to enjoy the all-inclusive breakfast buffet. They had everything from smoked salmon to freshly made omelets, fresh fruit and yogurt, pastries, and more. Compared to the over-cooked and often unrecognizable items served at the staff cafeteria, I savored every delicious bite. Juxtaposed to my normal day off back in Hua Hin, (which I had started to fondly refer to as the armpit of Thailand) I felt like I had died and gone to heaven.

After breakfast, I decided to relax and read for a few hours in their outdoor patio lounge. I was deeply engrossed in Elizabeth Gilbert's book, Eat Pray Love – a journey not unlike my own. I really didn't want to leave, but once 3 p.m. arrived, I figured I better get going and head to Hua Hin, back to my lifeless staff apartment building. I jumped on the sky train, which whisked me over the hustle and bustle of the busy streets below, and arrived back at the minivan station. I only had to wait about 15 minutes until it filled up, and then I begrudgingly sat back to endure the three-hour, stop-and-go trip back to my life in Hua Hin.

Chapter 13:
The Worst 'Healthy' Vacation Imaginable
May 2008

Over four months had passed since I'd arrived in Thailand, and I was feeling totally settled in. I had fallen into the groove of my six-day workweek and was enjoying my job of improving the health of my mostly rich, and a few famous, people at the resort. I was still anxiously awaiting news from my boss regarding if and when he would be meeting with the men from the stem cell company. The lack of a confirmed meeting date was frustrating. However, other than Philip, the first diabetic I had talked to who had received the treatment, I hadn't heard back from any of the others I had contacted, which didn't seem like a good sign. My excitement over the idea of becoming cured had taken a huge nosedive, although, I still had arguments in my head involving the optimistic part of myself trying to overcome my doubt.

Dave, Monica, and I, as well as the naturopaths from Australia, Katrina, Nadine, and Olivia, had all became quite close friends. I was grateful for their presence because talking with them in the cafeteria over meal times was pretty much the extent of my social life.

The only other social engagement I had was an AA meeting I went to each Wednesday night. Being someone who frequented these 12-step addiction support programs at home, I had found a meeting for ex-pats online, amazingly right down the street from my apartment. Most of the attendees were retirees who had struggled with alcoholism in their past, some more distantly than others. My 'drug of choice' has always been food and sugar, but it seems addicts can relate to each other's struggles, regardless of the chosen substance, so I felt grateful to be able to attend their meeting.

Anytime stress or loneliness showed up in my brain, the food addict inside me would become triggered and cause me to become preoccupied with food, especially sugar, regardless of my level of physical hunger. I believe this reaction comes from my deeply ingrained habit, likely established when I was a young girl, of using food to distract myself from feeling uncomfortable emotions. Ironically, overeating a bunch of sugar never left me feeling well (big surprise), especially given the fact I have diabetes. Thus having this group, who could relate to living with an overwhelming, out-of-control desire to ingest something in hopes of it taking away pain, yet it causing even more, was a wonderful means of support for me around this seemingly endless challenge in my life.

My hunger for connection was also being fed with regular calls over Skype with my mom and my fabulous aunt Mary. Being able to see their smiling faces on my computer screen on an almost daily basis was a lifesaver, given my ever-present hunger for connection. My mom and I spoke almost every morning, which was more frequently than we ever did at home. Each morning when I turned on my computer to check my email, I would immediately get a call from her because it would be 5 p.m. at home and her Skype account would alert her the second I came online.

As we did through medical school, aunt Mary and I scheduled a weekly check-in time where I would share with her everything that had happened in the previous week and in response, she would share with me some of her brilliant wisdom. Without fail her advice allowed me to see my challenges as wonderful opportunities for growth of my character. If I were feeling sad about being single, she would remind me that relationships built on a desire to take away loneliness do not create the steady foundation necessary for longevity; true love always starts from finding peace within. If I was feeling frustration about the health of my clients not improving as much as I knew was possible, she reminded me of a truth which applies in all relationships, that no matter how much information I share with someone, the other person is ultimately responsible for making the change, not me. People change only if and when they are ready. My main responsibility as a doctor is in giving the best information I can, and then let go of expectations.

In a nutshell, the rush of the newness of moving half way around the globe to Thailand and starting my new job as a physician at this ritzy, ocean side health spa had completely worn off. I started to notice how drained and exhausted I felt on a daily basis. I had felt this way throughout medical school and figured it was justified given the heavy load of classes I was

139

taking. Yet, now that I was finally in the groove of a somewhat normal life, I realized that locking my door to take a nap on my office floor in between clients on a regular basis was anything but normal. Being a doctor myself, I started coming up with various theories about what could be going on and decided my problem must be due to adrenal fatigue (a condition caused by long-term, consistent high stress and a resulting overproduction of the stress hormone cortisol). So I put myself on a blend of herbs known to nourish and strengthen the adrenal glands.

After a few weeks, I didn't notice any change. Getting out of bed in the morning had become a great challenge. I made sure I went to bed on time, exercised at the gym either before work or during lunch, but nothing seemed to help. I constantly felt heavy and tired. Luckily, my energetic and bubbly personality covered up how exhausted I actually felt when I was working with patients so they never had a clue. But I started getting worried and decided to ask for a week off and figured I just really needed some good rest.

My colleague Monica told me about a retreat center she had heard about that specialized in rejuvenation and cleansing. It was located on one of the beautiful islands down south, which I heard were so gorgeous they were a must-see for anyone visiting Thailand. She said she had heard nothing but positive reports about how fantastic the experience there was. It was a modest place, away from town, and was all about health and rejuvenation. Hearing her words made me so excited, it was enough for me to immediately call and make a reservation. I didn't even worry about doing any of my own research on the place because I was so excited to just have a week off (not always a good idea, by the way…).

I felt grateful to my boss because it only took a few days for me to be able to schedule the time off. I soon packed my bags and headed south. Although the trip to get there was anything but relaxing, I endured, knowing I was headed for ultimate relaxation. The journey started with an all-night bus ride where I desperately tried to get some sleep as I sat upright seated next to an elderly man with a roaring snore. Then a three-hour boat ride through stormy seas. The waters were so rough the staff handed out plastic bags to all the passengers in case anyone needed to throw up.

When we finally reached land, I was feeling much better. We were dropped off at a busy pier on a little tropical island called Koh Phangan. The swarms of taxi drivers frantically waved their hands at all the vacationers who had just disembarked from the boat. I picked a man who had a sweet smile and imagined him using his money to buy food for his family. I gave him the name of the retreat center, jumped on the back of his motorbike taxi, and we took off. The island was tiny, the perimeter reaching just over 30 miles around. It was basically inhabited around the shoreline and the center was dense jungle and steep hills, with just one road winding up and over reaching from east to west, and one from north to south. The arrival pier was on the west side of the island and the retreat center was located on the east shore so my ride proved to be quite the adventure.

Over the next 20 minutes, I was delighted by the most heavenly, visual encounter I'd ever experienced. The sights were straight out of one of those movies filmed on a picturesque tropical island. We started by winding up the steep hills over the center of the island, leading through the lush jungle with its Tarzan-like vines hanging over the road. At times the ascent was so precipitous, I wasn't sure if our little motorbike would make it and wondered if we were going to have to get off and walk. We didn't, and eventually reached the pinnacle of the island, emerging from the dense forest canopy to a spectacular 360-degree bird's eye view of the shoreline. The ocean was the most amazing crystal clear blue I had ever seen, and the white sand beaches literally shimmered in the sunshine.

We made our descent through the jungle on the other side of the island and then drove through the humble town of Had Rien. Had Rien is one of the best places in the world to see the full moon, and for many years now the beach there has become the home of a raucous, 'Full Moon Party.' Every month the entire beach becomes packed with hard-core partiers, musicians, fire dancers, tourists, and locals alike, who dance and dance until dawn. (It is also infamous for extensive drug use...I heard many stories of party-goers going missing.)

Before arriving, I read that this 'Full Moon Party' had become such a lucrative event for the locals they started holding a 'Half Moon Party' and then soon after, also added a, 'Quarter-

141

Moon Party.' Thus now there is a party every weekend, all year round. With as many tourists as there are in Thailand, the beach is apparently packed for this event week after week, rain or shine, moon or no moon.

However, my weary body was certainly not there to party and stay up all night, no matter how famous the 'Full Moon Party' was. (Yet given my ever-hungry spirit for adventure, I must admit the thought of attending crossed my mind once or twice.) My driver pulled up to a pier and pointed to a group of small boats. Apparently there were no roads to the retreat center thus it was only accessible via the sea. I paid my driver and walked over to the taxi boats. I was once again greeted by a swarm of smiling drivers, albeit a much smaller group than the one at the main pier, and stepped aboard the nicest looking one of the bunch. The boat was just like the private canal tour boat I rode in through Bangkok, and was unfortunately powered by one of those same ear-piercingly loud engines. I managed to figure out from the driver through his hand gestures that the ride would luckily only be about ten minutes.

We headed out of the bay, around the point, and arrived at the next beach over. It was small. To walk from one end to the other would probably take not even five minutes. Its shape curved inward and there were huge rock formations at both ends, creating a feeling of protection and being cradled into the safety of the bay. The beach was so over-grown with the lushness of the jungle I could barely see the cabins of the resort, which were set back from the shoreline. The only inhabitants of the beach were guests from the resort. (And the word 'resort' in this case is a far cry from the glitz and glamour of where I worked.)

Due to the absence of a dock, I took my shoes off to depart into the water and said thank you in Thai, one of the few phrases I could actually pronounce, "Khup khun ka."

I paid my boat driver his fare. I was greeted by a smiley Thai woman who motioned for me to follow her up the beach. She led me through the jungle on a windy, cobblestone path to a little stand-alone bungalow resting on four stilts. It had a deck with a hammock perfectly situated for admiring the vibrant red blossoms of a huge hibiscus plant, whose branches were bursting out over the deck.

The smiley woman left me to get settled in. The bathroom was on the ground floor of my bungalow and up the stairs was my humble room, with a bed and a dresser. I plunked myself down on the bed and smiled, stretching. Ahhhh, it felt fabulous to be there. A week of relaxation in the jungle. I couldn't imagine anywhere else in the world I'd rather be.

There was a big folder full of information about the resort on the bed, so I started to read through it. What I learned was not exactly what I had expected…The place was a detox center; to take a break from all the unhealthy foods, chemicals, polluted air, and stress. The folder was full of studies showing how polluted we are in today's world, with chemicals, such as pesticides, mercury, lead, antibiotics, Teflon, flame retardants, PCBs, DDT, and phthalates and BPA from plastic, and the huge toll on our health these chemicals are causing.

Having spent five years studying to be a naturopathic physician, this information was not new to me. During medical school I learned about the threat to our health these silent invaders are causing on a daily basis, but I never actually embarked on my own thorough cleansing regime because as the toxins are being released from the body, it can make you feel quite sick and tired. I never did it because I was already feeling so exhausted during school, I couldn't imagine putting myself through an intense regimen which would make me feel even worse.

What I realized in that moment was my week ahead was not exactly going to be the relaxing-by-the-beach and eating-an-abundance-of-healthy-foods vacation I had imagined. I turned to the page showing the daily schedule:

7 a.m. Colon cleansing via self-administered coffee enema
Breakfast: A shake of betonite clay and psyllium husks
10 a.m. Yoga class
Lunch: A shake of betonite clay and psyllium husks
2 p.m. A shake of betonite clay and psyllium husks
3 p.m. Fresh vegetable juice or coconut water
4 p.m. Colon cleansing
Dinner: A shake of betonite clay and psyllium husks
Evening snack: Vegetable broth

I wasn't going to be eating *anything*?! For a week?! A seven-day water fast and two colonics a day?! I didn't know whether to laugh or cry. I did a bit of both. My dreamy visions of sleeping late, eating a scrumptious and healthy breakfast, and then relaxing in the sunshine until it was time to enjoy another delicious meal flashed through my mind in a painful moment of shock and disbelief. Yet, my anguish was soon followed by an eager sense of anticipation. I believe there are no accidents in life so I decided to believe the reason why I ended up there was because this kind of 'detox' was exactly what I needed to improve my health and allow me to feel better.

I had made an overnight bus trip plus crossed rough seas to get there. I had already paid in full. I was there and I decided there was no turning back. I took a deep breath and embraced my new, unexpected reality. As aunt Mary always says, *"Trust life, Jody."* So I decided to trust I was exactly where I was supposed to be and started to unpack.

I spent my first night relaxing in the hammock on my serene deck, breathing in and out as I was doing my best to accept what lay ahead of me on my 'vacation.' I was able to deeply enjoy the sights and sounds of the jungle surrounding me, and eventually dozed off to sleep.

Morning arrived and I checked in for the 'new guest orientation' at 7:00 a.m. The guest lounge was a big wooden bungalow just a few feet up from the beach, covered in vegetation, open air (meaning it had shades that could be opened or closed instead of walls), full of hammocks and big cozy lounge chairs and a library of health oriented books. There were about 15 people of various ages, mostly Caucasian westerners, lounging about, either reading or chit-chatting. I was greeted with a warm welcome from Christine, the head staff member, who I learned was from England.

"Hello Jody! Welcome to a wonderful week of cleansing! Congratulations on embarking on such a challenging but beneficial experience for your body." I chuckled to myself and chose not to divulge the truth about how I had not made a conscious decision to do this rigorous program.

Christine and I spent the next hour going over all the details of my week ahead. She confirmed everything about the daily schedule and strongly suggested I follow it to the best of my ability. I was to arrive in the lounge at each of the posted 'meal' times to get my 'shake.' (From that day forward, my love for 'shakes,' albeit those made from ice cream, has forever had a new twist of meaning in my mind...) The purpose of the clay and psyllium husks was for their ability to bind and rid toxins from the body. The detox and cleansing capsules contained herbs meant to support the liver in carrying out detoxification. The purpose of not eating was so the extraordinary amount of energy the body spends digesting food on a daily basis would instead be used for removing toxins from the body (to have enough energy to do some 'spring cleaning,' you could say).

As I learned in medical school, the theory of performing an enema is to enhance the process of removing toxins from the body. When the colon does not release on a daily, or even meal-by-meal basis, toxins meant to be excreted from the body are reabsorbed back into the blood stream. Thus doing enemas greatly enhances the removal of toxins from the body.

Christine went on to inform me that enemas have been called *"one of the oldest medical procedures still in use today."* The earliest medical text in existence, the Egyptian Ebers Papyrus, (1,500 B.C.) mentions it. The Greeks wrote of the fabled cleanliness of the Egyptians, which included the internal cleansing of their systems through enemas. The Egyptians did this because they *"believed that diseases were engendered by superfluities of the food."* (A theory which certainly holds even more weight in today's toxic world, with all the chemicals we inadvertently ingest on a daily basis plus the amount of processed foods eaten nowadays!) For centuries, enemas were a routine home remedy to relieve a wide array of ailments. In the past century, the routine use of enemas has died out, except for the use of potentially dangerous barium enemas before colonic X-rays or before or after surgery and childbirth.

Yet, in the world of naturopathic medicine, they are still used frequently. So this whole colon-cleansing idea, although unexpected, was not a new concept for me. (I actually administered them during my clinical practice in medical school and they were offered back at the resort, not only for detoxification, but for relieving depression and strengthening the immune system as well.) Given that toxins can affect every area

145

of the body, naturopaths see enemas as an excellent measure of preventative medicine.

Christine continued on and explained to me the enema procedure employed at the retreat center. Twice a day a staff member would set up my bathroom in preparation for my enema. A long wooden board, called a 'colema board' would be placed on the front rim of my toilet and the other end would be placed on a chair a few feet in front of the toilet, allowing the board to have a bit of a downward slant towards the toilet. There were footrests at the end of the board, which rested on each side of the toilet. A ten-gallon bucket would be hung above the toilet with a five-foot tube connected to the bottom of the bucket. The bucket was filled with coffee....yet not for drinking! Coffee is a stimulant, as we all well know. But when used in an enema, it actually serves to stimulate the liver to release toxins. The instructions were for me to lie down on this board, put the tube you-know-where, and then let all the coffee drain in and out of my colon.

Christine finished her presentation to me. With a bubbly smile on her face, one akin to as if she'd just described all the exhilarating activities available to me at some fancy beachside resort, asked, "Any questions Jody?!"

Doing my best to drum up some enthusiasm, I replied, "Nope. I think I've got it. Thanks!"

Christine walked away and there I sat with my morning 'shake' and nothing but time. I sat down in one of the lounge chairs and introduced myself to the other brave souls who had already been there for a few days. There was a couple from England in their thirties, an elderly American woman, a young Canadian girl with her mother, and a 50-year-old man from Australia.

One of them asked, "So Jody, are you ready for this?"

I wasn't sure what to say so I lied, "Can't wait!"

For the next few hours, the group lounged about while sharing their experience thus far with me about going through the cleanse…"Oh my God, day two was the worst! I felt like I was going to die! I was so dizzy and felt like I needed to puke all day but never could since my stomach had nothing in it!"

"No way man, day four was the killer for me! I was so weak I could barely walk."

"I agree. Day four was hell. I've never felt so nauseous in my life."

"I'll never be able to drink a 'shake' again. I don't care what's in it because my mental experience of drinking a 'shake' will forever be tainted with the taste of clay."

"I'm dying for chocolate. I'm a total addict and usually eat it everyday. It's a frickin' miracle I've made it this long."

"You should see what comes out during my enemas!"

…My ability to accept my reality was rapidly taking a turn for the worst. Only an hour into day one, and I was already feeling sick to my stomach…

"Today is day six for me and I feel like a million bucks! I have never felt so energetic and clear headed!"

A wave of relief washed over me. "Tell me more," I pleaded to this suddenly angelic-like man from Australia.

He smiled and nodded gently, "This is my third time doing this program and I keep coming back every year because I feel absolutely amazing at the end of it and continue to for months afterward. Trust me! You'll be soooo glad you had this experience! Just hang in there past the first few days and you will experience bliss!"

I decided to hang all my faith on his optimistic statement. I chose to let go of my painful pang of dread, which I felt had already begun to eat a hole in the lining of my soon-to-be empty stomach. Then I changed the subject.

"So, what do you guys do all day?"

"You're looking at it. Most of us just chill out here in the lounge. They suggest for us to relax as much as possible to allow our body's energy to go towards cleansing and removing toxins. There are tons of great books lying around but if you get sleepy, the hammocks around the property are a great place to nap. There are some lawn chairs on the beach but you shouldn't spend too much time in the sun or go swimming. You'll probably be pretty low on energy until after day four but if you're up to it in the afternoon, the gentle yoga class is a nice treat."

Indeed, the intention for my vacation was to relax, but to literally sit around and do *nothing* all day long was going to be a challenge for my ever-adventurous, tired or not, personality. I somewhat welcomed my, yet another, 'opportunity' to practice accepting my reality as is, as opposed to how I wanted it to be….the valuable skill for life taught in Buddhism.

Our conversations soon transformed into silence and I found myself happily reclining in a super comfy lounge chair, peering out through the trees and admiring the peacefulness of the crystal clear ocean. Although my vacation was not unfolding anything like I had expected, I took a few deep breaths and filled myself with gratitude for the ability to have an entire week just to relax, surrounded by the beauty of the vibrant, tropical flowers, the palm trees, and the ocean. The chill-out vibe pulsating through the lounge soon caught me in its trance, as I drifted off to sleep.

The next few days consisted of: me drinking my five shakes, conducting my twice-daily enemas, and lounging in the lounge as I fell in and out of sleep countless times throughout the day. Truly, I wasn't even very hungry, surprising enough. Just exhausted and weak. My main daily 'activity' was swinging in a hammock and staring out at the ocean through the palm trees hour after hour.

Everything changed on day four, however. Day four was hell. Truly! How I was feeling, I'll get to that in a moment. But additionally, one fact about hanging out in the jungle is that people are *not* the only things who spend time there. So do bugs.

I was going stir crazy…My naps were constantly interrupted due to being eaten alive by the most monstrous-sized mosquitoes I'd ever seen. Not only was getting bit by them horrendously annoying, but I started resenting them, realizing they were having a smorgasbord on my blood, as I was starving.

The crickets constantly filled the air with the most obnoxious, high-pitched, screeching noise I'd ever heard. The sound pierced my eardrums. As for the humungous cockroaches, they weren't so bad. I'd only encountered two of them…one I found crawling on my toothbrush, and the other woke me up in the middle of the night as it was jumping around

148

on my head, trying to get free from being tangled in my hair...awesome.

But insect inconveniences aside, the last time I felt as ill as I did that day was when I suffered a torturous bout of food poisoning in Chile years before. I was so nauseous walking became difficult. I lay in my bed for hours, unable to find the least bit of respite from feeling horrendous. I figured my body was diligently purging out toxins, so I forced myself to drink as much water as possible. But the downside was that I had to garner all the energy I had to get to the bathroom every couple of hours. And since my urge to pee forced me to get up and make it to the bathroom, my persevering spirit somehow also followed through with my twice-daily enemas.

Day four was hell, and day five and six weren't much better. The fatigue I felt before arriving at that place was nothing compared to the utter weakness and exhaustion I was experiencing. As a diabetic, my normal insulin dose is about 30 units a day, more when I eat more and less when I eat less. I reduced my dose to two units per day and luckily my blood sugar levels stayed perfectly normal, albeit on the low side. So I couldn't blame feeling so poorly on erratic blood sugar levels, as I normally do.

According to the testimonials I had been hearing all week, everyone had experienced a day of hell on around day three or four, albeit not as intense as I was encountering. But everyone seemed to quickly get over the hump and enjoy various degrees of the clear headed, energetic bliss which the man from Australia had mentioned. My tenacious self was putting all my faith in the *fact* that would eventually happen to me too.

Yet lying in my bed on day six, I started feeling as if I were lying in a jail cell. I had been lying there feeling like hell for days, with the only exception being to use the bathroom to pee or do my enema. It's not to say the tropical surroundings of my bungalow weren't gorgeous of course, but I had become desperate to get outside and have a change in scenery. Regardless of the intense nausea I felt, I dragged myself out of bed and carefully carried myself down the stairs. Using the trunks of the palm trees to steady me, bit by bit, I made my way to the lounge and then carefully laid myself down in one of the lounge chairs.

149

A few others were napping and reading. I was glad for the absence of conversation because any noise would've made the painful pounding in my head that much more unbearable. I happened to notice a book beside me entitled, "The Cure for All Diseases." My curiosity was immediately piqued and brought a welcomed breath of altered focus to my experience. I picked it up. It was over 600 pages and had a chapter on almost every disease I could think of. Before diving in, I was curious about the credentials of the author. She had an undergraduate degree in biology and a PhD in cell physiology. Seemed credible enough to me.

After scanning the first few chapters, I got the gist of her message. Her main point was the root cause of many of today's diseases stems from bacteria and/or parasites, and toxins. She referenced a study which took blood samples from 50 adults across various career fields in a major city and found on average, there were over 100 synthetic chemicals, as well as heavy metals, circulating in their blood...such as pesticides, antibiotics, plastic derivatives, mercury, lead and more. Given how horrendous I felt, this correlation with toxins and disease made a lot of sense to me.

The information about bacteria and parasites caught my attention too. There I was doing this cleanse, i.e. giving my body a chance to rid itself of anything which does not belong inside of me, feeling eerily similar to my past bout with food poisoning. I couldn't help but wonder that if by starving my body, I was also starving and aggravating parasites and bacteria festering inside of me, thus causing me to feel like I was experiencing food poisoning again.

I turned to the chapter on diabetes and the first line read, *"Diabetics have a parasite in their pancreas found in raw meat."* I cocked my head in shock and disbelief. I had certainly never read that before. I have heard a lot of theories regarding why my immune system suddenly started attacking and killing my previously healthy insulin producing cells at the age of seven...such as introducing cow's milk at too early of an age, low vitamin D, lack of adequate breast feeding, post-viral infection, or a stressful emotional experience...but I had never heard about a potential parasite infection in my pancreas being the cause. I took a deep breath to try to wrap my head around this new theory.

Viruses living in an organ and causing damage to it is a valid condition accepted by the medical community, such as how the hepatitis virus attacks the liver. So the concept of a parasite living in my pancreas didn't seem too far-fetched, although I had never heard of such a theory throughout medical school. The countless under-cooked hamburgers I had eaten as a child suddenly started flashing through my mind. The load of bacteria and parasites in raw hamburger meat I imagine takes quite a toll on one's immune system and yet the immune system of a young child is not even fully developed. I wondered about the potential for bacteria and parasites to live in other organs as well and started to let my mind wander... *"Maybe they live in my brain tissue and contribute to my moodiness and poor memory. Maybe they're in my liver and intestines, thus why I have chronic digestive issues. Maybe they're in my ovaries, thus why my periods are always late..."*

As I continued reading, I was fascinated by what seemed to be a potentially logical explanation for so many health conditions, yet I was baffled as to why I'd never heard of these theories before. Most medical doctors rarely explain *why* certain symptoms are happening. I'm not sure if they ever ask that question themselves. The norm today is to just give drugs to eliminate symptoms. Personally, I've been given drugs to replace my missing insulin, to force my body to have a period, to change my neurochemistry attempting to create a better mood...Drugs. Drugs. Drugs....But not answers. This book seemed to be full of plausible answers as to *why* I was experiencing these issues.

My mind continued to spin. I thought about all the conditions people are chronically suffering from today which the medical community simply treats by giving pills. I thought about all the patients at the resort on their pain-killers, their anti-inflammatories, anti-depressants, antacids, pills to lower their cholesterol, to lower their blood pressure. Not one of these pills actually treats the root cause of why the problem exists in the first place. Nobody I've ever met is actually deficient in Prozac or Lipitor for example.

Then I turned to the chapter on fatigue. The first line read, *"Anyone with irregular blood sugar levels can experience extreme fatigue."* Anger started to bubble up inside of me. In my 30 years of countless doctors' appointments for diabetes, not one of them had ever made this correlation for me. Although my

151

fatigue seemed to be at its worst recently, I could think back and remember having complained about it for years, yet always blaming and shaming myself for not getting enough sleep or eating as well as I should (even though I usually get eight hours of sleep and generally eat pretty healthy). Then I turned to the chapter on brain health. It stated that depression, lack of concentration, and memory issues can also be related to parasites...additional concerns I'd complained about on and off through the years.

Another issue I've begrudgingly lived with for years is a high pitched, ringing sound in my ears, a condition called tinnitus. I turned to the section on this and read it can be due to pockets of bacteria festering behind root canals. I thought about it for a moment and figured the ringing started about ten years earlier and guess what procedure I had done ten years prior? Two root canals.

I experienced a mix of anger and excitement. Anger for all the years I'd struggled with fatigue and other issues without ever finding a good answer or resolution to them, even after becoming a doctor. But excitement for how this newfound knowledge could potentially allow me to feel as great as I've always hoped to feel.

I started thinking about the dramatic decline in the quality of meat production in the past few decades. Cows now live locked up in cells their entire lives, never seeing sunlight or a green pasture on which to roam. Industrial sized cattle farms do all they can to cut costs and thus feed the cattle who-knows-what in order to save money, even dead and infected cow meat, the very cause of mad-cow disease. I wondered how many other similar diseases may exist which we have yet to fully understand?

And then my mind drifted to all the chemicals in today's world and how our bodies never had to process them throughout the millions of years of human evolution, until just the last century. I started thinking about all the various ways we are exposed to them...in the toothpaste we put into our mouths; the soaps and detergents we wash our hands, clothes, towels, and sheets with; the flame retardants sprayed on our mattresses; in the carpet we line our homes with; in almost every material used to make a new car; all the pesticides sprayed on our food and the preservatives and colorings added to so many packaged foods...

I closed the book, feeling overwhelmed. Visions of toxins, bacteria, viruses, and parasites festering all throughout my body started swirling around in my head. I made a commitment to look up the author on the internet when I returned home, as I lay back in my chair and closed my eyes, hoping my extreme nausea would soon pass.

Day 7:
Everyone Experiences Suffering
August 2008

I woke up in awe…in awe that I had made it to day seven. Given the fact my activities over the past week had been absolutely nothing except sleeping, eating, and meditating, day one felt like it was a month ago. Four more days to go…I wondered what still lay ahead.

Yet I don't have much to say about the events of day seven. My ability to stay focused on scanning my body without interruption from thoughts had definitely improved (which means I still could only make it for maybe a minute). I practiced sitting motionless through some more pain, yet without any fanfare like the previous day. I experienced occasional jolts and accepted them just as something my body needed to do, for whatever reason. My mind oscillated throughout the day from being filled with joy from this awesome, unique experience, to total boredom and dread for what a waste of time it all was.

What else can I say about the day? Well, not much really. In its entirety, I ate breakfast, lunch, and dinner; went to the bathroom several times; walked around outside after lunch, not conversing with any of the others around me of course; and sat with my eyes closed meditating on my little cushion on the floor for around eight hours.

My favorite part of the day was the evening video. Goenka opened with a description of a woman who lived during Buddha's time. Her one and only life's dream was to have a child. She was married at the age of 15, yet after years of trying she was still without child at the age of 25. Thus when she finally became pregnant after her 26th birthday, she cried tears of joy. The entire nine months preceding the birth, she danced in celebration and gave thanks to God day and night.

The fulfillment of her life's dream finally arrived when she gave birth to a beautiful baby boy. Holding her newborn baby, a feeling of love and heavenly bliss radiated from her heart unlike she had ever experienced before. She never imagined she could feel such utter joy and happiness as she did in that moment.

Yet tragedy hit just three days later. As she gently picked up her baby after a nap, she realized he was cold and not breathing. The shock and terror shot through her body like a bullet. Holding her baby tight against her chest, she started screaming and wailing as she ran out into the street, desperately looking for help.

She found her way to the local doctor and after only a short evaluation, he pronounced her baby dead. With the fierce determination of only an obstinate mother, she rejected his opinion, picked up her baby, and stomped outside. She decided she must visit the Buddha himself, because certainly he would be able to make her baby well again.

She passionately ran through the countryside until finally arriving at Buddha's residence. She placed her precious son in Buddha's lap and as she knelt at his feet, desperately pleaded for him to heal her baby.

With an air of absolute calmness and tranquility, Buddha said he could only help her if she were to return with a handful of Banyan tree seeds collected from three different homes where death had never touched.

She profoundly thanked the Buddha and immediately ran back out into the streets. As she entered the center of town, she feverishly knocked on every door she could find. Yet much to her dismay, her burning fire of hope slowly began to become extinguished. After an hour of searching, she was unable to find even one home untouched by the stinging pain of death. She doggedly continued for several more hours, until finally, the reality of her failure to find even one home untouched by death crushed her ability to continue on.

Empty handed and heartbroken, she solemnly returned to the Buddha. In utter empathy and peacefulness, he put his hand on her heart as he spoke his wisdom to her.

"My blessed child, in life, there is suffering. Every human experiences it. You are never alone. Grasping this lesson will keep you from falling into the excruciating pit of anguish and despair. Embracing this realization is key for having a peaceful life."

This moving story made me ponder the times where I'd felt the most pity and anguish in my life, such as all the times I'd spent hating being single, the unsettledness of having divorced parents since the age of two, my roller coaster struggles with

155

food, and the challenges of living with diabetes...

As I fell asleep that night, I let the freeing reality sink in that none of my hardships were unique to me...and as I did this, a warm blanket of peace fell over me.

Chapter 14:
A Dreadful Return Home

My last day of cleansing had _finally_ arrived. I woke up in shock and amazement I had made it through feeling so horrendous for what had now earned the title of: The Most Hellish Week of My Life. I was extremely nauseated and wondered how I was ever going to make it through the dreadful boat ride and ten-hour overnight bus trip back home to the resort. I peeled myself out of bed and slowly started putting my belongings, one by one, into my suitcase.

The miracle came about an hour later…my nausea suddenly lifted! I cried tears of relief, yet my lack of ability to walk more than a few steps at a time due to feeling so weak remained. I was cautiously optimistic. I had hope I could get through the day as long as I just went slowly.

All the other participants at the retreat had made it through their day of hell and had reached that blissful, clear-headed state the man from Australia had described. Not me. I couldn't stop thinking about all I had learned from that book and assumed the reason why I was still feeling so horrible was due to a disgusting level of toxins, bacteria, and the like still festering inside of me. I couldn't wait to get home and track down the whereabouts of the author.

Once I had packed, I slowly made my way through the lounge to check out. There was something absolutely glorious I received once I turned my key in: lunch. I can honestly say I could never have imagined there would come a day when I would be overjoyed to drink vegetable broth and eat steamed broccoli. It had been seven days since I'd ingested anything other than my five daily 'shakes,' made solely of bentonite clay and psyllium husks. With every bite of my glorious meal, I felt little bits of energy returning to my frail body. I closed my eyes and savored the textures I felt and how the flavors tasted in my mouth. Eating in such a conscious way, so full of gratitude for every bite, I was able to stretch the time it took for me to finish my meager lunch to beyond 30 minutes. I had to chuckle, thinking of my lifetime of eating meals substantially larger, which took me less than ten minutes to finish and leaving me hungry for more.

I was supposed to have had at least three meals before leaving the retreat, to ensure a safe journey home. But I had been stubborn, hoping an additional day of fasting would allow my body to finally reach that state of bliss everyone else was experiencing, yet to no avail. After I finished my lunch, I had to make my way to the beach to embark on the arduous journey home.

In a nutshell, after the 15-minute taxi boat ride (with its obnoxiously loud motor that pounded through my head); the 45-minute motorbike ride that wound steeply up and then sharply down the center of the island to the main pier; and the rough, three hour boat ride back to the mainland, my level of utter exhaustion made it crystal clear to me I'd never be able to make it through the ten-hour, overnight bus ride.

After exiting from the boat onto the mainland, there was luckily a café next to the pier where I wearily sat down for a while to figure out my next move. I remembered hearing how some of the other guests at the retreat had flown in from Bangkok, so I knew there must be a small airport somewhere. I happened to see a man reading the paper who had a large piece of luggage next to him, so I hobbled over his way.

"Excuse me sir, by chance are you headed to the airport?"

He smiled, "Yes. I'm catching the afternoon flight back to Bangkok. I'm headed over there shortly."

My smile beamed. "Oh that is fantastic news! Do you know what the likelihood is there would still be a seat available?"

"I imagine there will be one. I take this flight regularly and it's never been sold out. I'd suggest you jump on a taxi and head over to the airport right now to be sure."

This news gave me a welcomed burst of energy, just enough to allow me to gather my things and head on the back of a motorbike taxi to the airport. And I was in luck. Not only was there a seat available, but I wasn't even going to have to wait an hour before take off. My smile beamed from ear to ear. Instead of taking the ten-hour, overnight bus ride from hell back to Hua Hin, I was going to be whisked to Bangkok in just an hour. Heaven! I would still have to take the mini-van ride from

Bangkok and head three hours south, but given my options, that previously dreaded mini-van ride suddenly seemed painless. Much to my relief, I eventually made it home, safe and sound.

***

Arriving 'home' to my lifeless apartment building had never felt so phenomenal. After successfully making the long trek home, I collapsed on my bed and slept a solid 12 hours. I had luckily planned to have a day to recuperate before going back to work so I had the day off. When I awoke, my nausea was gone, but my weakness remained. I eagerly turned on the computer to research about the author of that book, "The Cure for All Diseases," by Dr. Hulda Clark. From what I could find, she now only treats seriously ill patients, such as those with cancer or AIDS…at her clinic in Tijuana.

Tijuana? Hmmm. Many would say this is a red flag…that being located across the US border in Mexico means her protocols are not legitimate or even safe, thus the government does not allow her to practice in America. I admit, I was a bit disappointed she wasn't working at some well-respected, national institution, but I wasn't ready to immediately call her a fraud just because she was located in Mexico.

After working in pharmaceutical sales for three years before attending medical school, I learned first hand how much our 'health' care system is driven by financial motives. For example, as a sales rep, I was told to use certain studies to prove to doctors how effective my particular drug was, but as soon as the marketing department decided on a new angle from which to promote the drug, a box of studies in alignment with this new message would suddenly arrive on my front doorstep, and I was demanded to shred all previous studies (or else get fired). I came to the stark realization that just because a doctor or the US Center for Disease Control gives a recommendation, we should not immediately trust that it's in the best interest of our health. The public should understand there are often ulterior motives driving these decisions.

Furthermore, the pharmaceutical companies are in bed, so to speak, with the politicians. The magnitude of their lobbying power is enormous. The amount of money Americans spend on pharmaceutical drugs is one of *the* top drivers of the US economy. In my opinion, any finding threatening the 'health' of our economy by improving *our* health via a non-drug protocol has the potential to incur such immense red tape, it would never make it to the public. The greater its potential to alleviate the need for pharmaceuticals, the greater the legal roadblocks it will likely have to overcome. I am definitely not a glass half-empty person. But I admit, I am not optimistic that a major medical finding, if it threatens the massive use of pharmaceutical drugs in any way, would be released without years of legal impediments.

So the fact Dr. Clark was located in Tijuana almost gave me the opposite reaction. Instead of assuming she was a fraud, I imagined her protocols might be so amazingly effective that she was seen as a threat to the pharmaceutical industry, and instead of fighting them, she chose to relocate in Mexico.

As I continued my research, I discovered practitioners all around the world that use Dr. Clark's protocols. The exact protocols are even generously shared on many different sites. In a nutshell her anti-bacterial/viral/parasite protocol includes using a combination of herbs plus an electrical device meant to single out and kill unwanted pathogens in the body. As I read on, I found some very gripping information.

"The number of microscopic and non-microscopic invaders in the human body on a regular basis is truly astounding. What's even more shocking, though, is the fact the western medical establishment seems to be completely oblivious to their presence. The damage they do in the body is very real and is a major source of suffering for an almost completely unsuspecting public...

In the United States, we seem to believe parasites are only problems for poor people from third-world countries. We think we are too clean and civilized to have parasite problems. Think again! A recent study published in a major medical journal stated the average American is carrying around two pounds of parasites in their body. If you think you are immune to the problem, all I can say is ignorance may be bliss. Most people simple refuse to believe what is going on, in spite of the evidence to the contrary. And it's costing the American public dearly."

I found a website where I could order a full protocol of the recommended anti-parasite herbs and figured I'd give them a try. Having studied botanical medicine, the suggested herbs were familiar to me and were standard in anti-parasitic protocols…black walnut, clove, berberis, and wormwood. I had never tried any of them before, even after my bout of food poisoning in Chile, so I felt optimistic, not that my diabetes would be cured necessarily, but I was curious if my energy would improve.

But a key part of the protocol was also these strange electrical devices I was reading about. I was becoming frustrated though, because there were so many different 'zappers' and 'magnetic pulsers' to choose from. I had no idea which I should try nor could I decipher which website was even legitimate. I wasn't inclined to buy anything until I could speak with someone who had actually worked with these devices first hand.

I sent an email directly to the clinic in Tijuana to see if they considered Type 1 Diabetes a severe enough condition to treat. If I was really going to give this approach a try, I figured I should attempt to work with the best. I sent off the email with a smile of eager anticipation and decided it was time for food. I was hungry, to say the least.

My week back at work was challenging, to say the least. My strength was slowly coming back with each meal I ate but my exhaustion remained. Luckily, it was slow season at the resort so my schedule had plenty of open slots each day, which allowed me time to lock my office door and take a desperately needed nap on the floor. After having spent my life dreaming of how great I would look if I could lose ten pounds, I had now lost 15 in the previous seven days, yet felt very unenthusiastic about my new, gaunt appearance. Frankly, I looked ghostly. I reached to scratch my arm one afternoon and was literally startled because

161

all I felt was bone. I hadn't weighed as little as I now did since I was a pre-pubescent 14-year-old.

Weeks went by and I can only say that my energy ebbed and flowed, yet was more of the former. The anti-parasitic herbs arrived, but after completing the two-week protocol, I didn't notice any improvement in my energy. I never heard back from the clinic in Tijuana and gave up trying to figure out which electrical device to buy. All my enthusiasm of learning more about Dr. Clark's work vanished. As so often happens in life, what I was once so hopeful about quickly turned into a faded memory, replaced with doubt and disappointment.

The situation with the stem cell company wasn't going well either. They had met with my boss while I was away and he shared the news with our CEO, but he thought it sounded too risky and rejected the whole idea. They offered to give me the procedure if I flew to their office in the Philippines. Because they needed to collect data from another Type 1 Diabetic they offered it to me at no cost. Although my initial excitement had taken a nosedive, a flicker of curiosity and hope remained.

As I thought more deeply about the physiology of the procedure, a pressing question arose. If I were going to have stem cells put into my vein in hopes of them regenerating my insulin-producing cells, how would these cells know when they have done an adequate job and *stop* replicating? I sent an email to the head doctor asking if they had plans to follow those who had already received the procedure into the future in order to track if any contracted cancer. I never received a reply. That was the last piece of communication I ever had with them.

All that work to suppress my excitement when first hearing about this procedure unfortunately proved prudent. My hopes of a cure had become shattered once again, by yet another empty promise.

Feeling fatigued day after day in life is hard enough, but when living in a foreign country, it's enough to turn a once-in-a-lifetime opportunity into a dreaded, living nightmare. I became deeply homesick. I started hating everything. I hated my stark, lifeless apartment. I hated the greasy mystery food at the cafeteria. I hated not being able to buy my own groceries and have a kitchen where I could fix my own meals. I hated being stuck for nine hours a day in an air-conditioned box of an office.

162

I hated wearing my puke green uniform. I hated hearing my filthy rich clients complain about measly headaches or the five or ten vanity pounds they wanted to lose. I hated the humidity. I hated not being able to understand what the nurses were always laughing about in the back office. I hated trying to speak Thai and not being understood. I hated the trashy, touristy city I lived in. I hated not having a two-day weekend where I could hang out with friends. I hated being single and feeling hopeless about my chances of meeting a suitable mate. Then the day came when I even hated the beach...

I was desperate for fresh air one day after work so I headed straight to the beach. I was feeling sad and alone, and decided to go for a swim in hopes of it transforming my mood into something more positive. The sun had already set, and it was a bit dark, but I didn't care. I jumped into the murky water anyway. Within seconds of being in the ocean, I was startled by something brushing up against my leg. I was immediately stricken with fear. My heart was pounding out of my chest. All the stories of the guests at the resort in intense pain due to jellyfish attacks flashed through my mind. I stood paralyzed, knowing if I moved, I might be brutally stung.

I took a deep breath, doing my best to calm myself. Then I reasoned if it were a jellyfish, I would already be in pain. I wasn't. Then I noticed something floating in front of me. It was a plastic bag. I looked around and was aghast. I was surrounded by garbage. Plastic bags and plastic bottles floated everywhere, all around me.

In my disgust, I swiftly headed back to the beach, wading through the garbage, and threw myself onto the sand. The one last place I had depended on to bring solace in that foreign land had failed me. My loneliness and frustration suffocated me. I had to take gasps of air in between my sobs. I'm not sure how long I let myself cry, maybe ten minutes, maybe a half hour or more. But similar to a child having a temper tantrum, I eventually became too tired to continue crying and my desperation slowly dissipated.

After many deep breaths, my mind hungered for relief. Sitting there alone on the beach, a feverish debate began in my head regarding whether or not it was time for me to quit my job and return home.

I had been marinating for the past several weeks in the flavors of my discontent and did not like the taste of them. Yet when I pondered going home, instead of bringing relief, I was filled with apprehension.

"Jody, you dreamed about moving away from the dark, depressing Seattle weather for years and are now finally living in a place where the sun shines everyday, yet you want to move back?! You're crazy! You haven't even been here six months. What a loser you are if you quit so soon! And you LOVE meeting people from all over the world. Last week alone, you had clients from Australia, England, Germany, India, Japan, China, Malaysia, Dubai, Ireland...If you leave here, you'll never have another opportunity like this! If you go home, you'll be totally overwhelmed with the process of starting your own practice and it will take months before you even have more than a few patients a day. Since your first day here, you've been able to see at least six patients per day and thus have ample opportunity to do what you love. The endless opportunities for adventure afforded to you while living here in a foreign culture are priceless. As soon as you get home, you'll be bored and wish you were back here! You are making good money and don't even have to spend a single cent. You have no bills and all of your food is not only paid for but is prepared for you! You were so sick of making your own meals and couldn't wait to not have to cook, yet now you're changing your tune and say you miss cooking?! You obviously don't even know what you want in life! Heck, you're living a dream life, on the beach in Thailand yet aren't happy?! Maybe you don't even know how to be happy! You're screwed!"

The sunshine was long gone from view, literally and figuratively. Sitting there in the dark, all alone on the sand, it felt as if the blood in my head was boiling and that someone was taking a dull knife and stabbing it in and out of my heart. But then a calm and loving voice from my soul spoke out...

"Jody dear, you haven't felt energetic for years and have been pushing yourself through every day since even before you started the rigorous demands of medical school. You have money in the bank and a more than welcome invitation to stay in Seattle with mom. It would be a great time for you to truly allow your body to recoup and feel vibrant again. You have great skills as a physician you can take anywhere. You've been here for five months. It's been a great experience. What are you trying to prove by staying longer? Why do you think you should stay longer? Just for 'more?' More money? More time? More experience? Is 'more' really necessary? Or even healthy?"

A welcomed wave of peace washed over me as the kind voice in my head continued on.

"Having a strong sense of community and connection are one of the most important things to you in your life, and you have no interest in planting roots in Asia. If you would like to be married and start a family, it would be wise to live somewhere you actually enjoy being, in order to increase your chance of meeting a suitable mate. Summer in Seattle is approaching…what a great time it would be for you to go home."

But as soon as the loving voice finished its discourse, the counter voice swiftly echoed its convincing rebuttal. I sat there exhausted, not knowing which voice to listen to, feeling as if I were an ill-fated rope being pulled to shreds in a tumultuous game of tug-o-war.

I struggled back and forth and then realized I hadn't yet eaten dinner. I stood up, brushed the sand off, and headed to the cafeteria to get something to eat. Although I was genuinely hungry, and it was dinnertime, I was acutely aware of my familiar habit of wanting to eat, potentially uncontrollably, when feeling emotional.

But there was no avoiding my wrath. When I arrived at the cafeteria, the dinner rush was over, and the room was unfortunately empty. The kitchen closed each night at 7:30 p.m., but leftovers would be left out in big bowls for staff that worked late each night. I grabbed a plate and piled it high with everything I could. The rebellious part of me was pleased to have the room to myself so nobody could witness the massive quantities I was about to consume. I started shoving food in my mouth so fast that I didn't even taste it. It was as if I had gone unconscious. I was caught in the trance of this impulse for 15 or 20 minutes, returning to the food counter to refill my plate over and over. The growing pain in my over-stuffed belly didn't stop me. I just transitioned to a slower pace. I became conscious of how lost I was in this familiar, self-destructive habit, hungry for relief from painful emotions, yet I was unable to muster up enough willpower to step back from hopelessly stuffing my face.

The only thing which eventually forced me to stop was the fact the physical space in my stomach had literally filled to its max. I simply did not have room for even one more bite. Upon reaching this familiar point of shame and devastation, I finally dragged myself away from the food and headed to my lifeless room. Although I initially engaged in eating to distract me from my pain, my mental knowing of how this behavior in actuality always made me feel ten times worse was not enough to stop me from doing it...like a true addict. My drive to overeat felt like a primal urge, coming from an uncontrollable deeper hunger than my conscious mind had any control over.

Once I reached my bedroom, I threw myself on my bed in self-disgust, feeling lost, alone, and overwhelmed about what to do with my life. Furthermore, not only did I have an immense ache in my belly, but as a diabetic, I now had to calculate how many carbohydrates I had just eaten and then the appropriate dose of insulin necessary to bring my blood sugar back to normal. Given I had gone practically unconscious the entire time I was eating, I had no idea how much insulin I needed. I gave myself a 'shot in the dark' – enough to cover the minimum of what I was sure I needed, but not so much to put myself at risk of ending up in a potentially lethal, diabetic coma in the middle of the night.

The hunger in my belly had been indulged beyond any reasonable degree, yet the hunger in my heart felt as thirsty as a woman lost in the desert. Tears continued to stream down my face until my sorrow exhausted me into sleep.

***

Addiction to food is a difficult path – of course, addiction to *anything* is difficult. The irony is that society actually warmly welcomes and accommodates particular addictions, such as smoking rooms for smokers and the perfunctory 15-minute break twice a day to have a drag. As for alcohol, an over indulgence is often met with humor and even applause from the crowd. The drunk is the life of the party.

But food – well, there's no social space where it's appropriate to shove food in your face until your sick. There are no binging lounges found in airports. The person who overindulges in food is harshly judged and can even be openly ridiculed in western society.

The most obvious lesson in all of this is so simple. Human beings are not perfect. We are all missing key elements in our bodies and souls. To the extent we don't find the keys to our unique locks, we seek to fill the spaces with whatever comfort we can find. It is the human condition. Instead of judging one another's gaps or feeble attempts to fill them, it would be nice if someday everyone could simply recognize we ALL have imperfections. Recognizing them for what they are allows us to stop harshly judging others, as well as ourselves….and be much happier as a result.

***

I woke the next morning, grateful to have had eight hours of rest between me and the events of the night before, yet with a pounding headache. I felt as if I were hung over, but from overdosing on food, not alcohol. My blood sugar, as expected, was high as a kite. I gave myself another big dose of insulin, knowing in the next few hours my sugar level would finally be back to normal. Although the aftertaste of my shame and devastation from my behavior of the night before still lingered like the smell of a cigarette on a smoker's clothes, I gave myself a pep talk about how today was another day, another chance to make it a great one. Recounting some of aunt Mary's brilliant wisdom, I could hear her voice in my head.

"When you fall down Jody, don't stay down. Just get up, brush yourself off, and keep on walking forward."

I imagined the millions of people who had experienced and/or were in the same frame of mind as I in that moment…waking up feeling disgraced from their behaviors of the night before, yet with a responsibility to suit up and show up for their duties of the day ahead. After showering and putting on my puke green uniform, my tenacious self held my head high, put a smile on my face, and courageously headed out for another day at work.

Day 8:
Flowing With Life Increases Your Joy
August 2008

I awoke with a smile. It was day eight and the fortitude it had taken for me to arrive at this point delighted me. I was inspired by the peace I had garnered from Goenka's evening lessons as well as from my voluminous hours of mediation. I was also pleased with what a wonderful gift of relaxation and rejuvenation this retreat was for my body. The day ahead would underscore that even more.

As I was peacefully scanning my bodily sensations during the morning meditation session, my body started to sway. This of course immediately pulled my attention up into the world of thoughts spinning in my head. I was perplexed about whether I was somehow making this happen, as perhaps some sort of unconscious yearning to find a more comfortable position, or if this movement was being initiated by my muscles, without any impetus from my own, personal control.

I did my best to concentrate on letting go of every muscle in my body to ensure I was not initiating the movement. Sure enough, even in doing this, I continued to sway. My right shoulder leaned to the side, then rolled backward. Then my head started slowly rolling in circles and my torso followed. My left shoulder leaned forward as my right reached back, creating this luxurious, deep stretch across my chest.

My mind didn't know what to do with this experience. Part of me thought I should contract my muscles to make the movements stop so I could get back to practicing the meditation technique. But the more convincing part of my thinking decided to just focus on letting go of trying to force anything, and enjoy seeing where and how my body wanted to move.

My body apparently wanted to keep moving. I had become confident this desire was not coming from my mind so I enjoyed just letting it unfold however it needed to. My pattern of movement started feeling as if my muscles were literally unwinding. As my head spun slowly in circles, with each revolution my neck felt more and more relaxed. The same thing was true throughout my chest and back as my torso continued to sway.

At one point, my right shoulder lifted straight upward and then remained there for a few minutes, causing a kink in my neck. With all this organic movement going on, I had given up trying to keep my focus on methodically scanning my bodily sensations, but I still attempted to stay away from getting lost in my thoughts.

I put all my attention on the kink in my neck and did my best to stay away from analyzing it or having a mental discussion about how weird this whole experience was. I let go of the desire to move my shoulder back down and anxiously waited to see what my body was going to do next. Then suddenly, my shoulder dropped and the most peaceful wave of relaxation flowed through my back. It felt as if my upper back muscles had just let go of tension which had probably existed there for years.

Amazingly, after the session ended, I went outside during the break to test my theory my muscles had been literally unwinding and releasing from a state of chronic contraction. Generally, when I clasp my hands behind my back, my shoulders are so tight I can't lift my hands off my butt. This had always aggravated me in yoga classes as I watched everyone else raise their arms to a 90-degree angle, as I struggled to raise them even an inch. So I eagerly put my body to the test. I clasped my hands behind my back and started to raise them up.

Not only did I easily achieve an inch off my behind, but I was able to stretch them even beyond 90 degrees! I was stunned. I had literally *never* had the flexibility to do that before. It took a while for the reality to sink in that my shoulders and back were more relaxed than they had likely been in years. As I walked around the grounds during the break, I kept clasping my hands over and over and doing the same stretch again and again in order to get over my doubt and sure enough, every time, I was able to raise my hands above 90 degrees.

This experience of observing my body sway and unwind while meditating fascinated me and lasted the rest of the day. I was amazed to realize it had taken me over a week of stillness and meditation for my muscles to fully let go. It made me acutely aware of how much tension I must hold on a daily basis. My back felt phenomenal. It was more supple and relaxed than I could ever remember it being before.

After lunch I lay down on a bench outside and smiled as I enjoyed staring at the sky for the next hour. I pondered how contracted we humans can be, not just physically but mentally too…contracted in the sense of when we feel stuck in some aspect of our life and are unable to see a way out…albeit living in this massive, expansive world. I thought about how much suffering we generate when living in this state of self-induced contraction. I became convinced that every time I had resisted or felt pity about a fact of my life…such as the endless energy I'd spent hating my single status or having diabetes…I had created tension in my body, analogous to putting a rock into my metaphysical backpack.

I thought about one of my aunt Mary's key teachings… that 'life is trustable, even the parts we don't like.' I imagined truly embracing this concept and saw how much more ease and grace I would be able to enjoy from day to day. I realized if everything in life was trustable, how fruitless it was to waste time and energy fighting anything, especially when with resistance comes more suffering. This is not to say that taking action on things we don't like is not necessary at times, because it very well may be, but fighting and resistance are futile energies, which rarely accomplish anything anyway, except for more suffering.

I thought about the concept of yin and yang…of the necessity of the light and dark aspects of life in order to achieve balance. I had been brought up to believe that everyday was supposed to be happy and full of roses, and any day less than that pointed to something being wrong, or something needing to be fixed, or even the need for an anti-depressant, perhaps. Well, I had finally reached the conclusion that was all frankly a bunch of bull-s#*t!

I lay there and smiled at the thought of living my life from this open and trusting place, from enjoying the experience of flowing with whatever showed up in life, instead of fighting against it. A common childhood melody suddenly popped into my mind. After singing a few bars, I found myself laughing out loud at the realization of how much brilliance its lyrics expressed, and yet without ever grasping the lesson during the countless times I had sang it during childhood… *"Row, row, row your boat, gently down the stream. Merrily, merrily, merrily, merrily, life is but a dream!"*

Chapter 15:
In Search of Health and Peace

June 2008

My steadfast resolve to never give up when life's inevitable challenges appear carried me through the next few weeks. Yet, the relentless debate in my head continued … *"Jody, you'd be crazy to leave! The sun shines everyday, and you get to work with people from all over the world! This is a once in a lifetime opportunity! You sold almost everything you owned, rented out your house with a year's lease, and gave away your beloved cat, Jennifur…you absolutely cannot leave after only being here a few months! What a coward you would be! How stupid of you to even think about leaving!"*

But then the hunger in my heart to meet a wonderful man (who at least spoke English) would kick in and I'd be convinced I should return home…*"Jody, why the hell are you over here?! You're 35 and tired of being single. You have no interest in ever settling down in Asia, and you're not getting any younger. Except for chatting with your colleagues at meals, you have no social life here. Zero! You are exhausted everyday, and it's not getting any better. You need to go home. Now!"*

One day I'd be chatting with mom, telling her I was looking into flights to come home, and the next day I would be engaged in an animated discussion with my aunt about what an amazing adventure I was living and how I was committed to staying for a year, no matter what. My desire to overeat on the days I felt lost and alone continued. At least I had the 12-step meeting on Wednesday nights to go to for support in dealing with my seemingly uncontrollable urges to binge when my emotions were flaring up. It was helpful for me to be reminded each week of simple tools for staying away from destructive behaviors, such as simply calling someone when I was feeling down, instead of walking into the cafeteria to fill my hunger…which had nothing to do with food.

My lunch hour arrived one day. I was authentically hungry, and my emotions were in check. I had just enjoyed a quick workout at the gym to get that trusty exercise-induced mood boost, which for me has always been the most effective and instantaneous anti-depressant around. After all those depressing years selling and taking the drug myself, Prozac doesn't hold a candle to exercise in my book. It was going to have to be a quick lunch though, but I was happy to be in a good mental place and ready to enjoy a healthy meal. I filled my plate with a normal amount of food and scanned the packed room for where I was going to sit.

Lunchtime was always a delight. On many days, it was the only time I had to connect with my colleagues from home, Monica and Dave, and the other wonderful naturopaths I had grown to love from Australia, Katrina, Nadine, and Olivia. This particular day, much to my delight, they were all sitting at the same table. As I sat down, I tuned into their heated discussion about one of Monica's morning patients. Apparently this woman fully acknowledged she was obese and indulged in a nightly habit of drinking alcohol to excess, yet saw no reason to change because she stated she was deeply happy with her life as it was.

I was shocked and intrigued at the thought of *not* seeing indulging in food as a problem. Dave felt her testimonial was a load of crap because he alleged when one is enslaved to an addiction, freedom and full contentment cannot coexist within that state of slavery. Without sharing my own personal experience, although tending to agree with Dave, I decided to play the part of the devil's advocate…

"There are many different levels to the human psyche. Imagine she was a slave as child, locked up in a basement for years, and now as an emancipated adult, the freedom she feels on a daily basis completely fills her psyche with joy, thus she experiences her love for food and alcohol as positive. Remember," I said, pausing only to take a drink from my water glass, "happiness is relative. Perhaps being a slave was the most horrible experience she ever endured, and now being free, nothing can take away her joy, even eating and drinking to excess."

Monica piped in. "But she is blind to the fact she is not free. She is still a slave, only now to her addictions."

I held to my point. "Sure, she is an addict. But pain is also relative. Your pain, her pain, or my pain can never be measured like apples to apples. The entirety of ones circumstances determine how one views life. Any event in itself is never inherently good or bad, nor does it even have any inherent meaning for that matter. A perfect example is a movie. The critics hate it, yet you love it. Thus it's not about the movie at all. Life has everything to do with one's personal perception of events, less about the events themselves. Everyone loves a sunset, right? Well, what if you were stranded out in the cold and the sun was setting? Suddenly, a sunset becomes a death sentence. Such is true with everything in life. Furthermore, defense mechanisms are powerful realities, so powerful they make people believe even the most absurd lies. Pain? What pain? I am blissfully happy....And so it is."

Our lively discussion came to an unfortunate, abrupt end when the clock hit 12:50. We all had clients at the top of the hour and needed to head to our respective offices. I felt vulnerable, sitting with my colleagues talking about addiction. I had taken the stance that an addiction could be a pleasant experience, as if to talk myself into believing that opinion. Yet even if what I said were true for the woman in question, I knew it was not true for me.

I arrived back at my office and scanned the chart of my next client, a 50-year-old woman from England. She had come to the resort to lose weight.

She arrived at my office and before I could even introduce myself, flopped down in her chair and started yelling, "I must lose 20 kilograms! I hate my disgusting body! Please tell me what to eat and what I should do for exercise. How do I get rid of all of this disgusting cellulite?! Please tell me everything I can do to become beautiful again. Is there a weight-loss tea I can drink? This body isn't me. I am disgusting like this!"

I took a deep breath and assessed the situation, saddened by the thought of how many millions of women, and men too, around the world struggle with weight and food issues and have such distaste for the miracle of their body held within their very own skin. I wanted to dive into the deeper issue of how much self-hate she possessed. I wanted to explain if she really desired to make a lasting, healthy change, it would only be possible if she first started by being more kind to herself...since true change cannot last if the impetus comes from shame and punishment.

Yet the only thing she wanted from me was to tell her how to lose weight, and fast. The challenge of working in a resort setting was my clients only came for a few days and had paid a lot of money to achieve their desired results, thus I had to let go of what I thought was best for them and work with wherever they were at. So my approach with this woman, in the mere 50 minutes I had with her, was to just focus on answering her questions...

"To lose weight, the first recommendation I always give is to eat more vegetables. Adding more of something is always more enjoyable and effective than starting from a place of deprivation. Furthermore, vegetables are low in calories, high in energy-boosting nutrients, and high in fiber, which helps you feel full sooner and thus eat less. I recommend sticking with those lower in natural sugar, in order to keep your blood sugar levels balanced. High sugar, be it from junk food or even from fruits and some vegetables, can wreak havoc on your emotional health, cause fatigue, and even cause cravings for more sugar." I handed her a list of low and high sugar vegetables.

She eagerly grabbed the handout from me and started to scan it. "Pumpkin is high sugar?! THAT is why I am fat! I eat pumpkin all the time!"

I really had to dig my heels in and keep my mouth shut around wanting to delve into her obvious entrenched emotions around her weight. Yet I couldn't help but put a piece of bait out to see if she'd bite.

"Well, even though pumpkin is high sugar, weight gain is usually more complex of an issue than simply eating too much of a single vegetable." I let the end of my statement hang in silence for a few seconds, but she didn't take the bait.

The remainder of her appointment I sadly stuck with telling her what everyone already knows...eat more vegetables, drink more water, exercise regularly, reduce stress, reduce sugar, don't eat processed foods... I had to release my desire to explain the reason that *why* following these simple rules is so challenging is because of ones beliefs...the beliefs one holds about what they do and do not deserve in life, and emotions one is or is not willing to feel.

Of course, the funny thing about me giving out nutrition advice was the fact I certainly had my own struggles with food.

A great quote I luckily heard years ago which alleviated this contradiction for me was, *"What ones needs to learn most for themselves is a topic one teaches best."* Another is, *"He who fails most in any area becomes the expert in that subject because he intimately knows what does and does not work."* I was also pleased to learn years back that shamans of a particular tribe are those members who had become the most ill or burdened throughout their lives…because in order to help others through difficulties, there is no greater teacher than triumphing through one's *own* challenges.

I had not exactly fully triumphed through my own challenges at that point though. In fact, I was more like smack in the middle of their tide. As the weeks went on, my fatigue continued without any signs of lifting, which made navigating through the struggle of whether I should stay in Thailand or go home that much more bewildering. One day I would be authentically concerned that something was terribly wrong with me, and the next day, I would just blame myself for not doing a better job of eating perfectly and balancing my blood sugar levels, and thus blaming my fatigue on the irregular blood sugar levels of diabetes. But then I would tell myself there was no good reason why I shouldn't go home if I were ready to leave, and yet my thoughts would flip again as I berated myself for not being able to better handle the pressures of life, and affirm to myself I wouldn't be any happier if I returned home anyway.

Finally, one day, I had had enough. The levee broke. I finally decided on a nice compromise between the two opposing views endlessly swirling around in my head. I was not ready to leave Thailand, but I knew I needed a break. I needed a *real* vacation, not a week of starving and feeling like hell. I was not attached to whether or not I continued working at the resort so this allowed me to come up with a bold proposition to present to my boss. Although I was not eligible for any additional time off, I decided I was going to ask anyway. This idea alone was a very welcome antidote for finally extinguishing the feverish battle in my head about whether I should stay or go.

I wanted to have enough time to feel truly rested and energized. Two weeks didn't feel like enough; I wanted a month. Although I realized most people would never be so bold as to make such an audacious request, I don't look to 'what everyone else is doing' as a way to determine whether or not something is right for me. Of course, this does not mean my bold decisions don't come without having to work through my own fear and self-doubt. (Moving to Thailand being a perfect example.)

A new debate in my head started about whether or not I should really ask for that much time off, but I quickly came to my resolve. I realized we live in a world of opinions and man-made rules anyway, and what is 'right' often comes simply from whatever opinion belongs to the majority or whatever has been considered 'right' in the past. I thought about the state of affairs in today's world and came to the conclusion we would all be a heck of a lot healthier if everyone stopped for a moment to really discover what felt right and true, and then acted from that place. Furthermore, from my closed-door perspective of having clients truly share how crazy their lives were, we'd all be a heck of a lot healthier and happier if more people actually *did* ask for more time off.

Case in point: I had a 60-year-old Chinese woman in my office that week who had almost literally been working herself to death. She revealed to me she works 15-hour days, seven days a week, and couldn't remember the last time she had given herself a day off. Through her tears of exhaustion she admitted she had been working so hard her entire lifetime in hopes of receiving the approval she so desperately had been longing for from her dad, ever since she was a child. At the age of 60, she was able to finally let go and realize she was never going get the validation she was looking for from the outside world. It was time to give herself a long, overdue break. She was grateful and proud of herself for booking her vacation, because the other option she had been considering was suicide.

I decided to not feel imprisoned by the rule which said I had no more vacation time left. I listened to what I thought was a wise decision for my body and acted from that place. I had become so clear about what I wanted, nothing could've made me back down. Not being paid for a month was a non-issue since I had been putting my entire paycheck each month in the bank due to the fact the resort covered the entirety of my living expenses. When the moment arrived to approach my boss, I told him I realized a month was a lot to ask so if it was too much, then I guess I was quitting. If he wanted me back in a month, however, I'd be back.

I experienced a feeling similar to when the persistent dreary clouds of Seattle's dark skies would finally part, after weeks of non-stop rain, allowing the brilliant sunshine to beam through, when he gave me his reply: "Jody, you do great work here and I don't want to lose you. It's slow season so now is the perfect time. Leave on Monday. Take care of yourself and see you when you get back."

YES!

***

Blue skies for as far as the eye can see...the glistening ocean sparkling like diamonds...patches of clear blue water serving as windows to the bright hues of the coral below...monumental boulders rising up from the sea extending up the steep hillsides...swaying palm trees dancing throughout the hillsides...the rich fragrance of lumeria trees...the vibrant red of hibiscus flowers...freshly fallen papayas calling for me to enjoy their flesh....

This is lovely little Koh Tao, which means 'Turtle Island.' It is a tropical island off the east coast of Thailand measuring just 21-square kilometers and a population of only about 6,000 people. It's basically just a little, tropical island, way out on its own, in the middle of the Gulf of Thailand. When I was on my detox 'vacation' on the island of Koh Phangan, every traveler I met talked about how gorgeous and peaceful this island to the north was. It seemed like the perfect place to spend my month off.

When researching where I wanted to go for my month off, there were key features I desired and Koh Tao met them all. First, with my love for the water, staying beachside was a must. I wanted a remote place but didn't want to be totally isolated. I wanted a little variety in the daily goings-on, but not too much busyness. I wanted a place where my money could be comfortably stretched out for a month. Staying far away from the party-going, music-blaring, back-packer scene, common

177

throughout Asia, was a must. I wanted a quiet beach, but one with enough people around so I could have someone to talk to now and then. With how amazing the snorkeling is purported to be in Thailand, I definitely wanted to experience swimming among the colorful schools of tropical fish and witnessing the amazing varieties of coral....and Koh Tao happens to be one of the best places for snorkeling in the world.

When I arrived on the island, I was determined to find a quaint, little, beachside bungalow on a quiet stretch of sand. I had heard of a place which sounded perfect just 20 minutes from the main pier, called Tanote Bay. I jumped on the back of a motorbike taxi and was on my way. Immediately upon my arrival, I knew I had found the perfect spot. The beautiful white sandy beach, which stretched just a few hundred yards from end to end, was so pure in color, it sparkled like diamonds. The bay was deeply concave, with each arm of the cove creating a nurturing feeling of an embrace. At the 'hand' of each arm stood proud boulders, which gave an impression of the rocks' serving as vigilant guardians of the bay, ensuring safety to all inhabitants. The only commercial development included five, humble, bungalow operations, each with their own beachside restaurant. That was it. No town. No shops. No dance clubs. The rest was jungle. Overgrown plants and leaning palm trees covered the bungalow roofs and stretched out onto the white sand beach, while the glistening ocean waves rhythmically danced upon the shore.

As soon as I paid my taxi driver, I noticed some bungalows high up on the hillside at the north end of the beach, each sporting an unobstructed view of the bay and a hammock on the front deck. My heart skipped a beat with excitement. I didn't bother looking at the other four establishments. I had found exactly what I was looking for.

I headed over in its direction, via a heavenly walk in my bare feet through the sand, and arrived at the outdoor restaurant/front desk reception area. An elderly man, who spoke only a few words in English, handed me a key as he motioned for me to check out one of the available bungalows. I headed up the windy, cement path, beautifully adorned with vibrantly colored flowers along each side swaying in the cool ocean breeze. I stepped onto the deck and had to stop for a minute to take in the stunning view before me. The sun shining on the ocean created the appearance of shimmering diamonds on its surface. I took a deep breath and filled myself with gratitude for my remarkable opportunity to spend a month in paradise.

Although I was already sold on the place given the view from the deck alone, I put the key in and opened the door. The room was just big enough to fit the bed itself and there was an adjacent bathroom. It was humble and bare, but perfect. I headed back down to the reception to ask about the price. Since I would be staying for a month, he offered me the 'discount' rate. Instead of paying the full price of 500 Baht per night, my rate was 400 Baht...an equivalent of $13 per night! My joy practically exploded, making me wish I could give this quiet, reserved, frail and elderly Thai man a bear hug. Luckily for his sake, I restrained myself. I skipped back up the path with the energy of a child on Christmas morning, whistling along. I was definitely ready to settle into my new 'home.' I quickly unpacked and spent almost the entire rest of the day in bliss, rocking in my hammock and enjoying the spectacular ocean view.

I woke up the next morning, the first full day of my month in paradise, in utter joy. I rolled myself out of bed and in just three steps, opened the door and flopped myself into the luxurious hammock. Once again, I literally stayed there for hours, being cradled by the swinging motion and awed by the stunning view before me. I thought back to the five intense years I spent in medical school, when my perfectionist drive wouldn't allow myself even one day to take a break from studying and how it felt like my high-pressured life would never, ever end. This juxtaposition pleasantly reminded me of the truth that no matter how hard or eternal a situation in life may seem, it eventually must come to an end, because the only constant in life is change.

I was completely enthralled by the beauty of the ocean and the opportunity to let my body rest all day. I was mesmerized by the fact there was truly *nothing* I had to do, no obligations at all. I tried to think back to a time when I had felt as blessed and free as I did in that moment, but could not think of a single time in my adult life where I had experienced a similar occasion. Sure, I felt free as a child, but as is true with most of us when we were young, I did not have enough life experience to

179

truly appreciate the freedom I had.

Once I actually was ready for a change from lying in the hammock, I got up and flipped through some of the information in my room about Tanote Bay. The island's population, as one would suspect from a beautiful tropical island with crystal clear water, is concentrated around the beaches. Many of the beaches are only accessible by four-wheel-drive vehicles along one of the few, rugged, overland roads. The center of the island is lush, rocky, and hilly. Scuba diving and snorkeling are one of its biggest draws for tourists, as well as its many idyllic, beachside bungalows. The infrastructure is still pretty basic, but 24-hour electricity had recently been established to the majority of the island.

Being a full-bred westerner and having lived in a large home in a major US city since the day I was born, I am always amazed when I stop long enough to feel grateful for the seemingly inconspicuous luxuries I have been surrounded by throughout my entire life. *Not* living with electricity is a concept I don't think many westerners can even imagine.

The amount of gratitude I felt throughout that day was so immense at times it actually made me feel uncomfortable. Although I could take credit for personally creating many of my amazing life experiences, there was a lot just due to luck. My mind began to wonder... *"How did I get so lucky to be born into a family where food, shelter, warmth, and safety were never an issue? And likely never will be for the rest of my life? And the amount of freedom I have, not only as a human, but as a woman?"*

I spent most of my time that day pondering those amazing facts. Their truth astounded me, as they so often continue to do so today. After my eighth or ninth hour snuggled in my luxurious hammock, swinging in gratitude, I eventually stood up, took the three steps necessary to reach my bed and was amazingly able to fall into a deep slumber for the rest of the night.

✳✳✳

The first two weeks of my month in paradise flew by so fast I actually got a calendar out one day to confirm I had truly arrived 14 days prior. My daily routine had developed into the most peaceful way of life I could've ever imagined, and one I'd certainly never before experienced in my life. In the mornings, I would open my eyes at whatever time my body deemed appropriate. Some days it would be at ten, after having enjoyed a full 12 hours of sleep, and on other days it would be at six, the perfect time to see the glorious sunrise. Then I would roll out of bed, open the door, do a little yoga, and then flop into my luxurious hammock on the deck. I would swing back and forth for an hour or two while being entertained by the glorious show happening in front of me... the waves crashing against the rocks, the birds soaring high in the sky, the trees dancing in the wind, and the colorful fishing and dive boats coming and going in the bay.

As I swayed in my hammock, I would periodically close my eyes and visualize letting go of the stress I had been carrying around in my body for at least the last decade....the tightness in my neck and shoulders, the fiery knot between my shoulder blades, the ache in my low back, the tension in my belly... After enjoying allowing my body to be still for the first hour or two of the day, I would then get up and practice stilling my mind. I would sit up straight in the deck chair, close my eyes, and meditate for an hour. The joy of this practice was that by the end of the hour, my body was more relaxed than even after an hour of just swaying in the hammock.

After meditating, I would put my bathing suit, shorts, and t-shirt on and head down the beautiful windy path, passing by the fragrant plumeria tree, the hibiscus plants, and the countless other flowering bundles of joy and enter the beachside restaurant for a quick bite to eat before heading to the beach.

Once I arrived at the glorious white sand beach, it was usually around noon, and thus at the peak heat of the day, so my favored spot became this perfect little nook underneath one of the many palm trees serving as the demarcation between where the jungle ended and the beach began. I was thrilled to finally have time to read my beloved aunt Mary's book, which had been gathering dust on my nightstand for years. Entitled, 'The Gift of Our Compulsions,' she uses the word 'compulsions' to refer not only to the obvious ones, such as over-eating or drinking, but also to today's common compulsions of over-thinking, over-working, constant struggling, deleterious internet surfing, being

181

over-busy, etc.

Every afternoon I became enthralled with the endless pearls of wisdom she shared throughout her book. It was as if she was sitting right there next to me on the beach. One of my favorite lessons she shared was, when we find ourselves judging something within us as bad and hating ourselves for it, to instead use it as an opportunity to embrace our humanness and to practice unconditional love toward ourselves.

It made me think a lot about how much I hated myself every time I used food to cope with loneliness or anger or sadness, or any other uncomfortable emotion, and how berating myself made the situation worse, every time. The thought of being kind and loving to myself after I overate seemed totally counterintuitive. She and I had discussed this principle countless times during our weekly chats throughout the years, yet it's one of those lessons which takes hearing a thousand times or more before it sinks in.

In the book, she explained the key piece to this lesson is by learning to be compassionate and loving with ourselves at our weakest moments, we actually receive a gift of strength. She made an analogy to when a child has a temper tantrum. The only reason we do something harmful to ourselves is because there is a young part of ourselves feeling fearful and freaking out. So if we yell and scream at the child (or ourselves), does that approach make the situation better or worse? The answer is obvious when working with a child, yet isn't as easy when applying the principle to ourselves.

Mary explained that when we find ourselves thinking or acting in a harmful way towards ourselves, we need to realize we are only doing so because we're experiencing some sort of emotional pain, and thus it would be best to respond from a place of self-compassion. By doing this, we receive the gift of not perpetuating the cycle of self-hate, and instead, create peace within our heart.

Intellectually, it's brilliant. Realistically, being kind to yourself no matter what takes diligent practice. Every afternoon, I would sit on the beach and marinate myself in Mary's wisdom and make a pledge to do my best to incorporate her lessons into my life. Peace within my heart was something I'd been hungry for for years, yet even after fulfilling my lifetime dream of becoming a physician, it still often eluded me.

One of the fears I'd had about being on a tropical island by myself for a month was of being surrounded by madly-in-love, honeymooning couples, googoo-ing and gaagaa-ing over each other, chatting and laughing as they laid next to each other in the sand, sharing a bottle of wine at sunset (and let's not even mention what they likely did after dark). I can't tell you how many nights in the previous 20 years I'd spent feeling sad about being single. Yes, I love 'grabbing life by the horns,' but not having someone by my side to share my adventures with...well, it had become old. I have no problem being alone. I'd almost become too good at it. The issue was, at the age of 35, I simply wanted a partner.

Except for one 18-month relationship years prior, I had basically been single my entire life, wanting a boyfriend but never seemingly able to find one. Thus for years, every time I was around couples, most especially when they were being all lovey-dovey, the inevitable sharp pang of loneliness would stab me in the heart.

So on some days when I was sitting in my little, favorite nook under the palm tree, I would be lounging there in utter bliss, with a huge grin of gratitude beaming from ear to ear for having this amazing opportunity to have a month off in paradise. But on other days, when the beach was packed with lovers, garishly laughing and holding hands as they skipped into the sea, and I was the only loser sitting there alone, the familiar pain and longing in my heart would bring tears to my eyes.

On the days when tears streamed down my face, I would eventually pull myself out of my pile of pity by reminding myself of the words of wisdom Mary had shared with me during the countless times we had covered this topic...that there are no accidents in life...that every situation, especially the difficult ones, holds a great opportunity for becoming a better person, and, I always love this part...because crap is great fertilizer for growth. I would remind myself of the fact I always have the choice to either feel angry and resentful about being single and curse my years of failure in finding a mate or instead see it as a challenge to rise above and use as a means for personal growth. As I took a deep breath in, as if to capture her wisdom inside my body, I would then tenaciously turn my thoughts toward the immense gratitude I felt for being able to spend an amazing month in paradise.

By about three o'clock, I was ready to put her book down and head into the glorious ocean. I'd grab my mask and snorkel, eager to be astonished once again by the fascinating and vibrant life forms of the sea which continued to mesmerize me on a daily basis. Standing in the ocean at about thigh level, I'd spit into my mask and then give it a quick rinse (a fabulous tip for avoiding a mask fogging up, taught to me by my beloved grandfather Irving during our precious years vacationing in Hawaii when I was little). Then I'd fervently dive in and the adventure would begin.

After only a few seconds of swimming out, the view of the sand below came to an abrupt end as if the bottom had dropped out, and suddenly I'd have the feeling of looking over the edge of a ten-story building to an entire city below. Seriously, it was amazing! Huge, multicolored boulders stood tall like proud castles. Green splatter on the rocks looked like captivating pieces of modern art. Stunning coral fanned out from the sides of huge rocks as if acting as shade canopies to the life below. Various piles of bright green 'branches' stacked on top of each other resembled magnificent bonsai trees. Barren parts of white sand between the decorative rocks created the impression of serving to be the city streets and perhaps, open-air parks.

From afar, the coral looked as if it were just colored rocks. But when I swam up close, I could see the coral was actually alive. Looking closely at one of these magnificent pieces of life, I realized it was covered in thousands of tiny pulsating spores. Although it was tempting to touch, I had been told to restrain myself due to the fact the transfer of human bacteria can actually kill it, causing it to turn into an ugly pile of gray scraps – a horrible tragedy because of the amazing spectacle it was for those of us lucky enough to witness it in its full grandeur.

The coral was the most vibrant and varied I'd ever seen! There were huge round balls covered with squiggly and colorful lines creating the appearance of gigantic brains; bright green, circular 'platters' stretching six feet wide with every inch of their surface covered by 'fingers' sticking straight up; purple 'cauliflower' heads that ranged in size from tiny to gargantuan; random shapes resembling furry terrycloth bathrobes thrown into a pile on the floor; piles of 'deer antlers' with sharp projections pointing in every direction… and the vista of it all together was magnificent.

There were also huge, vibrantly colored 'clams,' somehow buried deep between pieces of adjacent coral, so the only part in view was their fluorescent colored 'lips,' which would snap shut anytime I swam up close to them. I floated past many long, jumbo-sized green 'hot dogs' (which looked like huge turds but are fondly known as 'sea cucumbers') and edges of 'buildings' decorated with tiny, bright red, blue, and green fuzzy balls, which would magically retract and disappear deep into the rock whenever I came close. Plankton, which looked like free-floating spider webs, hung everywhere, leaving the impression Spiderman must have recently swam by. Individual pieces of deep purple colored 'spaghetti' sticking straight up from the base of a rock floated back and forth in unison, resembling Bob Marley's dreadlocks, as if swaying to the beat of their favorite song, "What a Glorious Day in the Sea!"

The tropical fish were stunning, decorated in vibrant reds, blues and greens, some as big as salmon! A school of 20 or more of them would swim along next to me occasionally, each staring directly at me with their big, bulging eyes. Tadpole-sized fish would often dart into my view, swimming tightly next to one another as if to form one big mass. (I learned they do this in order to create the appearance of being a single, bigger fish, thus hopefully fooling potential predators and camouflaging the reality of their perfect, little, snack-sized body.) The mass of tadpoles would move like a freight train along in front of me. I literally had to stop once, as if waiting at a railroad crossing, before I could continue forward.

One day as I swam up to observe a huge school of six-inch fish, decorated with silver stripes and a bit of yellow on their fins, they seemed as interested in me as I was in them. One by one they swam directly toward my mask and made eye contact with me for a moment, as if to introduce themselves. After a few seconds, each would swim away to give the next guy a turn. But before I knew it, I wasn't just observing this school of fish, I was entirely engulfed by them!

I spun around and realized there were hundreds everywhere…to my left, to my right, underneath me, as well as above me. I stayed motionless and floated in absolute awe of the unique beauty around me. As they swam about, the sunlight shining through the ocean's surface transformed their appearance into a radiant field of sparkling diamonds, with beams of light bursting in every direction. This visual sensation absolutely took my breath away. I felt as if I myself had turned into a glowing and radiant being of light, being welcomed and surrounded by my new family. I stayed there for ages, just floating and floating and floating among this absolutely astonishing and captivating encounter.

Day 9:
The Power of Letting Go
August 2008

Was this really possible? Had I really made it to day nine? As I absorbed myself in enjoying every bite of my breakfast that morning, I had a moment of great self-appreciation and admiration. I was amazed at what I had accomplished in the previous eight days...fierce tenacity, determination, stillness, and extraordinary focus. After the countless moments in the first half of the retreat when day ten felt years away, I sat there in awe of the reality of how close it now was.

The morning meditation sessions were a breeze. I had truly strengthened my 'muscle' of concentration and was easily able to scan up and down my body, fully focusing on my physical sensations and not getting lost in thinking (at least, not too much anyway).

In the afternoon, I had, once again, another amazing experience. As I was calmly perched on my little cushion, eyes closed and meditating, I suddenly became aware of every part of my body tingling simultaneously. I had been focusing on the tingling in my pinky finger but then it suddenly spread throughout my entire body. I just sat there, no longer able to focus on a single area because my entire body had become one vibrating mass. As I tried to sharpen my focus back to my fingers, I realized I was unable to because I could no longer feel an edge to my body. It was as if the vibrating energy in my body had merged with the energy around me. It was amazing and this feeling lasted the entire afternoon.

At dinner, I constructed a theory about my incredible experience. I believed that as a result of letting go of so much physical tension, plus not engaging in doing really anything for the previous eight days... no working, no talking, no exercising, no communicating, no busyness, no nothing...I had truly let go of any blocks to simply being the vibrating mass of energy which I am, and everybody is, at our core.

Serendipitously, Goenka's lesson that night was about the power of letting go...letting go of fear, letting go of doubt, of worry, of wanting, and of struggle itself. He talked about how

187

our minds and thoughts can drive us crazy, causing us to contract and shut ourselves off from the natural flow of life. As we try to force life to go our way...craving things we don't have and longing to get rid of things we do...we cause ourselves suffering. In letting go of this fruitless battle, we free ourselves to enjoy a life full of peace and ease.

Having experienced the peace and joy from letting go on the physical plane, I completely embraced this lesson acknowledging the sheer wisdom in 'letting go' on the mental plane as well.

As I got ready for bed that night, I pondered my eternal resistance to being single. I tried to imagine letting go of both my aversion to it and my longing for finding a mate. I was entertained by how much my mind fought the idea of doing this. Thoughts flooded in about what a stupid idea it was and how it would be impossible anyway given how important this desire was to me.

But the wiser part of myself came to the realization of how all of my resisting and wanting had never brought me happiness, nor a partner in the first place. Aversion and longing had never changed my single status. So I realized, why not enjoy my life of singlehood, let go of the painful feelings of resisting and longing, and instead, put my faith in trusting that a mate will indeed come into my life someday. This felt good. Embracing the truth of the spectacular single woman I was, I did my best to fill myself with a profound sense of self-appreciation and unconditional love, as I fell deeply into a peaceful slumber.

Chapter 16:
Bad News

July 2008

7:00 a.m., Monday morning. Buzzzzzzzzzzzzz It was startling to have to force myself to get out of bed after my luxurious month in paradise, sleeping in day after glorious day. I actually felt a bit dizzy once I finally succeeded in ripping myself away from my sheets and made it to my feet. I took a cold shower to help me wake up and reminded myself that today was not about lounging on the beach and snorkeling, but about being a responsible physician and showing up for work. (Boo hiss!) I begrudgingly put my puke green uniform on and headed to the cafeteria for those long forgotten (or so I hoped) greasy, heat-lamp-warmed eggs. As I scooped some onto my plate, a sharp pain stabbed me in my heart, due to my longing for the freshly fallen papayas I used to enjoy for breakfast while sitting with my feet snuggled in the sand.

I took a seat next to my colleague Olivia, the most senior of the six of us. Due to the resort's custom of over-working the naturopaths and the resulting high turnover rate for our position, she had earned that title after being on staff for not even two years.

"Hey Jody! Welcome back! How was it?" I let out a sigh, "Truly amazing, Olivia."

"Well good for you. You're going to need to be rested because your schedule is packed for the next several weeks. And by the way, I've had it with this place and I'm quitting..."

It wasn't exactly the warm welcome I was hoping for. Olivia had become pregnant (she married a Thai a few months back) and didn't want to have to put up with the six-day workweek at the resort anymore, so she and her husband were planning on moving back to her home country of Australia.

Additionally, she proceeded to tell me our boss was fired two weeks prior and had been escorted off the premises after his mid-year review. Victor, our now ex-boss, was an American. He had hired me and my other two American colleagues, Dave and Monica. Victor didn't seem to get along too well with upper management, which had created this tension of 'the Americans'

189

versus everyone else. So upon learning that my biggest supporter was gone, it felt a bit like the captain of my ship had been thrown overboard.

Breakfast ended and I headed to my office with trepidation. After getting through my hundreds of emails from the last month, and seeing a few, luckily, quick and easy clients, it was already time for lunch. Having enjoyed all of my meals beachside, in utter peace and silence over the previous month, eating within the confines of the pea green walls of the staff cafeteria, as well as among the cacophony of the bustling conversations and the blaring television felt a bit too much to handle. I filled my plate and snuck up the stairs to enjoy my lunch sitting in the glorious sunshine up on the roof. Ahhhh. Back to a glimpse of the peace of my time off. I stretched, grateful to simply be outside.

That respite didn't last long, however. After finishing, I headed back downstairs to drop off my plate at the dish bin in the noisy cafeteria. As I was leaving, the head of HR came up to me and asked me to put my hand out.

She then slapped it and said, "That's for taking food out of the cafeteria, which you are not allowed to do," and promptly walked away.

…Hmmm, maybe the bungalows on my little island paradise would be interested in hiring a naturopath as a new service to their guests….

My first day back at work finally came to a very welcomed end. After learning Olivia was quitting, my boss has been fired, the resort was overbooked so guests were lining up to complain about not being able to enjoy their desired treatments, and my hand was slapped by the head of HR, I couldn't wait to just relax and have dinner with Monica, Katrina and Nadine. Being able to get caught up with them over a relaxing dinner away from the cafeteria would at least bring a peaceful ending to my tumultuous day, or so I thought.

After changing out of our puke green uniforms, we decided to splurge and head to one of the fancy, beachside restaurants. I was thrilled with this idea. As soon as we ordered though, Monica started to tell me about how there had been numerous predictions of an upcoming tsunami, which was expected to hit sometime within the next four weeks…and then they announced to me how each of them were considering quitting, and soon.

"Are you guys really serious?!"

They didn't have to answer my question; their stern looks said it all. I usually am not one to believe in 'the world is ending' predictions, but as they informed me of how much attention the press had been giving to this supposed, impending disaster, I too became worried. The tragic tsunami of just four years earlier in southern Thailand was still a fresh memory for us all.

So, it was not exactly the joyous night of reconnecting with my colleagues I had hoped for! I zoned out from the conversation for a while as all these questions began swirling around in my head…"*Where do I fit in the world? Where do I belong?*" All my friends back at home were married and busy being parents. I was single. No husband. No kids. I had spent decades longing to get away from the depressing, gray, Seattle weather, so at least I knew I didn't want to move back there. I had spent 30 years hungering for becoming a physician, a goal I had finally reached. What was my new goal? My new purpose? It had taken so much courage for me to sell almost half of my belongings, rent out my home, give away my dear cat, and say good-bye to my friends and family before moving to Thailand. Was I going to have to make a major move again? But where should I go?

Even among our heavy topics, we found plenty of reasons throughout the night to laugh, as we usually did when we were lucky enough to spend quality time together. We often laughed at the irony of how so many wealthy guests were unhappy, while the biggest smiles we'd ever seen beamed from the faces of Thais living in shacks on the side of the road. After we finished our meal, we walked along the beach back home to our respective lifeless apartment rooms and hugged each other good-night.

With a heaviness in my heart, I turned on my computer in hopes of receiving a note of love or good news from home. I scanned my inbox and was thrilled to see an email from the woman who had adopted my dear Jennifur. Although she wasn't my cat anymore, being able to receive emails now and again from her new owner made me feel like I was still in her life, like a grandmother who lived far away. I eagerly opened the email

191

but was suddenly jolted by the words I read. In my dismay, I had to read it a few times to be sure I was truly grasping the message correctly. *"...and so we had to give her away..."*

The events of the day had already primed my heart for breaking, and in receiving this news, it felt as if my heart had truly been broken in half. Apparently, now Jen was living with some stranger they had found through the internet classifieds. I flopped onto my bed and cried myself to sleep.

***

One thing I often find myself telling patients is how everyone in life has good days and bad. *Everyone.* It is inevitable that both ends of the emotional spectrum will be experienced throughout one's lifetime, over and over and over again. Thus realizing the truth, 'this too shall pass,' is a great tool for life, easing the pain of any challenging situation. Difficulties are just like the weather...the emotions and feelings will eventually float away, just like the clouds. And then the sun will shine....and then the rain will come...and then summer will arrive...and then winter will appear. Challenging events are all opportunities. Opportunities to either react to in a negative way, cussing and screaming and demanding, *"Why me?!"* Or in a more peaceful way, being tender with oneself for the realities of being human, and yet remembering the only constant in life is change.

But knowing all that rhetoric versus actually having the skill to put it into action, we all know are two different matters entirely. My challenge that evening was to somehow sit with my tumultuous emotions in a calm and mature way...and not head to the cafeteria for 'comfort.' Luckily I resisted that urge. But I lied on my bed and cried, wallowing in pity, fear, and despair. The tools I so skillfully teach my patients for how to stay calm through life's emotional storms were nowhere in sight.

Chapter 17:
Freedom at Last

July 2008

I woke up fuming the next morning. My head was spinning with fear and frustration about how much I hated my life and everything about living in Thailand. The familiar rant began: I hated my lifeless room. I hated the food in the cafeteria. I hated having to sit in my office all day without fresh air. I hated working six days a week. I hated not having a social life. I hated not being able to understand the local language. I hated the town. I hated the loud, crowded, dirty streets. I hated how impossible it was to find a peaceful place to walk. I hated how all the stray dogs struck me with terror every time they barked so feverishly at me. I hated not being able to take a relaxing stroll on the beach at sunset due to being told the beach was not safe for a woman to be alone on after dark....

I managed to overcome my internal fury enough to get dressed and head to work, yet I spent the day battling the raging voices in my head...

"Jody, you'll always hate life. It has always felt like a struggle to you...managing your diabetes day after endless day, feeling the starvation in your heart for love, and never knowing where you fit in life... It will always continue to be a struggle for you because you don't know how to live life any other way. And now you're getting old. You are starting to look like crap and it's just going to keep getting worse. Nobody is ever going to want to marry you..."

The negative voices in my head were relentless all day. Like a gift from God however, each of my patients that day happened to tell me how much they enjoyed working with me and the immense value they had received from their appointment. It was shocking and yet pleasing to me how, apparently, I was still such an effective physician, even while inside my head I was full of anger and couldn't stop thinking about how I wished I'd rather be curled up in bed with the covers over my head than at work.

The rant continued ...

"You can't even handle the littlest things in life, like eating in a sane manner. It's ridiculous how you consistently sabotage yourself by eating *just one wrong bite of food, which then screws up your blood sugar level and makes you feel like crap for hours. You're screwed no matter what job you have or what town you live in, because you'll always be lost in struggle. You're the same lonely girl you were when you were a teenager, yet now you look old and weathered. You're still sitting here dreaming of having a fricking boyfriend. What is wrong with you? All the biggest nerds you've ever known are married. How the hell have you become 35 years old and still have not had a significant person in your life? How stupid of you to be living in Asia when you want to so desperately find a man to share your life with…"*

I was mad at life. I was sick of feeling these feelings of depression, hopelessness, and despair. I was sick of listening to the old broken record in my head, yelling at me year after year about how messed up my life was. I was painfully frustrated by the consistency with which this state of mind had showed up throughout my life and was scared by the fact I had yet to be able to move beyond it once and for all.

And then, toward the end of my horrible day, to top it all off, I received the following email from the CEO of the resort:

Dear Naturopaths,

We cannot express enough our appreciation to you for the phenomenal job you do everyday. You improve the health of our guests and what you do is one of the most important jobs at the resort. Thank you.

Yet we are aware of the toll this demanding role can be for all of you. Each one of you has expressed to us how difficult it has been to get the rest you need given the six-day workweek, which is the norm here in Thailand.

After several years of unsuccessfully keeping our naturopaths as employees for longer than six months, we decided to send five Thai women to Australia for an 18-month holistic health curriculum. These women have completed the program as of last month and are now ready to take over the role as our resort naturopaths.

Please have your office cleaned out by the end of

194

today and then stop by the human resources office on your way out to sign paperwork and receive information about your compensation package, such as reimbursement for your flight back to your respective home countries.

We thank you for your tireless efforts over the months each of you have worked here and wish you well as you find a new job, more suitable to your needs of having two days off each week.

Sincerely,
Pat Tuliminda

I sat there in shock and disbelief. I read the letter at least five times in order to fully grasp the truth I was being laid off, not to mention via a group email. I took a few deep breaths to avoid the inevitable rage I was expecting to bubble up from inside of me, and realized in shock, it didn't.

The endless debate of whether to stay or go had been clearly answered for me. I discovered a feeling of joy and liberation radiating from my heart. It was as if the hunger behind all of my ranting and raving of the day, of how much I hated my life there, had suddenly been taken care of for me. I had received the green light to move on to the next phase of my life, wherever that may be.

I was free.

Day 10:
Hunger Fulfilled

August 2008

I woke up beaming. It was day ten! And I could smile at people today! The previous night, Goenka had announced that to ease our way back into communication, we were allowed to engage in body language on day ten. So at breakfast, I felt so much joy and excitement for all of us being so close to accomplishing this valiant task of meditating for ten days, I couldn't help but give great, big, bear hugs to everyone I happened to make eye contact with. It felt terrific to finally be able to look into the eyes of all these others whom I had shared this monumental journey with.

A beautiful thing was, even though I had not said a word to any of them over the course of our ten days together, nor did I even know who spoke English, it felt as if I already knew a bit about them. From the way they walked, how they dressed, the energy I felt when sitting next to them at mealtimes...all of these things carried a level of communication, which allowed me to get to know them. It is said only ten percent of communication is verbal anyway and that we get 75 percent of our information from others through non-verbal cues. Sitting there at breakfast, smiling at my still nameless, 'new friends,' that statistic certainly seemed accurate to me.

I proudly took my place on my little mediation cushion and closed my eyes. Full of triumphant joy and now well skilled in single-minded focus, I started my session by concentrating on the tingling feeling on the top of my head.

My day flowed with ease. Knowing I was so close to the end made my appreciation for each session, no matter how long at times it seemed to drag on, soar. Additionally, I experienced a final, remarkable experience that afternoon. As I was diligently and methodically scanning the sensations throughout my body, visions of my childhood started flashing through my mind.

In my life, it fascinates me why I feel compelled to drag up things which did not go well in my past over and over again, and yet do not speak with the same consistency of everything that _did_ go well when I was growing up, which was a lot! Who

196

knows how many times I've complained about having divorced parents, or how challenging my relationship was with my step mother, or how often I felt alone, or…

Yet, that afternoon, countless visions of all the happy times of my childhood vividly came to mind…the splendid joy I had every summer at camp, countless hours each summer waterskiing with my dad, clam digging at mom's cabin with her and my sister, playing soccer with all my girlfriends, playing hide-and-seek in the backyard, the day I learned to ride a bike without training wheels, singing songs with my campfire group, building forts in the living room with my sister, sleeping out in my tent in the backyard, making cookies with my friends…

Some of these recollections hadn't come to mind in years. Not only were my memories crystal clear, but it felt as if I'd been transported back in time; as if I was truly taking part in the event. My body felt as if I were a kid again. I felt vibrant. I felt energized. I felt joy radiating from my heart. I continued to sit there in bliss, as the countless happy visions of my childhood continued to flash through my mind, one after another.

At dinner, I came up with another theory to explain my experience. This time, my theory was that after having 'let go' of so much physically and mentally over the past ten days, I had truly reconnected with what I believe is the authentic and radiating joy I was, as is true of every human, naturally born with. After years of being alive, with all of life's inevitable challenges and disappointments, there is a tendency to carry the weight of these events into our present and future experiences. As a result, the negative memories act to suppress our ability to feel radiant joy as adults. We are likely not even conscious of the fact we are carrying the negative energy of these past events in our mind. This negative energy remains in our body and can affect us physically too…unless we are diligent at taking steps to consciously let go of it, not only from the past, but also as life's ups and downs continue to unfold.

After dinner, it was time for our last evening lesson. In the video, Goenka was still seated peacefully, cross-legged on the floor against the white-walled backdrop, with his devoted wife next to him, as he had been in all the other videos. He praised us for our determination and devoted practice. He then recounted the main lessons of the course…

1. *Do not believe everything you think…your brilliance lies beyond your thoughts.*

2. *The only constant in life is change…having attachments brings suffering because all things eventually will pass*

3. *Have compassion for yourself and others*

4. *Joy comes from within*

5. *Practicing meditation strengthens the ability to live in peace*

6. *By sitting with pain, not running from it, you allow it to be released*

7. *In life, there is suffering…you are never alone with your pain*

8. *Letting go of resisting what is and longing for what is not brings peace*

9. *Living in peace requires diligent practice to keep the mind clear of negative energy*

Sitting there cross-legged on the floor, on my little mediation cushion, somewhere out in the middle of nowhere in northern Thailand, with a group of people I had never even spoken a word to…I had truly never felt so peaceful. The exhilarating feeling I was experiencing was clearly not from having achieved my doctorate degree, nor from having a boyfriend, nor any other external circumstance.

The joy radiating from my heart in that moment was simply happening just because…because I had cleared away the blocks of physical tension and the suppressive clouds of negative thinking. I had strengthened my ability to be with what is, be it my joy or my pain, without judgment or resistance. I had become a compassionate witness to the breadth of all of my experiences, be they physical or mental, and trusted that 'this too shall pass.' My radiant smile beamed. I was in utter bliss.

***

The End

***

Prologue

A few of my friends gave me some wonderful feedback on this book in the last days before I sent it to print. One of the comments I heard with resounding volume was, "The end came so suddenly. You left me hanging Jody! Please include a prologue about what happened after Thailand."

To those of you who can relate in this moment of completing HUNGER, An Adventurous Journey of Finding Peace Within, you have them to thank! So here you go…

When I initially left Seattle in January 2008 for my 'dream job' at an elite health spa for the rich and famous in Thailand, I sold over half of my belongings, put what remained in storage, and rented out my house, not knowing when I'd ever live in the U.S. again. I had yearned to get out of rainy Seattle for so many years and now that I had landed a job as a doctor at a ritzy beachside resort, I figured I'd likely settle there for several years to come!

Well as you know, my time in Thailand didn't even last a year. My job ended concurrent with the start of the cold fall weather in Seattle. After enjoying more bright and balmy sunshine that year than perhaps I had experienced in my entire life combined, I decided it would most certainly NOT be a good time to return home.

Furthermore, I had become so inspired by writing about my adventures that I wanted to find a peaceful place to live for a while in order to turn my blog entries into this book. To follow in the footsteps of the best-selling author of Eat Pray Love, I decided to fly just a few hours south and live on the tropical island of Bali for a while. I found a lovely local family to live with for only dollars a day and bought a bicycle to get around town.

My life for the next several months was dedicated to creating this book. On some days I would write while lounging on my private balcony, afforded with views of lush green rice paddies and swaying palm trees. Other days I would write while perched on cushions at a local restaurant after receiving the thumbs up to sit there for as long as I wanted from the staff whom I quickly became on a first name basis with. And finally, sometimes I would prop myself up with yoga mats and sit on the floor of the local yoga studio for hours after class.

But truth be told, even living in paradise gets old. After five months in beautiful Bali and yet having been away from home for a total of eighteen months, I was getting the itch to return. I was hungry to be able to look directly in the eyes of my friends and family, and enjoy their loving embrace. I wasn't even close to being done with the book but once spring had sprung in Seattle, in June of 2009, I was ready to return home.

I put working on the book on hold as I struggled to figure out where to move and what the next chapter of my life was going to look like. To make a long story short, after six months of agonizing internal mental debating, I settled into living in a sunny town nestled in the mountains where I had vacationed countless times since childhood. I spent the next two years there setting up my private practice and creating my online programs...but not working on my book.

In July of 2011, the whispers from the book I had ignored for the previous years had transformed into a roaring demand for attention. I couldn't ignore my dusty manuscript any longer. Fortunately, one day I met a fantastic woman who had recently completed and published her own book, who said 'yes' to helping me complete mine.

With steadfast determination to finish, I called Sandra every Monday through Friday at 10 a.m. to commit to her at what time and for how many hours I would write each day...and I did this for months.

Some days, the writing would seamlessly flow out of me and I beamed with pride as I read over it. Yet other days, I would stare at my computer screen, in frustration of not knowing what the next sentence should be, or even how I was going to end the book.

A decision I had made when starting my book back in Thailand was that Oprah was going to love my book. I've said this to myself and to others countless times. I've said this so many times, it doesn't feel like a far-fetched dream at all. To me, it's just a matter of time before it comes true.

Well, within just a few days of my commitment to start writing again after my two-year hiatus, I heard Oprah was in town. As I was meditating one morning, I had a powerful thought that I must go to town to meet her. But I laughed it off, justifying I didn't know how or where that could happen, and just went about my day…or at least tried to.

As the day went on, this thought kept getting louder and louder until by 5 o'clock, I found myself driving to the hotel where I heard she was staying. I sat in the lobby and waited. To not waste my time and to avoid feeling like a stalker, I brought my computer and just spent my time working on the book.

Believe it or not, within 15 minutes, there she was. Oprah was within just a few feet of me casually walking through the lobby! I froze. I didn't truly think I'd see her! I just stood there in awe, as I watched her walk away from me into a private dinner party.

I sent my amazing news out on Facebook, texted and called everyone I knew. "Oprah just walked by me as I was writing my book!!!" And the gist of the responses I received was, "Cool! Did you tell her about it?!"

After my initial rush of excitement, I was disgruntled with my uncharacteristic lack of tenacity and lost opportunity to personally tell Oprah about my book. I tried to convince myself having Oprah walk by me in the very moment I was working on my book was a big enough victory worthy of celebration! After continuing to share my news with countless friends and family, I eventually walked to my car to go home.

Yet, the second I entered my car, there was that voice again.

"What are you doing Jody?! You've said for YEARS how Oprah is going to love your book. Well, go back in there and tell her about it!"

I had no choice. Without a second thought, I was propelled out of my car and headed back into the lobby. I took my stalker seat again and waited there for another hour or two. I was hoping she was still in the dinner party and would come out the same door as she entered, but I became uncertain.

I started to wonder if there was another exit door to the dinner party besides the front entrance. I decided to take the risk of leaving my post to go around the backside of the hotel to see if there was another way out of the private dinner party…but I was swiftly shooed away by a security guard.

Back to the lobby I went and sat back down in my stalker chair. If I were going to say something to her, I knew it would have to be something unique; something powerful enough to grab her attention. I didn't want to be just another idolizing fan.

Sure enough, my determination paid off. There she was, coming back out of the entrance of the dinner party with no one else immediately around her. This time, I was as ready as an eager cat, poised to pounce. (Well, not literally of course.)

I jumped up from my chair and confidently approached Oprah.

"Hello Oprah. Thank you for your courage and willingness to share your struggles with food with the world. I too share your struggles at times and am writing a book which addresses how we are always hungry for something much more meaningful than whatever external thing at times we may think we need."

With warm and direct eye contact, she smiled and replied, "That sounds wonderful. You are right-on about that. What is it called?"

"Hunger."

"Fabulous title! I love it."

I did it! I talked to Oprah and she loved the *title* of my book! We chatted for just a few more seconds before she was rushed by journalists. Grinning from ear to ear, I stepped aside glowing in utter triumph.

I now absolutely had all the motivation I needed to finish my book. After our serendipitous meeting that day, I knew I would someday meet her again...but I better have my completed book in my hand next time.

Now I *really* had to finish the book. I called Sandra everyday at 10am from July 2011 until spring of 2012.

The triumphant day finally arrived. After spanning over four years and countless hours compiling and transforming my writings while in Thailand, Bali, and now the US, on April 3rd, 2012, I at last typed the words, "The End."

But that is not the end of *this* story!

Summer 2012 arrived and I heard Oprah was in town again. This time, I had a real, hardcopy book to hand her! I cleared my calendar for the week she was supposed to be in town and anxiously sat in my exact same chair of the lobby where I had seen her the year before.

In the front cover I wrote: "Thank you Oprah for inspiring millions. My dream is that this book inspires you." In the back cover I wrote: "Oprah, if you are touched by this book, my dream is that you are moved enough to add it to your Book Club 2.0 reading list. Thank you!"

I brought my lunch and dinner, as well as water and snacks and sat there all day Monday, but no luck.

I returned Tuesday. No Oprah.

Wednesday. The edges of my beaming smile began to wilt.

Thursday. I started crying right in front of the FOX news reporter who was trying to commend me for my tenacity and determination.

Friday. I was called by security and requested to not return.

Saturday. Instead of wearing professional attire, I went incognito in my yoga clothes and a baseball hat.

Sunday. Practically with tears in my eyes, I left the book at the front desk and pleaded for them to deliver it to her room. They said they would, but their trite smiles didn't give me much faith.

'It was so easy to see her last year when I didn't have the book. Urgh! And now I've got the book in my hand, but no Oprah. Double Urgh!'

It is now the end of 2012. This story is not over...Stay tuned.

Acknowledgements

First and foremost I'd like to thank my parents. If it wasn't for you guys, I wouldn't even be here! Mom, thank you for loving me with the most unconditional love I have ever experienced. No matter if I'm feeling joy or sadness, looking beautiful or horrendous, living in the U.S. or heart-wrenchingly-to-you abroad, making six-figures or living at your place with no income and working on my latest outrageous career venture…you forever welcome me with open arms. I love you Mom!

Dad, thank you for passing on your adventurous, fun-seeking, I-can-do-anything attitude to me. Much of my braveness and boldness are because of you modeling that the world is my oyster. My travels around the world, my determination to become a doctor, my vision to inspire millions…I learned how to dream big because of you. I love you Dad!

Thank you to my sister Kristin for loving me no matter what. You listen to me go on in detail with whatever my latest exciting idea du jour is which I usually can't wait to tell you all about. In lieu of our differences, you always stand by my side. I love you sis!

Thank you to my friends whom I've known for decades and who continue to support me in whatever new bold adventure I decide to pursue. Even in lieu of moves, marriages, parenthood, and the like, I thank you for making the effort to stay in touch through the years. It means the world to me. To have friends that have known me through all the ups and downs of my life, and friends who I can just hang out with and not even have to say anything to is priceless. Thank you Jen, Marisa, Bridget, Kim, Jeane, Julie, and Tobey.

Friendship is by far one of the most significant and joyful parts of my life. Thank you to the wonderful women I have met in more recent years too…Shalynn, Diana, Joan,

Olivia, Kerry, Melissa, Batul, Kerenza, Ceisha, Mel, and Julie. I love you all!

Thank you to my Girls who shared this journey in Thailand with me! I would never have made it as long as I did over there if you guys weren't laughing and crying along with me during our year together. I love you Monica, Katrina, and Nadine! (BTW Ladies, we need to have a reunion soon!) And thank you to Manana, for your endless love and devoted support throughout my time abroad and beyond. Thank you!

Thank you to the biggest fan of my Thailand blog, who inspired me to turn it into this very book. Without your astounding words of praise and encouragement, Teeny, this book likely would've never even been written! I think it was actually you who planted the idea for me to do this, because of all the big dreams I have for my life, I've never had writing a book on my bucket list! Thank you Christine!

Thank you dear Sandra! After publishing your own book, you knew I needed a kick in the pants to help me finish mine. Being my accountability buddy, and allowing me to call you daily at 10 a.m. for months and months and months, to tell you at what time and for how many hours each day I would work on my book was truly the driving force I needed to finish this book. Thank you Sandra!

Thank you Kate! Allowing me to live in your masterpiece of a home these last few years as I finished my book allowed me the peace and tranquility I needed to complete this book. Your generosity will forever be appreciated and how we met will continue to be one of the greatest stories of my life. Thank you Kate!

Thank you to my Great Work sisters! Christine Arylo, Amy Ahlers, and Shiloh McCloud…thank you for sharing with me your valuable wisdom and advice, as well as modeling how to reach the masses with my message. Thank you to my fellow tribe of Great Women who all desire to reach the masses with our unique messages of inspiration...Batul, Bonnie, Cindy, Dinah, Jennifer, Julie, Holly, Kate, Rosa Linda, Shari, and Valentina. Your love and support are priceless!

Thank you to my editor Mary Agnes for putting up with my endless list of questions and further edits. You took a raw and verbose 500-page document and transformed it into this inspiring masterpiece. Thank you!

Thank you to those of you who read through my proofs and gave me such valuable feedback, especially catching typos that somehow had been missed from the previous several read-throughs...Cam, Leslie, Alison, and my entire book club. Thank you!

And of course, last but not least, thank YOU! My readers! I have a passion in my heart to share inspiration with the world. By reading this book, you allow me to make my dream of making a difference in our world come true. Thank YOU!

Appendix I:
The Lessons

Whenever you are feeling inspired to do so, I encourage you to take out a pen and paper and write a few of your answers to the following, life-transforming questions…

#1. Life is Trustable

Do you believe life is trustable? That the events of life are being orchestrated by a benevolent Higher Power? Why or why not? It is entirely up to you to choose what you believe in life. Are you choosing a belief that brings you joy? If not, are you willing to choose one that does?

#2. Focusing on Gratitude Expands Your Joy

Write as long of a list as you can of what you are grateful for in your life. Once you think you are done, come up with five to ten additional items. Note how you feel before and after. By doing this simple exercise throughout your day, you will increase your experience of joy. Bonus: Who do you have to thank for these? Reach out to at least two people in the next week to say 'thank you.'

#3. Self-love is Essential for Your Well-being

What do you love about yourself? Write as long of a list as you can and once you're done, come up with five additional items. What can you do today to acknowledge your amazing and wonderful self? You are a gift…celebrate it!

#4. Light and Dark are Necessary for Balance

Imagine if the sun never set, or winter never ended, or you never slept, or if you spent a day eating your favorite food non-stop all day...Come up with a list of three to five other examples of a good thing taken to the extreme, and note the suffering which results. Realizing this, where in your life are you resisting the necessity of both the light *and* the dark of a situation? Take a deep breath and relax into the knowing that both the light and dark elements of life are necessary to achieve balance.

#5. Easing Your Grip on Attachment
Enhances Feelings of Peace

What things, people, and situations are you most attached to in your life? Do you carry fear at the thought of losing any of these? Practice imagining yourself at peace, even in the face of losing something close to you. To help you with this, think back to a time where you lost something close to you and remind yourself how you were able to eventually heal from the loss. Lessening your grip of attachment will allow you to feel more at peace with the unknowns of life.

#6. Challenges Bring Growth

What are the greatest challenges you've experienced in your life? How have these challenges made you a stronger person? What value have these experiences brought to your life?

#7. The Four Pillars of Health
Create the Foundation for Your Life

How would you rate yourself in terms of the quality of nutrition you give to your body? If needed, write down a few simple steps you could take to improve this area.

Answer the above two questions for the other Three Pillars of Health: sleep, exercise, emotional well-being/stress level.

#8. The Health of the Environment
Directly Correlates to Your Own Health

Think for a moment about the amazing gifts of clean air, clean water, beautiful mountain vistas. Consider breathtaking sunsets over the ocean, brilliant flowers, stunning wild life and sea life... How do these priceless gifts from nature affect your health? Imagine if they did not exist? Rate your level of participation on a daily basis toward contributing to keeping the environment beautiful and pristine? What one step can you take today to contribute to this?

#9. Keep Death on Your Shoulder

Imagine someone is presenting your eulogy at your funeral. What would you like to be remembered for? How close are you to being in alignment with this image? What one step could you take today to be closer to this vision?

#10. Connection is Vital for Well-Being

Feeling connected to others and to your community is a key element necessary for achieving optimal well-being. Where and how do you connect with others in your life? How satisfied are you with this aspect of your life? What one step could you take today to increase your feeling of connection?

#11. Peace is Found Within

Think of a time when a happy event was going on around you, yet you did not feel happy. Now, think of a time when nothing particular was going on around you, yet you felt joyful anyway. Lastly, think of a time when a person or a thing made you happy, yet over time, it no longer had that effect. Take a moment to ponder or write about this concept in your life: lasting peace comes from within your own heart, regardless of outside circumstances.

#12. Be Compassionate

"Be kind to everyone you meet, for inside everyone lies a great battle." What is your relationship to the word 'compassion?' How would you rate your level of compassion towards others? And how about towards yourself? By increasing self-compassion, you automatically increase your compassion towards others. Where in your life could you practice acknowledging your humanness...the fact that it is okay to make mistakes and that perfection is never the goal...and be more kind to yourself? What one step could you take today to express more kindness to yourself?

#13. By Practicing Patience and Persistence, You are Bound to Be Successful

Think of a time when you worked hard to achieve a goal. Was the effort you put in worth it to you? Do you have dreams or aspirations which you have attempted to achieve in the past but gave up on? Are you willing to try again, practicing more patience and persistence toward reaching this goal? Imagine how you would feel achieving this dream.

#14. By Courageously Sitting with Pain, You Allow it to Be Released

"What we resist persists." Do you have areas of your life which feel painful when you think of them? If so, consider writing a letter to express your thoughts and emotions about this situation, without intending to give it to anyone. Allow yourself to write freely, without any filter or judgment. This exercise allows you to release emotions which you've likely been carrying around in your subconscious and thus are affecting your life in a negative way. After writing the letter, create a ceremony to release these painful emotions, such as burning the letter and releasing the ashes into the wind.

#15. Don't Believe Everything You Think

What are some of the most common thoughts you have from
day to day about yourself and your life? Do these thoughts make
you smile or cause angst? The ones that cause you angst, are they
provable facts? If not, realize you have the power to no longer
listen to them and choose more self-loving thoughts.

#16. Everything is Inherently Meaningless

Sunsets are beautiful to everyone, right? Not so…imagine if you
were stranded out in the cold. What strong beliefs do you have
about life in general? About yourself? About others in your life?
Ponder the fact you are entirely in charge of choosing these
beliefs…and thus you are also entirely in charge of changing
your beliefs at anytime. Replace one negative belief you have
with a new, positive one and practice embracing this new belief
for one week. You will likely feel like you are fooling yourself
but practice embracing the new belief anyway…this is simply the
process for how to adopt new beliefs.

#17. Life is Lived in the Present

The only place to really ever be is in the now. Past and future
never truly exist, only as thoughts in your mind. It is said the
large majority of worries never come true. When in worry, you're
cut off from the joy present in the moment because you are lost
in thought. When you find yourself lost in thought today, recite
two to three things you appreciate about the moment to bring
you back to the present. It can be as simple as the fact you are
warm, clothed, fed, dressed, safe, etc…then take a deep breath
and on the exhale, imagine breathing out your unnecessary
thoughts and worries.

#18. Fear is Usually Only a State of Mind

What are your greatest fears? How many of your past fears have
come true? Write a list of fears you have had in the past and how
they resolved. Are you willing to let go of your present fears and
replace them with thoughts which bring you joy instead? Try
right now to transform at least one.

Appendix II:
Notes on Meditation

Meditation, although practically a foreign word to most westerners, has been growing in popularity throughout the US for decades. It certainly isn't some rare and esoteric activity given the fact it's been a part of numerous world religions since the dawn of time. I was turned on to it during medical school, when my colleagues would constantly talk about the many physical and mental benefits it provides (yet it seemed impossible for me to find even ten minutes a day to do it among all the time I spent studying).

The word 'meditation' can mean so many different things, similar to how the word 'God' has so many interpretations. 'Meditation' to me simply means being still with my eyes closed, as I focus my attention on the in and out motion of my breath.

With the non-stop lifestyle I had been living for many years (which is certainly not something unique to me these days!)....studying for hours, then running here, driving there, planning this, organizing that, making a mess, cleaning the house, changing this, fixing that, cooking food, eating the food, texting dad, calling mom, and spending an embarrassing amount of time fruitlessly attempting day after day to someday clean out my email inbox...I had realized that perhaps why I'd been feeling so fatigued for so long was simply because my mind and body had become desperately hungry to BE STILL! Does this resonate with you?

When I first started meditating, lassoing the focus of my mind to simply focus on my breath for an hour was no easy task (as is still true today). Watching the mad dash of my fleeting thoughts and the realization I had almost no power to tame them was quite a humbling revelation. I decided my brain must have been born that way. I imagined I had spent the first few minutes of life thinking, 'I'm hungry! No, I think I need a nap. I'm confused. I think I'll cry! Actually no, I'd just like some milk...'

Once I finally started practicing meditation, if I was able to enjoy even one minute of focus without thoughts floating in, I felt successful. Yet then I learned meditation should never be about attempting to achieve 'success.' In Buddhism, 'non-attachment' is a key principle to live by, thus simply practicing the act of meditation is enough. There is no such thing as a 'good' session or 'bad' session per se. Applying judgment creates a craving for it to always be a particular way and an aversion to when it is not that way. Yet living in this manner creates suffering because nothing ever stays the same. The only constant in life is change thus if we crave something to always be a particular way, we are setting ourselves up for disappointment. So just regularly sitting still, regardless of what thoughts are floating through your mind or not, is good enough.

Thus the majority of my time meditating is often spent watching how busy my mind is, and then continually refocusing my attention on my breath, using my mantra, *"Breath in. Breath out. Breath in. Breath out. Breath in…"*

I encourage you to give it a try, if only for three minutes a day to start. Consistency is more important than length of time. By cultivating a daily mediation practice, you are bound to feel more peace and calm in your life.

Appendix III:
Notes on Conservation

Koh Tao, the name of the island where I spent my month in paradise, literally means 'island of turtles.' So I should tell you about all the turtles I saw, right?! Well, I wish I could. A very sad reality is turtles are no longer seen there. To have a name like 'Turtle Island,' you can imagine that once upon a time there were hundreds of them frolicking around. Well, throughout my entire month, I did not see a single turtle on Turtle Island.

The influx of tourists over the previous 20 years has made life impossible for them. They've either been scared away or poisoned. The non-stop activity on the beaches deprives them of the needed peaceful areas in the sand for laying their eggs. All the boats and people moving around in the sea scare them away, as they leave in search of more peaceful surroundings. Furthermore, they end up ingesting the poisonous, man-made toxins floating around in the water. Urgh! Every time I saw someone throw their toxic cigarette butt or plastic water bottle into the ocean, I couldn't help but feel anger. On this note, I must take a moment to digress...

A few weeks earlier as I was getting ready for work one morning, I was watching the world news on BBC and there was a story about what a massive problem the accumulation of waste around the globe, most notably from plastic, has become. There were video clips from countries all around the world showing landfills overflowing with towering mountains of plastic garbage.

One major city in Africa incurred a devastating flood after a rainstorm due to littered plastic bags, which had clogged the city's sewer drains. And kudos to them! This city has now outlawed plastic bags. (One of the things about life that always baffles me is how the impetus for change seemingly does not occur until the effects of a major problem demand it to happen.)

It doesn't just accumulate on land either. Annually, six million tons of trash ends up in our oceans (as I experienced first hand on that dreadful day when I thought I was being attacked by a jelly fish, yet it was just a bunch of trash), 80 percent originating as litter, which enters the ocean as a result of being propelled from land via wind and water runoff. Consequently, 100,000 marine animals such as dolphins, whales, seals, and turtles choke or become entangled in our waste every year, as was part of the issue on beautiful no-turtles, Turtle Island.

I was shocked when I heard the news story share about the fact that land is so cheap outside the US that garbage from America is now often shipped overseas. Heaven forbid the biggest waste producing country in the world live next to their own waste! (Urgh) It certainly makes more sense to spend millions of dollars on gas to fuel a barge to pollute its way across the ocean, carrying all of this American waste to some other 'more deserving' country. That day when I was surrounded by plastic garbage, who knows, maybe it was trash that had originated from the US.

Realizing this enormous waste problem, I made the transition a few years ago to always use my own bags, but it certainly didn't happen overnight. I thought about it for many months, about how I should really stop using all these plastic bags. Then I finally kept canvas bags as well as reusable mesh produce bags permanently in my trunk...and always walked into the store forgetting them. But eventually, I finally made it to the point where sometimes I won't even buy things unless I have my own bags. I also keep silverware in the glove box of my car to avoid using plastic silverware every time I eat take-out.

As for bottles and other plastic, have you heard of the huge quagmires floating out in the ocean full of plastic debris? The BBC news story continued on with details of how there are seven of these massive, floating, plastic islands around the globe. The current only flows inward in these particular areas thus allowing the accumulation of non-biodegradable matter, most notably plastic. But it's not in big, recognizable chunks.

Plastic, although it never entirely disintegrates, eventually breaks down into tiny specks. Sea life interprets these specks as food. So they eat them, not knowing in due course after repeated feedings, the plastic will accumulate in their body and eventually kill them...which was one of the issues contributing to the disappearance of the turtles around Turtle Island. Even I got confused. For example, one day as I was snorkeling, I noticed a bright, white shell in the shallow water. So I picked it up and gee, it was not a shell. It was a broken plastic spoon.

The BBC news story went on to point out how plastic waste is just one 'small' source of this global, burgeoning, garbage problem. They shared how residues of pharmaceutical drugs are now being found in city water. Think about what this means! It means that millions of people are taking drugs → urinating residues of them into the toilet → this contaminated water somehow ends up back in our city water → and then we are cooking our vegetables, cleaning our clothes, drinking, and bathing in this 'clean' water. (As a naturopath, here is but another one of the many reasons why I like to help people reduce the use of prescription drugs!)

So I'd like to take this moment to make a plea…If we each just took tiny steps to reduce our production of waste, we could dramatically reduce this very real and drastic problem! I'll make it super easy for you. Here's a small list of very easy and simple steps which if everyone did just a few, we could make a significant, positive impact on our oceans and maybe even allow a few turtles to come back to Turtle Island! THANK YOU!

#1-Please say no to a bag if you don't really need it. Keep reusable shopping bags in your trunk and you'll eventually get in the habit of using them. Stock up on full sized bags as well as mesh produce bags. Or, just keep all those plastic bags you have stuffed in some drawer in your kitchen instead in your trunk and reuse them. Alternatively, if you're in the store and have forgotten your bags, just grab some out of the plastic bag recycle bin and use them.

#2- Buy beverages in glass over those in plastic. Use your own water container and refill it, instead of buying plastic water bottles. (The water in them is toxic anyway due to plastic residues you end up drinking!) Get a simple counter-top water filter which screws into your kitchen faucet. Here is the one I recommend: http://www.healthegoods.com/premium 10-stage-countertop-water-filter-new-wave-enviro.html

#3- Use your own, reusable coffee mug or ask for a 'for here' mug when you intend on staying in the coffee shop. Additionally, whenever you have the option to use a washable mug or a paper cup, choose the mug.

#4- Be mindful of how many paper napkins you use. Restrain from grabbing a huge stack. One or two will usually do the job.

#5- Contact the companies you do business with and request communication be via email only...monthly statements, bills, insurance info...If you hold stock, you can also request to have all that bulky quarterly company earnings stuff and proxy material sent electronically.

#6- When choosing between two similar items at the store, buy the one packed in less packaging.

On that last point, another bit of food for thought is when you choose non-manufactured thus non-packaged foods, (such as fresh vegetables and fruit) not only are you avoiding contributing to our waste problem by avoiding packaging, but you're also improving your health by avoiding the chemicals found in processed foods. Cool, right?!

On a positive note, I was impressed with how many 'What You Can Do to Preserve our Ocean' posters were tacked up around the beach on Turtle Island. They were full of educational information, such as pointing out how cigarette butts contain plastic and other toxins thus need to be thrown away in proper bins; a reminder to buy locally made goods since they don't have excessive packaging (among other benefits); dispose of trash properly so it doesn't get blown into the ocean...

To sum this up, if you're so inclined, take a look at this great video that beautifully sums up this entire issue: **www.thestoryofstuff.com**

By each of us taking little steps to reduce this massive problem, in the future when you find yourself enjoying a tropical island vacation, there will be a good chance you won't have to swim through garbage, but instead be surrounded by a wealth of joyful turtles!

THANK YOU!!!

Let's Stay in Touch!

Here's How:

I hope you enjoyed HUNGER, An Adventurous Journey of Finding Peace Within. Thank you for reading!

One of my greatest joys in life is to inspire others to do what it takes to feel great physically, as well as have a life you love. If my book had this affect on you in one way or another, I thank you for suggesting it to your friends! Or better yet, buy a few copies and give them away as unexpected gifts. Generosity improves your health!

To continue to be inspired by my informative and practical information for how to have a healthy body and create a life you love, I would be honored for you to interact with me in any or all of the following ways:

1. Go to www.DrJodyND.com and enter your email address in the box on the home page to **receive my weekly health email**, 'The Vitality Vibe!...Juicy Tidbits of Healthy Wisdom from Dr. Jody.'

2. Follow my daily health tips on **Facebook** at www.facebook.com/DrJodyND and **Twitter** at www.twitter.com/DrJodyND

3. Go to www.DrJodyND.com and **send me a note to let me know where you are with your health versus where you'd like to be.** Upon availability, you will be scheduled for a free phone session with me to determine if and how working together would be a good fit for you. I'd love to help you!

4. Enroll in my **online eCourses** at: www.DrJodyND.com (As of Jan 2013, I am in the process of creating my first few classes. I have plans to roll out several more in the next year on topics such as Optimal Nutrition, The Four Pillars of Health, How to Avoid the Cold & Flu

Naturally, and eBooks on how to treat asthma, allergies & more naturally.)

5. **Contact me about being a speaker** for your group or organization! I am a dynamic and engaging presenter, sure to be a valuable source of health information and inspiration. I can present on a wide-array of heath topics…covering physical health, as well as mental wellbeing. I am a fire-cracker of motivation to say the least! Fill out the contact form on my website and describe your audience and what topics you're interested in.

6. **Contact me about leading your own private health retreat**. Organize your friends or family, pick the date and place, and tell me when and where you want me to arrive! Beforehand, we will custom design each element of your health retreat per whatever you desire in terms of nutrition, exercise, meditation, and more. Go to my website, www.DrJodyND.com and fill out the contact form to share with me your initial ideas.

7. **Schedule a series of private appointments** to receive guidance for how to treat your health condition naturally. Fill out the contact form on my website and describe to me how you would like to improve your health.

8. **Enroll in my elite life-transforming program**, 'Boost Your Vitality! 180 days to Change Your Life.' By signing up for this one-of-a-kind health and wellness program, you will receive:

   a. A private call with me each week, where I will design an individualized program for strengthening your 4 Pillars of Health…your nutrition, exercise, sleep, and emotional well-being

   b. A weekly 'Success & Support' call with the others in the program + an accountability partner

   c. Access to the private Facebook page where you can share the inspiring stories of success and transformation you will be experiencing as a result of giving yourself the gift of enrolling in this program

   d. The option of having me fly to you to take an educational trip together to the grocery store, and then spend the day transforming your kitchen to one bursting with health and vitality

   e. The most intimate access to me and my vast knowledge of health and wellbeing of any of the above options!

By being healthy in mind and body, you give yourself the gift of having a life you love. I would be honored to support you in turning this into your reality! I encourage you to take advantage of my above list of offerings. I promise, you will gain tools for having a body and a life you love.

To your health!
Dr. Jody

And one last thing...

In regards to my beautiful cat Jennifur! ...I am sending this note out in hopes her new owner will read this book and then contact me! All I know about you, the owner, is that you found Jen over Craig's list in Seattle in 2008. I think you were a woman who lived on a lot of land, maybe even a farm. Jen is mostly black, with white paws, a white nose, and a white neck, and her long fur is as smooth as silk. She hates other animals and has the personality of a dog...she demands a lot of attention and will come when you call her. If this sounds like your cat, I would be eternally grateful for you to reach out to me so that I may hear how she is doing!!!

Thank you!